Wheaton Theology Conference

The BEAUTY of GOD

Theology and the Arts

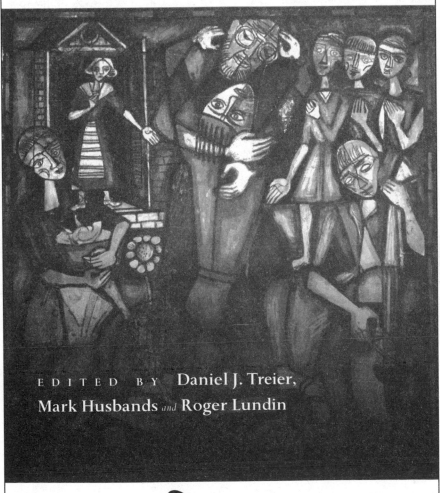

EDITED BY Daniel J. Treier,
Mark Husbands *and* Roger Lundin

IVP Academic

An imprint of InterVarsity Press
Downers Grove, Illinois

InterVarsity Press
P.O. Box 1400, Downers Grove, IL 60515-1426
World Wide Web: www.ivpress.com
E-mail: mail@ivpress.com

InterVarsity Press® is the book-publishing division of InterVarsity Christian Fellowship/USA®, a student
movement active on campus at hundreds of universities, colleges and schools of nursing in the United States
of America, and a member movement of the International Fellowship of Evangelical Students. For
information about local and regional activities, write Public Relations Dept., InterVarsity Christian
Fellowship/USA, 6400 Schroeder Rd., P.O. Box 7895, Madison, WI 53707-7895, or visit the IVCF website at
<www.ivcf.org>.

Scripture quotations, unless otherwise noted, are from the New Revised Standard Version of the Bible,
copyright 1989 by the Division of Christian Education of the National Council of Churches of Christ in the
USA. Used by permission. All rights reserved.

"The Sickness and the Magnet" from Alaskaphrenia by Christine Hume. © 2004 by Christine Hume. Used by
permission of New Issues Poetry and Prose.

The poems "The Procession," "Nunc Dimitti" and "Benedictus" by Jill Peláez Baumgaertner first appeared in
Christianity and Literature 52, no. 3 (2003): 409-16, and are used by permission.

"Come Sunday" by Duke Ellington, copyright © 1966 (Renewed) by G. Schirmer, Inc. International copyright
secured. All rights reserved. Reprinted by permission.

"Never" by Micheal O'Siadhal from Micheal O'Siadhal: The Gossamer Wall (Bloodaxe Books, 2002).
Used by permission.

"Cosmos" by Micheal O'Siadhal from Micheal O'Siadhal: Poems 1975-1995 (Bloodaxe Books, 1999).
Used by permission.

Lines from "A Man Walked Out" are from Ghost Pain by Sydney Lea, published by Sarabande Books, Inc.
© 2005 by Sydney Lea. Reprinted by permission of Sarabande Books and the author.

Richard Wilbur's "Love Calls Us to the Things of This World" from Things of This World, copyright © 1956
and renowed 1984 by Richard Wilbur, reprinted by permission of Harcourt, Inc.

Design: Cindy Kiple
Images: Victoria & Albert Museum, London/Art Resource, NY
ISBN 978-0-8308-2843-2

Printed in the United States of America ∞

Library of Congress Cataloging-in-Publication Data

Wheaton Theology Conference (15th : 2006 : Wheaton College, Ill.)
    The beauty of God: theology and the arts / edited by Daniel J.
Treier, Mark Husbands, and Rober Lundin.
        p. cm.
    Includes bibliographical references and index.
    ISBN 978-0-8308-2843-2 (pbk.: alk. paper)
    1. Christianity and the arts—Congresses. 2. Aesthetics—Religious
aspects—Christianity—Congresses. I. Treier, Daniel J., 1972- II.
Husbands, Mark, 1961- III. Lundin, Roger. IV. Title.
    BR115.A8W44 2006
    261.5'7—dc22

                                                        2006101565

P	18	17	16	15	14	13	12	11	10	9	8	7	6	5	4	3	2	1
Y	22	21	20	19	18	17	16	15	14	13	12	11	10	09	08	07		

CONTENTS

INTRODUCTION

Daniel J. Treier, Mark Husbands and Roger Lundin

After a period of considerable neglect in modern religious thought and church culture alike, beauty has begun to reclaim its rightful place in the larger scheme of Christian theology. For many centuries, along with goodness and truth, it formed part of the triad of transcendental ideals that the Christian tradition inherited from the classical age and appropriated for its own uses. From the beginning of the Christian era to the dawning of the modern world, a rough consensus about the interrelationships of beauty, truth and goodness governed Western conceptions of everything from the workings of language to the intricacies of creation and the mysteries of providence. "Beauty is the splendour of truth," observes Stephen Dedalus in James Joyce's *A Portrait of the Artist as a Young Man,* and to explain his passion for beauty, Stephen draws upon the thought of Plato, Aristotle and Thomas Aquinas, among others. In doing so he crisply outlines the synthesis of nature and grace that for centuries had assured beauty of a central role in Christian reflection on the nature of God and the drama of redemption.[1]

Under a number of pressures, that synthesis gave way in the early modern period, and the theological interest in beauty entered a period of slow but steady decline. Over time the ideal of beauty seemed increasingly irrelevant to the new realities that science, economics and politics were either discovering or creating at the dawn of the modern age. Discoveries in astronomy and in physics, for example, made it all but impossible to recon-

---

[1]James Joyce, *A Portrait of the Artist as a Young Man* (1916; reprint, New York: New American Library, 1991), p. 210.

cile classical ideals of symmetry with a dawning awareness of the sprawling and ragged particularity of the physical universe. In turn, advances in scientific understanding fed a rapidly growing appetite for technological mastery, which to this day remains unsated. Add to this mix a growing eighteenth- and nineteenth-century emphasis on individual particularities and cultural differences, and it seems in retrospect hardly surprising that the classical ideal of beauty was displaced from the center to the periphery of modern thought.

Regrettably, the forces unleashed by the Protestant Reformation played a key role in the drama of beauty's displacement. To say that is not to claim that the Reformers were blind to the appeal of beauty. On the contrary, John Calvin and Martin Luther were masters of prose style and showed a keen awareness of beauty's nuances and meaning. In like manner, during the eighteenth century, the Methodism of Charles and John Wesley evidenced vibrant alertness to the substance of spiritual beauty, the writings of Jonathan Edwards focused with intense brilliance on "the excellency and beauty of God," and in music the glorious example of J. S. Bach gave evidence of a deep sensitivity to beauty in the Reformation tradition.

Nevertheless, as brilliantly as they embodied the beautiful in their own works, the likes of Luther, Bach and Edwards could do little to counter the disregard for beauty that marked much of Protestant theology and experience. By shifting the focus from the intricate harmony of the outward creation to the virtuous passions of the inner spirit, Protestant culture, perhaps unintentionally, fostered indifference to beauty beyond the self. In the fundamentalist tradition of the early twentieth century, in particular, beauty was seen to be suspect, and close attention to it was discouraged on biblical, theological and eschatological grounds.

Eventually, as the evangelical descendants of fundamentalism began to pursue faithful engagement with the complex realities and apologetic significance of cultural life, attention to the God-given possibilities of beauty returned quite naturally. While signs of profound aesthetic weakness remain, sources of hope have also begun to appear within contemporary theology as well as academic and cultural life at large. In Roman Catholic theology, for example, Hans Urs von Balthasar spent half a century developing a comprehensive theological aesthetics, and his work continues to open up fruitful lines of inquiry. Protestant contributions regarding beauty have been modest since Edwards, but recent works by Nicholas Wolterstorff,

Frank Burch Brown, Edward Farley and others provide examples of developing strength. If metaphysics played the role of first theology or philosophy in premodern ages and epistemology took first place in the modern era, then it seems that axiology—a general theory of values, whether in terms of ethics or aesthetics—could dominate after the postmodern turn. Theologians may be catching up.

The 2006 Wheaton Theology Conference set out to gauge the current status of Christian thinking and practice in the arts, as well as seeking to suggest fresh theological and artistic possibilities for the future. The conference brought together scholars from several disciplines and artists from a wide range of media and styles. Several others presented fine papers that we cannot include here for reasons of space, but we owe them our gratitude all the same. The essays included in this book give evidence of the guiding concern of the conference, which was to balance theological sensitivity to the vibrant worlds of art with aesthetic alertness to the centrality of the Scriptures and the primacy of the cross.

In the modern world, efforts at engaging the arts theologically have appealed to the doctrines of creation and incarnation for support. Particularly within Catholic and evangelical Protestant aesthetics, recent decades have witnessed considerable interest in a so-called "sacramental" view of the arts and an "incarnational" view of reality. In certain regards the renewed emphasis on incarnation and sacrament has allowed vital elements of Christian truth to emerge. Yet the gains here have come at some cost, for when doctrinal categories are abstracted from their confessional contexts, they can readily become skewed or distorted, forced to serve ends quite apart from their proper meaning.

For example, this has proved to be the case with the terms *sacramental* and *incarnational* in contemporary Protestant aesthetics. All that God created is indeed good, and through that goodness God has given a mandate for cultural life and artistic production. Furthermore, through the life, death and resurrection of Jesus Christ, God reaffirmed the dignity of creation and the cultural vocation of human beings. In Christ the sacraments link the creation with the incarnation, as through them we receive those "gifts of God for the people of God" which supply tangible means of celebrating and sustaining our union with the risen Lord.

If applied without theological discernment or restraint, however, the doctrine of creation can be used to foster any activity that appeals to a culture at a particular time and place. In making use of this doctrine, then, we do well to remember that because of the fall into sin, the created order remains in "bondage to decay" (Rom 8:21). As a result of the effects of sin, God has given us a redemptive mission as well as a cultural charge. Far from suggesting that the arts are or should be primarily evangelistic tools, the reality of sin and the claims of the gospel mean that artistic forms stand under judgment and in need of grace as fully as human ideas and actions do.

To bring the doctrines of creation and redemption together, we turn to the person and work of Jesus Christ. Yet in isolation the incarnation has fared equally poorly in aesthetics as has the doctrine of creation. At times, Protestant advocates of the arts in particular have promoted the incarnation as a general concept of the divine blessing of the world rather than as a doctrine of the specific redemptive activity that God has accomplished through the person and work of Jesus Christ. The incarnation, after all, is a truth about his particular reality and not about us, except insofar as we are the human objects of the saving action of the divine subject. Moreover, the Bible tells us that the incarnate Lord was not beautiful in some earthly respects (Is 53:2), and apparently his apostolic messengers, such as the apostle Paul, need not be aesthetically effective either (see 1-2 Cor). All of which raises the question, Have "incarnational" approaches to the arts taken sufficient account of this?

Both God's providential sustenance of creation and the redemptive particularity of the incarnation call for dynamic rather than static approaches to beauty, and they seem to disallow generic endorsements of the arts as inherently sacramental activities. In Scripture the sacraments are signs of God's saving activity, and they possess both temporal and spatial density. The idea that all of nature is a sacramental repository of grace is problematic inasmuch as it trades on a static conception of value as something that is fixed in objects and readily accessible to the human imagination. Similarly, for such a view the particularity of the biblical sacraments and their essential connection to the work of Jesus Christ easily fade into the background or disappear entirely when eclipsed by a general theory of revelation. If everything becomes sacramental, then nothing is sacred—or to be sacred means nothing much in particular.

If the doctrines of creation, incarnation and sacrament are to have authority for Christian approaches to aesthetics, then we must attend to the reality of the Fall; the dynamics of the life, death and resurrection of Jesus; and the workings of the Spirit in the life of the church. In short, all our theological reflections on the arts require the constant reminder that when we turn our eyes upon Jesus, we see his face turned toward Jerusalem and his gaze fixed upon the cross as the joy set before him (Heb 12:2). If God is most glorified, according to John, when Christ is lifted up to be crucified, then whither Christian approaches to beauty?

Beyond turning our eyes upon Jesus, the Bible also enjoins us to focus on our hearing. In connection with faith, the scriptural privilege is accorded to hearing, along with some wariness about sight. As some premodern Christians such as Augustine recognized, the beauty of the natural world can distract us from the God revealed in Christ's weakness. In a sense we ought to "use" creation for God's glory rather than "enjoying" the world for its own sake. The costly self-sacrifice of Jesus Christ not only heralds the value of the material world but also highlights what ultimately matters, and in so doing calls us to look for the new creation. Because we hope for what we do not yet see, beauty has a certain Logos-centeredness which acknowledges that the forms of this world are passing away.

Church fathers may have overlooked the ways in which enjoyment of God's created gifts can be an act of worship. And Protestant Christians may have heralded the divine Word to the eventual neglect not only of sacrament but also of beautiful art. Later, some puritanical Protestants may have even denied the value of ordinary life that the Reformers sought to recover. Yet, even still, Scripture warns us against lusting with worldly eyes and worshiping the creature rather than the Creator, thus eclipsing our anticipation of the new creation with the present form of this world. Even in the eschaton, after all, we will not see God per se but rather revelation remains the dialectical unveiling-with-veiling of the spoken Word.

Far from precluding robust Christian engagement with the arts, these evangelical hopes for theological discipline regarding aesthetics should inspire chastened yet full appreciation of creation's beauty even as it remains unperfected. Indeed, the following essays reflect the riches of music, the visual arts such as painting and film, and various forms of literature. The movement of the essays follows not only these categories of artistic media but also the flow of the biblical story from creation to new creation. Yet, as we consider the aesthetic implications of a trinitarian approach to creation, we must acknowledge human brokenness and creaturely suffering, seeking redemptive approaches to culture that involve bearing not only evangelistic witness but also alternative visions of artistic excellence.

We enjoyed artistic excellence as Jeremy Begbie offered music interspersed throughout his two keynote addresses that open this volume. Musical traces remain in the published versions, first of all as he explores beauty in relation to Bach. Reminding us that for Christians beauty must reflect our understanding of the triune God, Begbie sees beauty as dynamic, tied to other-centered love. Yet created beauty will testify to God's otherness as well. Matter matters, and creation participates in the glorification of Jesus Christ rather than some static, immaterial, Platonic necessity. The Holy Spirit elicits openness to particulars and to change. These truths Begbie then illustrates and deepens by attending to the stunning invention and unmistakable coherence of Bach's music.

In the subsequent essay Begbie explores the relation between beauty and sentimentality. At times the arts have fostered sentimentality's evasion or trivialization of evil, emotional self-indulgence and avoidance of costly action. Indeed, this is even the case in Christian worship. Moreover, arts such as music might seem to offer paradigms that harmonize evil into some kind of necessary progression. Yet it does not have to be so. Begbie points us again to the Christian story, specifically to the three days of Easter. Rather than isolating either the cross or the resurrection, he finds that we must go through Holy Saturday as well, in order to see the glory to come from the standpoint of waiting without knowing the full ending. God's beauty is not sentimental, for God has engaged the most horrible evil in all its ugliness— while demonstrating the beauty of justice.

Bruce Benson lends another voice with reflections on music from philosophical theology. Drawing on the work of Jean-Louis Chrétien, Benson's theme is the way that call and response structure our creaturely lives, with implications for art. God's call in creation precedes beauty, which therefore takes the character of response. As our response manifests divine beauty, it forwards the divine call to others, who then respond and call. And so forth. As a result, we cannot shrink art down to creativity or making, but must also see the improvisation of practical wisdom as artistic. In fact, Benson explores the improvisation of black spirituals and jazz as one instance of what characterizes art in general: repetition, not just innovation. Such "signifying" highlights the reality of "broken beauty," for in many communities—or for many in all our communities—improvisation addresses both suffering and hope. So it must, if for Christians art is a form of action.

The call for a "broken beauty" resonates with all three essays that follow concerning the visual arts. John Walford offers an art historical perspective connected with the Dutch Reformed tradition. He contrasts the Neo-Platonic and Aristotelian influences on art, as seen in the idealized visions of Michelangelo or Poussin, with the realism of Rembrandt and others from the Netherlands. In such a perspective, portraying truth can be beautiful, whether or not the truth adheres to classical ideals of form. Walford explores some contemporary examples of Christian artists who pursue "broken beauty" as well, while reflecting on whether art most fittingly addresses the ideal divine, the real and human or their point of intersection.

Bruce Herman, deeply involved in the recent exhibition of figurative and representational art titled "A Broken Beauty," likewise argues for a form of realism. Finding in Keats's "Ode on a Grecian Urn" the equation of beauty with adolescent eros never to be fulfilled, Herman explores the import of this characteristic equation in contemporary culture. He suggests that Christians ought to define beauty in light of the realism of marriage. Wounds and imperfections surface and cannot be hidden, yet in this covenant relationship eros is requited and finds real beauty. Marriage forms us morally and offers us a biblical model for understanding relationship with God—hence, there we find truth and goodness as well in a manner consistent with the message of the cross.

When we turn to film with the work of Roy Anker, the message remains fairly consistent. Some have tried to deal cinematically with the divine along the lines of "bigger is better." Anker criticizes such appeals to spectacle and sentiment, arguing that they illuminate little about God and seemingly engage in desperate idolatry. Conversely, others—notably Europeans—have pursued spartan minimalism and thereby highlighted moments of existential drama. Anker criticizes this approach too, however, finding its implied metaphysic to exclude or at least hide the divine dualistically from everyday life. Accordingly, he champions the efforts of a few to suggest that the luminous transcendent is indeed present amid the ordinary and broken, if only we had eyes to see. In Krzysztof Kieslowski's *Three Colors: Blue,* for example, moments of beauty are extraordinary but only come to pass in relation to profound brokenness.

The same quotation from Gerald Manley Hopkins that provides Anker's title—"the world is charged with the grandeur of God. / It will flame out, like shining from shook foil"—appears in our next essay as well. Turning our attention to text and to poetry in particular, Jill Peláez Baumgaertner highlights the importance of language for experiencing the divine. Yet here too beauty must account for brokenness: "the Christ Hopkins describes with 'darksome devouring eyes'—it is this Christ that reveals the beauty of a God that we in this post-Holocaust age can hold onto by our fingernails" (p. 153). The Christian poet's vocation is to revitalize language—not with the self-obsession and self-enclosed inscrutability that characterize some contemporary verse but via the message of the cross, as Baumgaertner skillfully illustrates.

Practices of Scripture reading are the focus of James Fodor's essay, as he too offers an aesthetic caution. For Fodor, theology's artistic revitalization requires a return to "memory" as practiced by Augustine, Bonaventure and so many other ancients. Such *memoria* is not merely stiff recall but imaginatively productive—for helping us to learn and live out a scriptural vision. Again the cross figures prominently, this time in Bonaventure's "The Journey of the Soul into God," with its attention to Francis of Assisi's vision of a cruciform man amid a six-winged seraph. Here restrained use of the Platonic ascent motif opens into a larger theme: Fodor believes that theology's aesthetic recovery must stem from a certain neglect of "the arts" as a province of high culture. Rather, if we would be led back to God, we must recognize the arts of the ordinary, ways that scriptural signs focus our attention on the One we should enjoy rather than holding our attention within the creation we use for such delight.

In Roger Lundin's essay we travel beyond the Middle Ages to the modern. Lundin explores the eighteenth-century origins of "aesthetics" as a Western discipline, prompted by modern cosmology and historical consciousness. As art became further and further separated from reason, and thereby too from the natural world that was now taken to be silent, beauty became an alternative faith. Seen as the realm of freedom opposed to nature, aesthetics could substitute for bygone Christian religion now that nature was not a type of transcendent reality but a trope for human creativity to exercise. Lundin counters, however, this vision of which Nietzsche so clearly understood the implications. Following Karl Barth and Hans Urs von Balthasar, he urges Christians to keep Christ at the center of cultural aspirations. In so doing we will oppose dualisms between spirit and matter or humanity and the natural order. Instead, recovering a sense of the *drama* of redemption, we will engage in the arts as play, seeing for what it truly is the reality of life in the face of death and of death in the face of resurrection.

Such an aesthetic vision offers much for our alienated Western culture. Edward Oakes concludes our volume by continuing to engage issues of cultural apologetics, while surveying the thought of Hans Urs von Balthasar in particular. European nihilism and its rise in America seem to obliterate beauty's evangelical incentive: how can one hunger for the gospel who has never really known what it is to hunger for anything truly desirable? Despite the extent of this challenge, Balthasar sought to reunite the transcendentals while placing beauty prior to goodness and truth in the order of coming to God. First we desire, next we commit to action, and then we can reflect upon what we have come to know—a reversal of Kant's modern pattern. So it is also with Christian mission: first prayer, next proclamation and only then dialogue with the world. Such a pattern of beauty, goodness and truth united stems from the reality that Truth is a person—God as revealed in Jesus Christ. Again, at the end of this book just as at the beginning, Christian reflection on the arts must address trinitarian theology. As Oakes demonstrates, keeping Christ the center is crucial for all cultural enterprises, including our witness to the beauty of God.

We trust that this brief introduction and the essays themselves can convey a small sense of the blessing we enjoyed in April 2006 at the conference itself. Beyond the speakers, we owe heartfelt gratitude to others whose gracious support and encouragement make the Wheaton Theology Conference possible—for particular assistance we thank Liz Klassen, Peter Kline as well as Bruce Knowlton and the staff at the media resources department. David Hooker organized a wonderful art exhibit with the cooperation of Buswell Memorial Library. Fellow theologians at Wheaton continue to provide wise counsel and ongoing support in many ways; David Lauber was especially helpful with this project.

Furthermore, the conference and work of scholarship represented by this volume would simply not happen without the financial assistance of Inter-Varsity Press and, in particular, the friendly advice of Bob Fryling, publisher, and Gary Deddo, associate editor for academic books. Finally, we express our thanks to the dean of humanities and theological studies, Jill Peláez Baumgaertner and the associate dean of the biblical and theological studies department, Jeffrey Greenman, for their ongoing care and attention to fostering theological scholarship at Wheaton College.

PART ONE

Music

Responding to the Beauty
of the Triune Creator

CREATED BEAUTY

The Witness of J. S. Bach

Jeremy S. Begbie

Among the millions of words spoken and written about J. S. Bach's *Goldberg Variations* of 1741, few are as intriguing as those of the musicologist Peter Williams when he stands back from this dazzling *tour de force* and reflects:

> I think myself that it "feels special" because, whatever antecedent this or that feature has, its beauty is both original—seldom like anything else, even in Bach—and at the same time comprehensible, intelligible, coherent, based on simple, "truthful" harmonies.[1]

Most of what I want to say in this chapter[2] is suggested by that observation (even though Williams himself would probably demur at the theological slant I shall be putting on his words). The matter he brings to the surface is the interplay between two types of beauty: on the one hand, the beauty which is in some sense already "there" in the nature of things (the beauty of "truthful" harmonies), and on the other, the beauty human beings make (the "original" beauty of a piece like the *Goldberg*). Put more theologically, there is the beauty directly given to the world by God, and that which we are invited to fashion as God's creatures. Taking our cue from Williams, the question we shall be pursuing in this chapter is: how might an engagement with Bach's music, especially as considered in its time and place, assist us in gain-

---

[1] Peter F. Williams, *Bach: The Goldberg Variations* (Cambridge: Cambridge University Press, 2001), p. 1.

[2] I am very grateful to Dr. Suzanne McDonald and Dona McCullagh for their very valuable comments on an earlier draft of this chapter.

ing a clearer theological perception and understanding of these two senses of created beauty, and of the relation between them?

Theological Bearings

We shall turn to Bach in due course. The first task, however, is to say something about the concept of "beauty" itself, to clarify what we might intend by this fluid and much-contested notion, and in particular, what might be entailed in a specifically *theological* perspective on it. With limited space, I cannot attempt anything like a comprehensive "theology of the beautiful," but we do at least need to gain some theological bearings—that is, highlight key features of the theological landscape that are especially relevant to a responsible Christian account of beauty and the ways in which such an account is affected by them.

Our primary orientation, of course, will not be to an experience of the beautiful, nor to an aesthetics, but to the quite specific God attested in Scripture—the gracious, reconciling, self-revealing God of Jesus Christ. If an account of beauty is to be *theo-logical* in Christian terms, its *logos* or rationale will take its shape primarily from the being and acts of this *theos*. Crassly obvious as this may seem, even a casual survey of religious treatments and theologies of beauty over the last thirty years will frequently show a marked lack of attention to the identity of the deity or deities being presumed. Difficulties are compounded if the de facto basic allegiance is to some prior and fixed conception of beauty, especially if it is allied to a metaphysical scheme whose consonance with the testimony of Scripture is anything but clear. If we are to think of the phenomenon of beauty, at least initially, in terms of the main strands that inform the so-called "great theory" (and I see no compelling reason not to do so)—in other words, *proportion and consonance of parts, brightness* or resplendence, *perfection* or integrity, and as *affording pleasure upon contemplation*[3]—then these strands need to be con-

---

[3]See Wladyslaw Tatarkiewicz, "The Great Theory of Beauty and Its Decline," *The Journal of Aesthetics and Art Criticism* 31 (1972): 165-80. (Nicholas Wolterstorff rightly points out that although Tatarkiewicz sees consonance of parts as identical with due proportion, not all the writers Tatarkiewicz cites presume this [Nicholas Wolterstorff, *Art in Action: Toward a Christian Aesthetic* (Grand Rapids: Eerdmans, 1980), p. 162].) I am not suggesting, of course, that these strands together constitute a *definition* of beauty—but they do at least indicate some of the most prominent lines or themes in mainstream Western thinking about beauty. See also Jerome Stolnitz, " 'Beauty': Some Stages in the History of an Idea," *Journal of the History of Ideas* 22, no. 2 (1961): 185-204; Edward Farley, *Faith and Beauty: A Theological Aesthetic* (Aldershot: Ashgate, 2001), pp. 17-26.

stantly re-formed and transformed, purged and purified by a repeated return to the saving self-disclosure of Scripture's God.

Needless to say, this will sound to some like an appeal for a sectarian retreat into a Christian ghetto, an isolationist "fideism" that rules out conversation with all but Christians. Nothing of the sort is intended. The point is not to close down dialogue about beauty with those outside or on the edges of Christian tradition, nor with the vast corpus of philosophical writings on beauty. The issue is at root about the norms shaping our language. If a conversation about "beauty" is to be fruitful, one cannot *but* care about the criteria governing the deployment of such a historically loaded and polysemous word—for how can speech bear fruit if it has ceased to care about its primary responsibilities? And to care about these criteria, for the Christian at any rate, is ultimately to care about the God to whom the church turns for the reshaping of all its words.

A Christian account of beauty, then, will be oriented to a particular God. Let me press the matter. According to the Christian tradition, this God has identified himself as irreducibly *trinitarian*. The deity celebrated in Christian faith is not an undifferentiated monad or blank "Absence," but a triunity of inexhaustible love and life, active and present to the world as triune and never more intensively than in the saving life, death and resurrection of Jesus Christ. If, then, we are to speak of God as primordially beautiful—however we may want to qualify this—then strenuous care must be taken to ensure it is *this* God of whom we speak.[4] If we speak of divine proportion

---

[4]It was a rigorous concern for the specificity of theology's God that made Karl Barth so circumspect about ascribing beauty to God—perhaps excessively so (Karl Barth, *Church Dogmatics* 2/1, trans. G. W. Bromiley and T. F. Torrance [Edinburgh: T & T Clark, 1957], pp. 650-66). As so often with this theologian, the fear is of an intrusive a priori that in some manner constrains God, a "transcendental" to which God is made answerable—and the particular anxiety here is Hellenism. So Barth insists: "God is not beautiful in the sense that he shares in an idea of beauty superior to him, so that to know it is to know him as God. On the contrary, it is as he is God that he is also beautiful, so that he is the basis and standard of everything that is beautiful and of all ideas of the beautiful" (ibid., p. 656). Hence Barth will not allow beauty to be a "leading concept" in the doctrine of God. It is secondary to God's glory, an "explanation" of it; beauty is the "form" of God's glory—that about his self-revealing glory which attracts rather than repels, which redeems, persuades and convinces, evokes joy rather than indifference. One might wish Barth had developed these views rather more extensively, and especially in relation to creaturely beauty, but his *methodological* concerns, I would suggest, are to be seriously heeded. (One of the most puzzling things about David Bentley Hart's substantial recent book on the aesthetics of Christian truth—*The Beauty of the Infinite: The Aesthetics of Christian Truth* [Grand Rapids: Eerdmans, 2003]—is that he is frequently very close to Barth methodologically, yet what few remarks he makes about Barth are extraordinarily dismissive. Among

and consonance, can these be any other than the proportion and consonance of this triune God? If we speak of divine brightness, integrity or perfection, can these be any other than the brightness, integrity and perfection of the trinitarian life? Everything depends here on refusing all a priori abstractions and maintaining a resolute focus on the saving economy of God in Jesus Christ. Divine beauty is discovered not in the first instance by reference to a doctrine (still less to a philosophy of beauty) but by strict attention to a movement in history enacted for us—supremely the story of Jesus Christ the incarnate Son, living in the Father's presence in the power of the Spirit. Trinitarian beauty has, so to speak, been performed for us.[5]

To begin to unfold the implications of this: if beauty is to be ascribed primordially to the triune God, and the life of God is constituted by the dynamism of outgoing love, then primordial beauty is *the beauty of this ecstatic love for the other.* God's beauty is not static structure but the dynamism of love. The "proportion and consonance" of God, his "brightness" or radiance, his "perfection" and his affording "pleasure upon contemplation" are all to be understood in the light of the endless self-donation of Father to Son and Son to Father in the ecstatic momentum of the Spirit. Hence we find Balthasar insisting that it is to the economy of salvation that we must go to discover God's beauty (and thus the ultimate measure of all beauty), since the incarnation, death and raising of Jesus display God's love in its clearest and most decisive form; here, above all, we witness the mutual self-surrendering love of Father and Son in the Spirit for the healing of the world.[6] This linking

---

the reviews I have read, only Robert Jenson's points this out ["Review Essay: David Bentley Hart, *The Beauty of the Infinite: The Aesthetics of Christian Truth,*" *Pro Ecclesia* 4, no. 2 (2005): 236].)
[5]So Hans Urs von Balthasar writes that we "ought never to speak of God's beauty without reference to the form and manner of appearing which he exhibits in salvation-history." And later: "God's attribute of beauty can certainly . . . be examined in the context of a doctrine of the divine attributes. Besides examining God's beauty as manifested by God's actions in his creation, his beauty would also be deduced from the harmony of his essential attributes, and particularly from the Trinity. But such a doctrine of God and the Trinity really speaks to us only when and as long as the *theologia* does not become detached from the *oikonomia,* but rather lets its every formulation and stage of reflection be accompanied and supported by the latter's vivid discernibility" (see Hans Urs von Balthasar, *The Glory of the Lord. A Theological Aesthetics,* vol. 1, *Seeing the Form,* trans. Erasmo Leivà-Merikakis [Edinburgh: T & T Clark, 1982], pp. 124, 125).
[6]Speaking of God's saving economy, Balthasar writes: "should we not . . . consider this 'art' of God's to be precisely the transcendent archetype of all worldly and human beauty?" (ibid., p. 70). In this respect we can also join Jonathan Edwards when he writes of "primary beauty," whose chief instance is God's own triune benevolence, the mutual generosity and "infinite consent" that constitutes the life of God. See Roland A. Delattre, *Beauty and Sensibility in the*

of beauty with outgoing love requires giving a full and crucial place to the *Holy Spirit* in connection with beauty—as we shall see many times. Insofar as the Spirit is the personal unity of the mutual outgoingness of Father and Son, the impulse toward self-sharing in God's life, we might well describe the Spirit as the "beautifier" in God.[7]

Giving the trinitarian character of God its formal and material due means *we will resist the temptation to drive apart beauty and the infinite,* something that is so much a mark of modernity and postmodernity. Here we can have some sympathy with John Milbank and others who lament what they see as the modern rupture of beauty and the sublime, evident especially since the eighteenth century.[8] As understood in the tradition represented by Kant, the experience of the sublime is an awareness of being overwhelmed by something uncontainable, beyond our grasp. In Kant this is either mainly "mathematical"—when we are overwhelmed by size and are confronted with the limits of our sense perception (such as we might experience under a starry sky or when suddenly faced with a mountain massif), or "dynamical"— when we are overwhelmed by a power that makes us acutely aware of our own finitude and physical vulnerability (such as we might feel in a raging storm).[9] On this reading, it should be stressed, the sublime is unrepresentable to the senses and the imagination, and as such can provoke not only awe and wonderment but also unease and even terror. Beauty, by contrast, is radically tied to the ordering of the mind. The experience of beauty, for Kant, is the experience of the cognitive faculties of the imagination and the

---

Thought of Jonathan Edwards: An Essay in Aesthetics and Theological Ethics (New Haven, Conn.: Yale University Press, 1968), chaps. 7-8; Amy Plantinga Pauw, *"The Supreme Harmony of All": The Trinitarian Theology of Jonathan Edwards* (Grand Rapids: Eerdmans, 2002); Farley, *Faith and Beauty,* chap. 4.

We recall the woman pouring expensive ointment over Jesus' head. Jesus rebukes his disciples for complaining: "She has done a beautiful thing to me" (Mt 26:10). Her "giving everything" has been provoked by, and perhaps even in some manner shares in, the divine self-giving in and through Jesus.

[7]For a thorough exposition of the Spirit in relation to beauty, see Patrick Sherry, *Spirit and Beauty: An Introduction to Theological Aesthetics,* (London: SCM Press, 2002).

[8]John Milbank, "Beauty and the Soul," in *Theological Perspectives on God and Beauty,* ed. John Milbank, Graham Ward and Edith Wyschogrod (Harrisburg, Penn.: Trinity Press International, 2003), pp. 1-34; "Sublimity: The Modern Transcendent," in *Religion, Modernity and Postmodernity,* ed. Paul Heelas (Oxford: Blackwell, 1998), pp. 258-84; Frederick Bauerschmidt, "Aesthetics: The Theological Sublime," in *Radical Orthodoxy: A New Theology* (London: Routledge, 1999), pp. 201-19; Hart, *Beauty of the Infinite,* pp. 43-93.

[9]Immanuel Kant, *Critique of the Power of Judgement,* trans. Paul Guyer and Eric Matthews (Cambridge: Cambridge University Press, 2000), pp. 128-59. See Paul Crowther, *The Kantian Sublime: From Morality to Art* (Oxford: Oxford University Press, 1991).

understanding engaging in free play; the pleasure of the experience is derived from those powers that enable us to arrange a plurality of sense data.[10] The Milbankian argument is that in its approach to beauty and sublimity, the logic of postmodernism is essentially Kantian.[11] Beauty is downplayed (even "annihilated") as formed, tame, ordered and controllable, affecting us through harmony and proportion, whereas the sublime is extolled as formless, untamable, indeterminate and uncontrollable. Transposed into theology: infinite divine transcendence is understood in terms of negation: "modernity and postmodernity tend strictly to *substitute* sublimity for transcendence. This means that all that persists of transcendence is sheer unknowability or its quality of non-representability and non-depictability."[12] As such, the sublime is a *formless* divine presence,[13] devoid of love or goodness, and thus potentially oppressive.[14] In response to these lines of thinking, it is rightly insisted that the sublime should never have been divorced from beauty in the first place, that *beauty* should be thought through first of all in terms of infinity, but that since this infinity is none other than the infinity of the Trinity, it is not formless or shapeless or wholly unrepresentable, but the form-ful beauty of intratrinitarian love revealed in Jesus Christ, and as such can never be oppressive or dehumanizing but only life-enhancing. To quote Rusty Reno, "we are not overpowered by God as a sublime truth; we are romanced by God as pure beauty."[15]

With this primary orientation to the triune God in mind, whose own life is primordially beautiful, we can now turn more specifically to created beauty—and at this stage we will concentrate on created beauty in the first

---

[10]Kant, *Critique of the Power of Judgement*, pp. 89-127.

[11]"Even when Kant's sublime is not directly invoked, its logic (at least, construed in a certain way) is always presumed" (Hart, *Beauty of the Infinite*, pp. 44-45).

[12]Milbank, "Sublimity," p. 259. According to Hart, the key metaphysical assumption is "that the unrepresentable *is;* more to the point, that the unrepresentable . . . is somehow truer than the representable (which necessarily dissembles it), more original, and qualitatively *other;* that is, it does not differ from the representable by virtue of a greater fullness and unity of those transcendental moments that constitute the world of appearance, but by virtue of its absolute difference, its dialectical or negative indeterminacy, its no-thingness" (*Beauty of the Infinite*, p. 52).

[13]"It is just this attempt at once to reconcile and preserve a presumed incompatibility between form and infinity that recurs, almost obsessively, in postmodern thought" (ibid., p. 47).

[14]Hart argues that the entire pathology of the modern and postmodern can be diagnosed in terms of "narratives of the sublime": the differential sublime, the cosmological sublime, the ontological sublime and the ethical sublime (ibid., pp. 52-93).

[15]R. R. Reno, review of *The Beauty of the Infinite: the Aesthetics of Christian Truth* by David Bentley Hart, *Touchstone* <www.touchstonemag.com/archives/article.php?id=17-07-048-b>.

of our two senses, the beauty of the world as created by God.

First, a theological account of created beauty will speak of creation as *testifying to God's beauty, but in its own distinctive ways.* Much here turns on doing full justice to a double grain in Scripture's witness: the Creator's faithful *commitment* to the cosmos he has made, and his commitment to the cosmos *in its otherness.* Creation testifies to God's beauty, but *in its own ways;* or better: God testifies to his own beauty through creation's own beauty.

To take each side of this in turn: there is God's irreversible dedication to all that he has fashioned, a dedication grounded in the intratrinitarian love, "the love that moves the sun and the other stars" (Dante). Basic to this is the Creator's commitment to physical matter, something that blazes forth above all in the incarnation and resurrection of Jesus, where God's first "and it was good" in Genesis is stupendously and decisively reaffirmed. This means spurning any gnosticism that devalues created beauty (including that of the body) on the grounds, say, of its physicality, or out of a mistaken belief in the inherent formlessness of matter. We will resist treating physical beauty as something through which we ascend to immaterial beauty if this means leaving creation's physicality behind as something supposedly lacking reality or essential goodness in the sight of God. Creation's beauty is not, so to speak, something that lives in a land beyond the sensual or behind the material particular or beneath the surface, or wherever—*to which* we must travel. Creation's beauty is just that, the beauty *of creation.* The beauty of a coral reef *is* its endless variegation, play of color, patterned relations; its beautiful forms are the forms *of its matter.*

No less important, however, is acknowledging God's commitment to the flourishing of the world *as other* than God, this otherness arising from and testifying to the otherness of the trinitarian Persons.[16] Creation is indeed "charged" with divine beauty because the Creator is at work through his Spirit bringing things to their proper end in relation to the Father through the Son. But it is charged in its own creaturely ways, according to its own rationality and ordering processes.

There is therefore no need to deny a priori that the beauty of creation can correspond to God's beauty, reflect and bear witness to it, but care is needed

---

[16]Hart, *Beauty of the Infinite,* pp. 249ff. Wolfhart Pannenberg is one of many who want to trace the roots of the distinctiveness of the created world from God in the differentiation of God's intratrinitarian life. See Wolfhart Pannenberg, *Systematic Theology,* vol. 2, trans. Geoffrey W. Bromiley (Grand Rapids: Eerdmans, 1994), pp. 20ff.

if we are to do justice to creation's integrity. Special caution is needed if we find ourselves thinking along Platonic lines: of God as the Form of beauty in which beautiful particular things participate. If we do attempt to discern creaturely signs of God's beauty in creation, we should be careful not to do so on the basis of some presumed *necessity* of created beauty to resemble God's beauty or to resemble it in particular ways, but only on the basis of what God has actually warranted us to affirm by virtue of his particular and gracious acts, climaxing in Jesus Christ. The naiveté of assuming we may simply "read off" God's beauty from creation is most obvious when we are confronted with the creation's corruptions and distortions (however we are to understand these), and when we forget that our perception of creation *as* reflecting God's beauty depends on the work of the Holy Spirit.

It is for these reasons that if we are to speak of creation's beauty "participating" in God's beauty (on the grounds of creation as a whole "participating" in God), we will do so with some hesitation, despite the popularity of this language in some circles.[17] John Webster has drawn attention to the hazards of the "participation" metaphor, especially insofar as it is allowed to carry inappropriate Platonic overtones: for instance, that we will overlook the irreducible Creator-creature distinction and the asymmetry of the God-world relation, that we will fail to understand God's ways with the world through the lens of the particular saving acts of God in the history of Israel and Jesus Christ, that we will forget that any capacity of the creation to reflect or witness to the Creator is graciously given by the Creator.[18] Nevertheless, it is not at all obvious that we need reject the participation model altogether, for arguably there are ways of employing it (as history shows) that can highlight very ef-

---

[17]The notion of participation is central to the "Radical Orthodoxy" movement, with its commitment to a rehabilitated, Christianized Platonism, and its eagerness to overcome any implication that a part of created territory can be thought as independent of God. However, it is far from clear that Radical Orthodoxy's notion of the "suspension of the material" in the divine can do justice to a biblical, dynamic ontology of grace that upholds the irreducible Creator-creature distinction. For discussion, cf. James K. A. Smith, *Introducing Radical Orthodoxy: Mapping a Post-Secular Theology* (Grand Rapids: Baker Academic, 2004), pp. 74-77, 189-95; "Will the Real Plato Please Stand Up? Participation Versus Incarnation," in *Radical Orthodoxy and the Reformed Tradition,* ed. James K. A. Smith and James H. Olthius (Grand Rapids: Baker Academic, 2005), pp. 61-72; Adrienne Dengerink Chaplin, "The Invisible and the Sublime: From Participation to Reconciliation," in *Radical Orthodoxy and the Reformed Tradition,* pp. 89-106.

[18]Webster's objections to the language of "participation" as applied to humans' fellowship with God are succinctly set out in "The Church and the Perfection of God," in *The Community of the Word: Toward an Evangelical Ecclesiology,* ed. Mark Husbands and Daniel J. Treier (Downers Grove, Ill.: InterVarsity Press, 2005), pp. 91ff.

fectively the gracious, prior agency of God, and the contingency of the world upon God's triune life, and without falling into the traps Webster fears.[19]

Second, a theological account of created beauty will return repeatedly to *Jesus Christ as the one in whom creation has reached its eschatological goal.* If Christ is the measure of divine beauty, so also of created beauty. In Jesus Christ, divine beauty has, so to speak, got to grips with the wounded and deformed beauty of the world; in the incarnate Son, crucified, risen and now exalted, we witness God's re-creation of the world's beauty. The one through whom all things are upheld (Heb 1:3), by whom all things are held together (Col 1:17), by whose blood all things are reconciled to God (Col 1:20), is "the firstborn of all creation . . . the beginning, the firstborn from the dead" (Col 1:15, 18), the one in whom all things will finally be gathered up (Eph 1:10). In the risen and ascended Christ, creation's beauty has reached its culmination. Here we see physical matter transformed into the conditions of the age to come, granting us a preview of that age when the earth will be filled with the glory of God as the waters cover the sea.

Third, a theological account of created beauty will return repeatedly to *the Holy Spirit as the one who realizes now in our midst what has been achieved in the Son, thus anticipating the future.* (This is the prime antidote to the pathology of nostalgia of which Bruce Herman speaks in his essay in this volume.[20]) A Christian account of created beauty is thus charged with

---

[19]See the trenchant treatment of Calvin's handling of the theme in Julie Canlis, "Calvin, Osiander and Participation in God," *International Journal of Systematic Theology* 6, no. 2 (2004): 169-84; and the wider discussion of participation in relation to theological language in Alan J. Torrance, *Persons in Communion: An Essay on Trinitarian Description and Human Participation* (Edinburgh: T & T Clark, 1996), pp. 307ff. The critical point is this: the first and primary control on the semantics of "participation" should be the New Testament notion of *koinonia,* not the Platonic concept of *methexis* (the participation of particulars in eternal forms)—whatever wisdom may be justifiably gleaned from the latter. The large issue lurking in the background here is that of the "analogy of being" *(analogia entis),* the analogical correspondences between divine and created reality, a notion that in various forms has exercised considerable influence on philosophies and theologies of beauty. For an exceptionally clear-headed treatment of this matter, cf. Alan J. Torrance, *Persons in Communion,* pp. 356ff. Torrance properly urges that we do not presume an ontological continuity between the divine and created realms that is conceptualized apart from and independently of God's self-revelation in Christ. There are subtle and important differences between Balthasar and Barth on this matter; cf. John Webster, "Balthasar and Karl Barth," in *The Cambridge Companion to Hans Urs Von Balthasar,* ed. Edward T. Oakes and David Moss (Cambridge: Cambridge University Press, 2004), pp. 248ff.

[20]This dimension is brought out strongly in Eberhard Jüngel's penetrating essay on beauty, " 'Even the Beautiful Must Die'—Beauty in the Light of Truth. Theological Observations on the Aesthetic Relation," in *Theological Essays II,* ed. John Webster (Edinburgh: T & T Clark, 1995), pp. 59-81.

promise. It is not chiefly determined by a sense of a paradise lost but of a glory still to appear, the old beauty remade and transfigured, the beauty of the future that has already been embodied in Christ: "the beautiful is only the pre-appearance of the coming truth . . . [it] carries within itself the *promise* of truth to come, a future *direct* encounter with truth . . . the beautiful is a *pre-appearance directed to a goal.*"[21] Here there is much to be said for the ancient wisdom of Basil the Great (c. 330-379) for whom the Holy Spirit "perfects" creation, enabling it to flourish in anticipation of the final future.[22] Beauty we apprehend now is a Spirit-given foretaste of the beauty still to be given, in the midst of a creation that languishes in bondage to corruption, groans in anticipation of a glory not yet revealed (Rom 8:20-22). Hence the dazzling mountain scene that takes our breath away should not provoke us to try to seize and freeze the moment, but to give thanks and look ahead to the beauty of the new heaven and the new earth, of which this world's finest beauty is but a miniscule glimpse. We delight in the world's beauty *as* we lament its transience. To borrow William Blake's words:

> He who binds to himself a joy
> Does the winged life destroy;
> But he who kisses the joy as it flies
> Lives in eternity's sunrise.[23]

What is true of joy here is no less true of beauty.

Fourth, a theological account of created beauty, oriented to Christ and the Spirit, and thus to a trinitarian God, will delight in *a diversity of particulars.* If beauty's integrity involves a "proportion of parts," these parts are just that, distinct parts or particulars in various measured relations with each other. And these particulars, in order for beauty to be manifest, are not normally identical but will manifest diversity as they relate to each other, at least at some level. In Gerard Manley Hopkins's words, creation's beauty is a "pied" beauty: "dappled things," "skies of couple-colour as a brinded cow," "rose-moles all in stipple upon trout that swim," "Fresh-firecoal chestnut-falls; finches' wings"—all these things "Praise him."[24] Creation sings *laus Deo* in

---

[21]Ibid., p. 76.
[22]Sherry, *Spirit and Beauty,* chap. 7. For a recent treatment of the Holy Spirit as the one who frees creation, see Sigurd Bergmann, *Creation Set Free: The Spirit as Liberator of Nature* (Grand Rapids: Eerdmans, 2005).
[23]"Eternity," in W. H. Stevenson, ed., *The Complete Poems—Second Edition* (London: Longman, 1989), p. 189.
[24]Gerard Manley Hopkins, "Pied Beauty" (1877).

and through its ineffaceable diversity of particularities. Here again the ministry of the Spirit comes to the fore. The Spirit is the "particularizer" (sadly, something not seen strongly in Hopkins): unifying and uniting, certainly, but in so doing liberating things to be the particular things they are created to be. The beautiful unity that the Spirit generates is not one of homogenized harmony or bland replication, but one in which the unique particularity of things is enabled and promoted; it is the Spirit's office "to realise the true being of each created thing by bringing it, through Christ, into saving relation with God the Father."[25] The spring of this is of course to be found in the Godhead, whose unified life is not monadic sameness or an undifferentiated oneness more fundamental than the Persons, but a life of divine "particulars-in-relation," in which the Spirit (we may tentatively suggest) "particularizes" the persons of Father and Son, constituting and realizing them as persons-in-communion.

Fifth, a theological account of created beauty will be *wary of closed harmonies*. We may indeed articulate beauty in terms of proportion and perfection or integrity, but if beauty is to be rethought out of a center in the being and acts of the triune God, we will be guarded about accounts of created beauty that interpret such notions primarily or exclusively in terms of balance, symmetry and equivalence. As far as divine beauty is concerned, if the "measure" of beauty is outgoing love for the sake of the other, it will not be long before we are forced to come to terms with *excess* or *uncontainability*, the intratrinitarian life being one of a ceaseless overflow of self-giving. There is still proportion and integrity, but it is the proportion and integrity of abundant love.

Creation, by grace, is given to share in this "excess"—indeed, creation's very existence is the result of the overflow of divine love—albeit in its own creaturely ways. So God's beautiful extravagance takes creaturely form in the oversupply of wine at Cana, the welcome Jesus shows to outcasts and sinners, the undeserved forgiveness in the first light of Easter Day. This is how creation's deformed beauty is remade, not by a repair or "return to normality," but by a re-creation exceeding all balance, by a love that is absurdly lavish and profligate, surplus to all "requirement," overflowing beyond anything demanded or expected, generous beyond measure.

---

[25]Colin E. Gunton, *The One, the Three and the Many* (Cambridge: Cambridge University Press, 1993), p. 189. This is a strand of pneumatology explored very fully by Gunton; see ibid., especially chap. 7.

This in turn means taking the creation's *contingency* seriously, giving due recognition to the unpredictable, to that which does not simply flow out of the past but which is nonetheless consistent and fruitful, to the new devel- opments that God is constantly bringing forth from his world. Those work- ing at the borderlands of contemporary science and theology have not been slow to engage with such ideas, giving rise to various proposals for a meta- physics of "contingent order."[26] Whatever weight we give to this or that emerging cosmology, the widespread questioning of closed mechanistic models in the natural sciences should at least give us pause for thought. Once again, a danger often lurking here is a defective account of the Holy Spirit, in which we describe the Spirit's role chiefly (solely?) in terms of ef- fecting return and closure, completing a circle. This has the unfortunate ef- fect of neglecting the Spirit's role as improviser, bringing about a faithful novelty, fresh improvisations consistent with what has been achieved "once and for all" in Christ.[27] The other great danger of overharmonious models of beauty is that they will be singularly ill-equipped to take the evilness of evil seriously, evil's sheer irrationality (this matter I address in chapter two).

Sixth, an account of created beauty will recognize that beauty *elicits desire*—a desire to dwell with and enjoy that which we experience as beau- tiful. This links up with those currents in the "great theory" that speak of beauty's brightness (and thus attraction), and the pleasure it affords upon contemplation. There is, of course, a massive literature in Christian history on the attractiveness of God's beauty, and the love and desire *(eros)* that God's beauty evokes in us. Understandably, many are nervous about the al- liance of beauty and desire, especially in a theological context. From a philo- sophical perspective those in the Kantian tradition will suspect that desire spells the end of aesthetics (and, indeed, ethics), for to allow "interest" a constitutive role in aesthetic enjoyment is to destroy its character as contem-

---

[26]For different examples, see T. F. Torrance, *Divine and Contingent Order* (Edinburgh: T & T Clark, 1998); J. C. Polkinghorne and Michael Welker, *The End of the World and the Ends of God: Science and Theology on Eschatology* (Harrisburg, Penn.: Trinity Press International, 2000), chap. 1; A. R. Peacocke, *Creation and the World of Science* (Oxford: Clarendon, 1979); Jean-Jacques Suurmond, *Word and Spirit at Play: Towards a Charismatic Theology* (Grand Rapids: Eerdmans, 1994).

[27]In this regard, with respect to human history, Ben Quash makes some pointed critical com- ments about Balthasar, especially in relation to his theodramatics, questioning whether he has allowed the "epic" character of his thought to engender an approach to history that cannot do justice to the humanly contingent (*Theology and the Drama of History* [Cambridge: Cam- bridge University Press, 2005]).

plative dispassion. From a theological perspective the suspicion may well derive from a sharp contrast sometimes made between "desire" and "love," *eros* and *agape*, the former understood in an instrumentalist sense as possessive and consuming, the latter as selfless self-giving for the sake of the other as other. To permit *eros* a place in Christian faith, it is said, is to open the door to the subjugation of the other, to an inevitable violation of the other's integrity.

Much recent writing has sought to counter these suspicions.[28] Without space to enter a complex field, I might at least say the following. Just as the triune God lives as an endless movement of attraction and delight, so God does not make himself available as an object for dispassionate scrutiny but in an overture of enticement, through which by the Spirit's agency we are made to long for God's presence, indeed, thirst for him. God "attracts our attention" by the outgoing Spirit, enabling us to respond, catching us up into the divine life. Indeed, can we not say that to experience the allure of God *is* nothing other than to experience the Spirit reconciling us to the Father through the Son and thus reordering our desires?[29] No wedge need be driven between *agape* and *eros* provided the latter is not allowed to introduce notions of subsuming the "other" under manipulative restraint; indeed, as David Bentley Hart puts it, God's love, and hence the love with which we come to love God, is "eros and agape at once: a desire for the other that delights in the distance of otherness."[30] As far as created beauty is concerned, beauty in the world that glorifies this God will also evoke desire—a yearning to explore and take pleasure in whatever is beautiful. There need be no shame in this provided our delight is delight in the other *as other*, and as long as we regularly recall that our love for God is the *cantus firmus* that enables all other desires to flourish.[31]

Bach and Created Beauty

With these theological bearings in mind, expressed all too briefly, we may

---

[28]See, e.g., Karl Barth, *Church Dogmatics* 3/2, trans. G. W. Bromiley and T. F. Torrance (Edinburgh: T & T Clark, 1960), pp. 279-85; Timothy Gorringe, *The Education of Desire: Towards a Theology of the Senses* (London: SCM, 2001); Paul D. L. Avis, *Eros and the Sacred* (London: SPCK, 1989); Hart, *Beauty of the Infinite*, pp. 19-20, 188-92.

[29]Cf. Balthasar, *Glory of the Lord*, 1:121. Balthasar is rightly eager to reshape certain Platonic and Neo-Platonic conceptions of *eros* in the light of God's own self-communication in the economy of salvation.

[30]Hart, *Beauty of the Infinite*, p. 20.

[31]Dietrich Bonhoeffer, *Letters and Papers from Prison* (London: SCM Press, 1972), p. 303.

turn to the music of J. S. Bach (1685-1750). How might an engagement with
Bach's music, especially as considered in its time and place, help us gain a
clearer theological perception and understanding of created beauty—beauty
of the sort we have just been adumbrating? To avoid methodological confusion, two preliminary points need to be made. First, in an exercise of this
sort, the controlling truth criteria are not provided by music; Bach's music
does not and cannot be allowed to provide norms for beauty that are more
ultimate or determinative than those given in the self-disclosure of the triune
God in Jesus Christ. Nevertheless, and this is the second point, it is quite
legitimate to ask whether, *within* the theological bearings provided by these
criteria (some of which we have just outlined), music might make its own
unique contribution to the perception and understanding of created beauty.
And this is my concern here. Such an approach depends on (1) acknowledging that music is an art that is irreducible to the verbal forms of theological discourse, yet (2) allowing for the possibility that it might nevertheless
be able to engage the realities with which that discourse deals, and in ways
that afford genuine discovery and truthful articulation of them.[32]

We can focus down our concern by asking: what kind of cosmos, under
God, might Bach's music provoke us to imagine, and thus what vision of
created beauty? Is there anything to support Hart's bold claim that "Bach's
is the ultimate Christian music; it reflects as no other human artefact ever has
or could the Christian vision of creation"?[33]

To begin with, we need to clarify some of the features of the way this
composer typically operates. Of special importance is something that Lau-
rence Dreyfus has recently argued was central to Bach's art, namely "invention" *(inventio)*.[34] Many pianists' first introduction to Bach will be one of his
two-part "inventions."[35] The composer tells us these were designed to serve
as models for "good inventions" and "developing the same satisfactorily."
What does he mean?

The word *inventio* derives from classical rhetoric, and in Bach's time was

---

[32]For discussion of what is entailed here, see Jeremy Begbie, *Theology, Music and Time* (Cambridge: Cambridge University Press, 2000), chap. 10; "The Theological Potential of Music:
A Response to Adrienne Dengerink Chaplin," *Christian Scholar's Review* 33, no. 1 (2003):
135-41.

[33]Hart, *Beauty of the Infinite*, p. 283. I am strongly indebted in this section to Hart's short but
superb discussion of Bach (ibid., pp. 282-85).

[34]Laurence Dreyfus, *Bach and the Patterns of Invention* (Cambridge, Mass.: Harvard University
Press, 2004).

[35]See J. S. Bach, "Inventions and Sinfonias," *Aufrichtige Anleitung* (BWV 772-801).

widely used as a metaphor for the basic musical idea, the unit of music that formed the subject matter of a piece. Not only this, it denoted the process of discovering that fundamental idea. The key for Bach was to find *generative* material, an idea that was capable of being developed in a variety of ways, for "by crafting a workable idea, one unlocks the door to a complete musical work."[36] So the method of finding an invention was inseparable from thinking about how it might be developed—*elaboratio,* to use the rhetorical term. Hence Bach's concern to show us models of good inventions *and* of their development.

So, for example, the first of the two-part inventions begins:

Figure 1.1. The first of Bach's two-part inventions

Section "A" marks an invention.[37] Bach has found that the opening figure of this invention can be turned upside down (inverted) in a musically convincing way. So the seven-note figure in the first measure

Figure 1.2. Seven-note figure in the first measure

in the third measure becomes

Figure 1.3. Inverted seven-note figure

---

[36]Dreyfus, *Bach and the Patterns of Invention,* p. 2.

[37]An invention is thus not a "theme" in the modern sense of the word—in this case the invention includes the same theme played twice. An invention is *the entire unit of music* that will provide material for development.

Indeed, this inversion is itself part of a secondary invention (beginning in the third measure). Both these core inventions have been chosen with a view to what can be elaborated from them. They can be subjected very effectively to voice exchange, melodic inversion, switching from major to minor and so forth—as Bach goes on to demonstrate. I cannot here trace all the elaborations displayed in this one piece.[38] What needs stressing, however, is Bach's intense interest and skill in this elaborative dimension. The evidence suggests that most of his contemporaries viewed *elaboratio* as among the most unexciting parts of composing and could treat it almost casually. Bach appears to have thought about extensive elaboration even from the start, when choosing the initial material. As Dreyfus puts it, "One might even be tempted to say that in Bach's works both invention and elaboration are marked by an almost equally intense mental activity. . . . In no other composer of the period does one find such a fanatical zeal directed so often toward what others considered the least interesting parts of a composition."[39] Indeed, Bach seems to have had an almost superhuman eye for how relatively simple sets of notes would combine, cohere and behave in different groupings. His son, C. P. E. Bach, famously testified to how his father used to hear the main theme of a fugue played or sung by someone else, predict what would be done with it and then elbow his son gleefully when he was proved right.[40] In short, as Christoph Wolff puts it, the principle of elaboration, "determines like nothing else Bach's art and personal style."[41]

With these preliminary remarks about *inventio* and *elaboratio* in mind, we can begin to open up the theological dimensions of our inquiry by highlighting certain features typical of the musical fabric of a vast number of Bach's pieces.

First, we hear an *elaboration governed not chiefly by an external, pregiven logic but first and foremost by the musical material itself.* Dreyfus's research

---

[38]For a full treatment, see Dreyfus, *Bach and the Patterns of Invention*, pp. 10-26.

[39]Ibid., pp. 22, 24.

[40]"When [J. S. Bach] listened to a rich and many-voiced fugue, he could soon say, after the first entries of the subjects, what contrapuntal devices it would be possible to apply, and which of them the composer by rights ought to apply, and on such occasions, when I was standing next to him, and he had voiced his surmises to me, he would joyfully nudge me when his expectations were fulfilled" (C. P. E. Bach, in *The New Bach Reader: A Life of Johann Sebastian Bach in Letters and Documents,* ed. Hans T. David, Arthur Mendel, and Christoph Wolff [New York: W. W. Norton, 1998], p. 396).

[41]Christoph Wolff, *Johann Sebastian Bach: The Learned Musician* (New York and London: Norton, 2000), p. 469.

has shown that, whatever the precise order in which Bach composed a piece, it is highly inappropriate to envision him starting with a fixed, precise and unalterable "form" and then proceeding to fill it with music; rather we would be better understanding him *searching for inventions with rich potential, and accordingly finding an appropriate form.* In other words, this is an art in which the musical material is not forced into preconceived strict grids but structured according to the shapes that appear to be latent in it and thus apt for it. For Bach, we recall, *inventio* and *elaboratio* were the chief disciplines; *dispositio*—the disposition or arrangement of the elaborations in a particular order—was a subsidiary process (as was *decoratio,* the art of decorating or embellishing).[42] This is not, of course, to claim that Bach had only a passing interest in large-scale structure, or that he never worked with basic formal outlines. The point is rather that he does not seem to be driven chiefly by prior structural schemes that require strict adherence in advance, but far more by the local and specific material he handles. A fugue, for instance, is more like a texture with conventions than it is a PowerPoint template.[43]

It is this aspect of Bach that has been obscured by some scholars' fascination with number schemes and mathematics in his music. There is little doubt that Bach was greatly charmed by numbers, that he used some number symbolism in his music and that some of this symbolism is theological.[44] But this has not only led some scholars to construct vast and fanciful theories on the flimsiest of evidence;[45] it has also led to a neglect of the extent to which Bach, even in his most "mathematical" pieces, includes material that is anything but

---

[42]Dreyfus: "if a passage was to be transformed several times during the course of a piece, Bach must have planned at least some of its transformations in advance." In other words, "there is every reason to suppose that he composed some of it *out of order*" (Dreyfus, *Bach and the Patterns of Invention,* p. 13).

[43]This is why genre was far more important than large-scale form for Bach and why so many of Bach's pieces modify and even disrupt traditional forms; "form was seen . . . as an occasional feature of a genre, and not the general theoretical category subsuming the genres that it later became" (ibid., p. 28).

[44]The "Sanctus" ("Holy, Holy, Holy") from the *Mass in B Minor,* to cite one instance, is pervaded with threeness. Calvin Stapert remarks: "if Bach did not use number symbolism, there are a remarkable number of remarkably apt coincidences in his music" (Calvin Stapert, "Christus Victor: Bach's St. John Passion," *Reformed Journal* 39 [1989]: 17).

[45]Some, for example, hold that Bach frequently employs a number alphabet, each number corresponding to a letter, such that the number of notes, rests or bars or whatever, carry theologically coded messages or allusions. This has been roundly criticized, and in any case, the particular connections drawn between numbers and music in Bach are often of meager theological value. For further discussion, cf. Ruth Tatlow, *Bach and the Riddle of the Number Alphabet* (Cambridge: Cambridge University Press, 1991).

mathematically elegant. So, for instance, although we find ample evidence in the *Goldberg Variations* of mathematical sequences and symmetries, we find these interlaced with striking and surprising irregularity.[46]

In sum, Bach seems far more intent on exploring the logic and potential of the musical material in hand than being driven by extramusical schemes of organization.[47] If we allow this aspect of his music to provoke a vision of the creation as God's handiwork possessed of beauty, it is one in which creation is not, so to speak, a text that hides a more basic group of meanings. Rather than theological schemes in which forms are given an eternal status in God's mind,[48] or schemes in which God initially creates ideas or forms and then subsequently creates the world, or schemes in which matter is created first and then shaped into forms, is it not more true to the biblical affirmation of the goodness and integrity of creation to affirm that it is created directly out of nothing, such that *it has its own appropriate forms,* forms that God honors and enables to flourish as intrinsic to the matter itself?[49] This links directly to what I have said about creation possessing its own creaturely beauty to which the Creator is wholly committed; creaturely beauty testifies to God's trinitarian beauty, certainly, but in its own distinctive ways. Creation's forms are beautiful as the forms *of its matter;* only after acknowledging this can we ask about how these might witness to the beauty of the triune God.

Second, we are provoked to hear, in a way that has perhaps never been surpassed, *difference as intrinsic to unity.* Bach's skill in deriving so much music from such tiny musical units means that he can offer intense experiences of the simultaneous combination of extreme unity and extreme com-

---

[46]Williams helpfully lists some of them: "The opening and closing irregularity of the dance-arabesque-canon sequences; the sheer difference in musical genre between the movements, irrespective of their part in the sequence (e.g. whether or not they are canons); the exploring of both twos and threes, both to the ear and the eyes; the irregular placing of the minor variations and slow movements; the variety in the arabesques (not always two voices) and canons (not always threes); the absence of other symmetries that would have been easy to organize (e.g. if the canons at the perfect fourth and fifth are *inversus,* why not the canon at the perfect octave?)" (Williams, *Bach: The Goldberg Variations,* p. 46).

[47]To borrow some words from John Milbank on baroque music, "Structural supports are . . . overrun by the designs they are supposed to contain" (*Theology and Social Theory: Beyond Secular Reason* [Oxford: Blackwell, 1990], p. 429).

[48]On this, see the perceptive discussion in Colin E. Gunton, *The Triune Creator: A Historical and Systematic Study* (Edinburgh: Edinburgh University Press, 1998), pp. 77-79.

[49]I am not, of course, suggesting Bach was creating out of nothing; the point is about "working with the grain of the universe," seeing form as intrinsic to matter.

plexity. Even the resolutions in his music rarely undo its richness: the reconciliation at the end of the "Dona Nobis Pacem" fugue at the end of his *Mass in B Minor,* for example, does not cancel out any of the diversity of this huge work. Indeed, Bach is adept at helping us perceive rich complexity *in* the apparently simple. In the *Goldberg Variations,* we are given thirty variations on the bass line of a lyrical and stately sarabande. After an hour and a quarter of *elaboratio,* he asks for the aria to be played at the end, *da capo,* note for note. It is hard, if not impossible, to hear it without the memory of the variations, of all that has been done with the aria's bass line. In other words, we now hear the aria *as* varied, replete with diversity, full of humor and sadness, merriment and melancholy. At this point, the aria, we might say, *is* its *elaboration;* it is not more real than its diverse variations. (For Bach, we recall, *elaboratio* is no less important than the invention. If Dreyfus is right, Bach heard simplicity *as* elaborated simplicity.)

The links with our earlier theological material on creation's beauty—seen through the double lens of Christ and the Spirit—will be clear. The diverse particulars of creation are not an elaboration on some more profound, more basic, uniform simplicity, any more than the threefoldness of the Creator is the expression of a more basic singularity (as in modalism). In Hart's words, "The 'theme' of creation is the gift of the whole."[50] And this diversity of particulars-in-unity is not negated in the new heaven and the new earth, but there finds its full and final glory: the beauty of that endless day is surely not the beauty of one note, but of an eternally proliferating "polyphony."

Third, we are provoked to hear the *simultaneous presence of radical openness and radical consistency.* With almost any piece of Bach—although perhaps most of all in the solo instrumental works—the music will sound astonishingly contingent, free of necessity. Not only does Bach constantly adapt and reshape the forms and styles he inherits; even within the constraints he sets for himself for a piece, there is a remarkable contingency—Peter Williams even uses the word "caprice" of this aspect of the *Goldberg Variations.*[51] There is a wildness about Bach's beauty.

This is why I have deliberately avoided the word *organic.* Tempting as it might be to say that the elaborations "organically" emerge from the inventions like plants from seeds, there is in fact rarely anything organic about Bach's music—in the sense of the quasi-inevitable, smooth, continuous, un-

[50]Hart, *Beauty of the Infinite,* p. 282.
[51]Williams, *Bach: The Goldberg Variations,* p. 46.

folding of an idea or motif. Dreyfus ruthlessly exposes the inappropriateness of "organicism" as applied to Bach, arguing that such models are too closed, too prone to the logic of necessity, suppressing the place of human agency and historical circumstance.[52] Even without demonstration of this sort, however, we can perform a simple experiment to grasp the point: listen to almost any of the pieces for solo violin, stop the CD midway through a movement, and unless we happen to know the piece well, it is virtually impossible to predict what comes next. Yet what does follow is filled with sense: "each note is an unforced, unnecessary, and yet wholly fitting supplement" to the one that has come before it.[53]

It is this enticing interplay between constraint and contingency that has enthralled so many Bach scholars and players. An 1805 review of the first edition of Bach's works for solo violin described these pieces as "perhaps the greatest example in any art form of a master's ability to move with freedom and assurance, even in chains."[54] Put differently, much of Bach's music sounds improvised. This was one of the things about Bach that so intrigued the nineteenth-century composer and virtuoso Franz Liszt (1811-1886)—who himself transcribed and arranged many of Bach's works[55]—and that captivates many jazz musicians. (It is no accident that Bach was a superb improviser.) Again, I hardly need to point out the links with what I was saying earlier about the danger of thinking of beauty in terms of "closed harmonies," about the particularizing, proliferating ministry of the Holy Spirit, effecting faithful but unpredictable improvisations on the harmony achieved in Jesus Christ.

Fourth, a closely related observation: we are provoked to hear *an apparently limitless abundance of development.* Even at the end of the *Goldberg Variations*—to take one of numerous examples—the music is by no means structured toward giving the impression that it *has* to stop when it does. Although these pieces do involve mathematical structures that require specifically timed closures (both on the small and large scale), as I noted earlier, there is much in the music that works against this.[56] The "logic" is "open," as

---

[52]Dreyfus, *Bach and the Patterns of Invention,* esp. chap. 6.

[53]Hart, *Beauty of the Infinite,* p. 283.

[54]*Jenaische Allgemeine Literaturzeitung,* 282 (1805), as quoted in Wolff, *Johann Sebastian Bach,* p. 471.

[55]Martin Zenck, "Reinterpreting Bach in the Nineteenth and Twentieth Centuries," in *The Cambridge Companion to Bach,* ed. John Butt (Cambridge: Cambridge University Press, 1997), p. 228.

[56]See n. 46.

if the variations were only samples from a potentially limitless range of options. It is thus not surprising that this has led some to speak of "infinity" being evoked in pieces of this sort. This would need carefully qualifying, but, cautiously, we might say that insofar as this can be heard as an evocation of infinity, it is not the infinity of monotonous continuation but much more akin to the infinity of proliferating novelty, the ever new and ever more elaborate richness and bounty generated by the Holy Spirit as creation shares in the excess of God's own abundant differentiated infinity, and this itself might be heard as a glimpse of the nontransient novelty of the future transformed creation, "in which new occurrences are added but nothing passes away."[57]

Fifth, Bach's music can provoke us to hear *a beauty that can engage with and transform dissonance.* I have already alluded to this aspect of creation's beauty, and I will say much more about it in chapter two. Here we need only note that one of the marvels of Bach is the way in which he treats dissonance, in some pieces exploring it to quite unprecedented and alarming degrees (such as the famous twenty-fifth variation of the *Goldberg*), yet never in such a way as to grant it any kind of ultimacy.

Sixth and finally, to state the obvious, and picking up on our earlier point about beauty and desire, Bach's music, as a creaturely reality, has proved an endless source of delight for three hundred years; its beauty has a rare attraction, provoking a desire among millions to be "with" the music whether as listener, dancer, jogger, singer, player or analyst.

Standing back, then, what kind of cosmos, under God, might this music provoke us to imagine, and thus what vision of created beauty? A cosmos and a vision, it would seem, highly congruent with the sort we brought into relief in the first part of this chapter. This is not to claim, of course, that all of Bach's music has this capacity—were the argument to be developed, we would need to be far more specific; nor is it to claim that no other composer's music could do similar things; nor is it to deny that there are features of some of Bach's music that move in rather different directions. The claim is only that there is music here that can justifiably be said to embody some of the main features of a theological vision of created beauty, and as such, in its own musical ways, help us perceive and understand that vision more deeply and clearly.

---

[57]Richard Bauckham, "Time and Eternity," in *God Will Be All in All: The Eschatology of Jürgen Moltmann,* ed. Richard Bauckham (Edinburgh: T & T Clark, 1999), p. 186.

It may well be asked: if we are on the right lines, are the links merely fortuitous? Bach, after all, even if not remarkably or exceptionally devout, was a strong Lutheran, biblically well-educated. Is there anything to suggest that he himself would have conceived his music as giving voice to creation's beauty, or indeed that this might have been part of what he intended? This kind of question, of course, is deeply unfashionable these days. And to demonstrate what Bach might have believed about his music does not of itself imply that such beliefs are correct. And as we are constantly reminded, "the road to hell is paved with authorial intention."[58] Nevertheless, here we need only register that even a modicum of historical-theological research in the case of Bach does show that our invitation to hear his music in a certain way does at least have historical propriety—it would not have been fanciful to Bach himself and may in some cases reflect his intention—and this can be highly illuminating.[59] For the linking of music and the cosmos at large was anything but foreign to the Lutheranism of his period. As Joyce Irwin has shown, among theologians the ancient tradition of seeing music as articulating the divinely gifted order of the cosmos may have weakened considerably by Bach's time, but among musicians it was by no means dead.[60] Although Bach was not a theorist or theologian of music (how interested he would have been in detailed metaphysics is moot),[61] there is plenty to suggest that the notion of music bringing to sound an engrained God-given cosmic beauty and thus offering "insight into the depths of the wisdom of the world" (words used on Bach's behalf),[62] would have been anything but for-

---

[58]The phrase comes from N. T. Wright; *The New Testament and the People of God* (London: SPCK, 1992), p. 55.

[59]To those who cry "intentional fallacy" at this point, it is worth remembering that when William Wimsatt and Monroe Beardsley offered their classic exposition of the intentional fallacy, their main point was that the "intention of the author is neither available nor desirable as a standard for judging the success of a work of literary art" (W. K. Wimsatt and M. C. Beardsley, "The Intentional Fallacy," in *The Verbal Icon: Studies in the Meaning of Poetry*, ed. W. K. Wimsatt [Lexington: University of Kentucky Press, 1954], p. 3). That is quite different from claiming that research into what a composer may have believed and intended is always doomed to failure or is invariably irrelevant for understanding or benefiting from a musical text. One of the refreshing things about Dreyfus's work is his refusal to be hidebound by theorists who turn limited, instructive insights into inflated, all-encompassing claims (the "death of the author," etc.). Cf. Dreyfus, *Bach and the Patterns of Invention*, p. 171.

[60]Joyce L. Irwin, *Neither Voice nor Heart Alone: German Lutheran Theology of Music in the Age of the Baroque* (New York: Peter Lang, 1993), esp. chaps. 4, 11.

[61]Dreyfus, *Bach and the Patterns of Invention*, p. 9; Wolff, *Johann Sebastian Bach*, pp. 337-39.

[62]J. A. Birnbaum, as quoted in Wolff, *Johann Sebastian Bach*, p. 338.

eign to him.[63] In this light it is not at all inappropriate to listen to the forty-eight preludes and fugues of the *Well-Tempered Clavier,* for example, as a stunning exploration of the properties and possibilities of a God-given sonic order, for they are derived from that physical "universal" built into the physical world, the "harmonic series."

Yet matters cannot be left there. The implication would be that all Bach is doing, or thinks he is doing, is bringing to light and representing the order of the natural world. It is patently obvious that he is doing very much more. If

---

[63]See John Butt, *Music Education and the Art of Performance in the German Baroque* (Cambridge: Cambridge University Press, 1994), pp. 33ff.; Wolff, *Johann Sebastian Bach,* pp. 1-11, 465-72. For example, there is a much-quoted saying attributed to Bach about the "thorough-bass" (a foundational bass line with accompanying chords, very common in baroque music) which relates this device to the God-given created order. John Butt calls this a "late flowering of the Pythagorean view of well-composed music as natural harmony" ("Bach's Metaphysics of Music," in *The Cambridge Companion to Bach,* ed. John Butt [Cambridge: Cambridge University Press, 1997], pp. 46-71, 54). Relevant also is the witness of J. A. Birnbaum, almost certainly acting as Bach's mouthpiece, who appeals to "the eternal rules of music" and of polyphonous music as an exemplar of the unity and diversity pervading the cosmos (ibid., pp. 55-59; Wolff, *Johann Sebastian Bach,* pp. 5-6). (There are elements in the Birnbaum document, however, that suggest he believes nature was sometimes *lacking* beauty, something that does not seem to trouble Wolff et al.) In 1747 Bach joined a learned group, the Corresponding Society of the Musical Sciences, one of whose members could write: "God is a harmonic being. All harmony originates from his wise order and organisation. . . . Where there is no conformity, there is also no order, no beauty, and no perfection. For beauty and perfection consist in the conformity of diversity" (as quoted in Wolff, *Johann Sebastian Bach,* p. 466). During his last years Bach wrote music that would seem to be highly consonant with the theories current in this circle, especially that of music as "sounding mathematics"—e.g., the *Canonic Variations on "Vom Himmel hoch da komm ich her"* and most famously, the *Art of Fugue* (Malcolm Boyd, ed., *Bach* [Oxford: Oxford University Press, 2000], pp. 205-6). Nevertheless, to align Bach closely with the rationalist cosmologies of the German Enlightenment, as some have attempted, is highly questionable. Recently, Wolff has contended that Bach's output is usefully interpreted in the light of the concept of musical "perfection," a characteristically Enlightenment notion used in Birnbaum's defense of Bach (see Wolff, *Johann Sebastian Bach,* pp. 466-67; see also John Butt, " 'A Mind Unconscious That It Is Calculating?' Bach and the Rationalist Philosophy of Leibniz and Spinoza," in *The Cambridge Companion to Bach,* ed. John Butt [Cambridge: Cambridge University Press, 1997], pp. 60-71; Ulrich Leisinger, "Forms and Functions of the Choral Movements in J. S. Bach's *St. Matthew Passion,*" in *Bach Studies 2,* ed. Daniel R. Melamed [Cambridge: Cambridge University Press, 1995], pp. 70-84). However, Dreyfus shows that these lines of argument pay insufficient attention to the role of human agency in Bach's practice—I have already spoken about the dangers of interpreting Bach in terms of "closed" systems. See Dreyfus, *Bach and the Patterns of Invention,* pp. 26-27, and chap. 8. And the contention that Bach would have leaned heavily on Enlightenment thinkers such as Leibniz and Wolff is unconvincing. (Even Leisinger has to admit that "no documentary evidence can be presented that Johann Sebastian Bach ever possessed or read any of Leibniz's or Wolff's treatises"; see "Forms and Functions," p. 84.) As far as aesthetics is concerned, Dreyfus argues that Bach is better understood as a subtle *critic* of Enlightenment thought than a solid supporter of it (see *Bach and the Patterns of Invention,* chap. 8).

he *is* eliciting creation's own beauty, he is doing so *through an active process of making:* principally through *inventio* and *elaboratio,* both of which are themselves constructive exercises, involving combining tones, making music. Inventions do not tumble out of nature like apples off a tree; they have to be worked at, constructed, and the elaborations likewise. Indeed, frequently we find Bach having to adjust the elaborations slightly to make them "fit" his constraints. Even at the very basic acoustic level, there are modifications: the *Well-Tempered Clavier* is indeed based on the twelve-note chromatic scale that does indeed derive from the "natural" fact of the harmonic series, but the scale he used and the slightly differently-tuned one we commonly use today, are in fact adjustments, "temperings" of what nature has given us.[64]

In fact, Bach reshaped almost everything he touched: from simple motifs to whole styles and genres. He is one of the least "passive" composers in history. Thus we are led to the second main sense of "created beauty" I distinguished at the start—the beauty humans make. If "natural" beauty is being discovered and turned into sound by Bach, this happens *as* it is shaped and reshaped, formed and reformed, through the ingenious use of a vast array of often highly sophisticated compositional techniques.

We are thus confronted with perhaps the central paradox of a Christian view of creativity: in and through the act of strenuous making we discover more fully what we have not made. The inability to hold these two together in our thinking—"given" beauty and "generated" beauty (in this case, artistic beauty)—the tendency to see them as inherently opposed, is, I submit, one of the cardinal marks of modernity, captivated as it has so often been by the notion of the godlike artist, forging order where supposedly none can be trusted or even found. Postmodernity has fared no better, typically collapsing "given" beauty into "generated" beauty without remainder (what beauty could there be except that which we construct?). Reactions to both of these visions sometimes take the form of a "return to nature," as if any modification of nature is to be seen as a corruption of it. But this trades on essentially the same competitive, bipolar outlook—human creativity as necessarily pitted against the natural world. Bach's music would seem to point us toward—and, arguably, embodies—a vision of the relation between natural and artistic beauty that does not assume an intrinsic tussle between them. Significantly, Bach's obituary spoke of Bach's "ingenious and unusual ideas"

---

[64]For explanation, cf. Stuart Isacoff, *Temperament: How Music Became a Battleground for the Great Minds of Western Civilization* (New York: Alfred A. Knopf, 2001).

and his extraordinary grasp of the "hidden secrets of harmony" without so much as a hint that the two had to be at odds.[65]

This is why attempts to line up Bach with the German Enlightenment's aesthetics of his day are so questionable, with its ideals of transparency and representation, where music is thought to be best when it shows least human artifice. Bach seems less interested in representing than he is in shaping his materials respectfully, and *in that way* expanding our awareness of those materials, the world we live in and our place in it.[66] At the same time, though of course Bach was astonishingly "original," we should avoid interpreting him through the lens of the self-conscious creativity of the Romantic *Künstler,* the individual genius who mediates order to the world through his unique art.

What Bach's music provokes us to imagine, then, when set in its context, is a subtle relationship between natural and artistic beauty, where the two are not seen as fundamentally incompatible, but where natural beauty is the inhabited environment, trusted and respected, in which artistic beauty is born, even if born through sweat and struggle. The vision of making beauty is not one that sees the artist as striving for creation out of nothing, fashioning and foisting order where none is given, or pursuing a fetish for originality (the wholly underived act); still less is it one of defiantly challenging God.[67] But nor is it one in which we simply "let nature be," merely follow

---

[65] *The New Bach Reader: A Life of Johann Sebastian Bach in Letters and Documents,* ed. Hans T. David, Arthur Mendel, and Christoph Wolff (New York: W. W. Norton, 1998), p. 305.

[66] This is arguably where Christoph Wolff comes unstuck *(Johann Sebastian Bach).* He acknowledges that Bach shows astonishing novelty and originality, but he is still *over*enamored with trying to show Bach's supposed indebtedness to certain Enlightenment notions of music's transparency to nature's harmony and order, and with these the notion that Bach's elaboration is a quasi-scientific exploration and discovery of nature's beauty (fueled by a comparison with Newton that is probably more questionable than illuminating). For discussion, cf. John Butt, "The Saint Johann Sebastian Passion," *The New Republic* 10 (2000): 33-38, and of the wider issues, Dreyfus, *Bach and the Patterns of Invention,* chap. 8.

[67] In a review of Wolff's book, Edward Said suggests that Bach (however unconsciously) appears to be engaged in a kind of rivalry with God. Is there not a "cosmic musical ambition" here, Said asks, "epic" in nature, even "demonic," especially in the late pieces where the composer unleashes such an awesome array of creative powers that we are bound to question (or at least qualify) traditional views of Bach's devotion to and reverence for God? "One can't help wondering whether all the piety and expression of humility before God weren't also Bach's way of keeping something considerably darker—more exuberant, more hubristic, verging on the blasphemous—at bay" (Edward Said, "Cosmic Ambition," *London Review of Books* [2001]: 13). Said does not seem to notice how anachronistic the guiding assumption behind this kind of suspicion is: Bach and most of his contemporaries would not have seen anything unusual in holding at one and the same time that God provides the already structured materials for the composer *and* that this same God *invites* and *delights in* an energetic elaboration of these materials on the part of a composer. And why should we?

its resonances and rhythms the way one might follow a river through a valley or the grain of a piece of wood. The vision is rather of the artist, as physical and embodied, set in the midst of a God-given world vibrant with a dynamic beauty of its own, not simply "there" like a brute fact to be escaped or violently abused but there as a gift from a God of overflowing beauty, a gift for us to interact with vigorously, shape and reshape, form and transform, and in this way fashion something as consistent and dazzlingly novel as the *Goldberg Variations,* art that can anticipate the beauty previewed and promised in Jesus Christ.

2

BEAUTY, SENTIMENTALITY
AND THE ARTS

Jeremy S. Begbie

> Beauty . . . disappeared not only from the advanced art of the 1960s, but from
> advanced philosophy of art of that decade as well. . . . [It] rarely came up in
> art periodicals from the 1960s without a deconstructionist snicker.[1]

Why the embarrassed chuckle when beauty is mentioned in the presence of
art's connoisseurs? Is this merely condescending elitism, a disdain for anything with popular appeal? "Beautiful" art, after all, sells very well. I suspect
that in most cases, in the midst of the scoffing will be a profound misgiving
about beauty, and one we would do well not to brush aside—a suspicion
of *sentimentality* to which beauty, it will often be assumed, inevitably opens
the door. In this chapter, I shall argue that sentimentality is neither a super-
ficial nor an inconsequential matter but a deep, pernicious strand in contemporary culture and in the church, and that the arts have often played a leading part in encouraging it. However, I shall contend that though it may often
be associated with beauty, the tie is not a necessary one. What I stressed in
chapter one needs to be restressed here: all depends on being prepared to
think and rethink beauty in the light of the acts and being of the triune God,
and in this context that means paying particular attention to the narrative of
Good Friday, Holy Saturday and Easter Day. Only in this way will we be
able to disentangle the pursuit of beauty from sentimentality, and, moreover,
begin to discern how the arts might contribute to generating a countersentimentality in our day.

---

[1]Arthur C. Danto, *The Abuse of Beauty* (Chicago: Open Court, 2003), p. 25.

The Pathology of Sentimentality

First we need to examine what sentimentality involves. There has been a flurry of philosophical writing on the theme recently,[2] even a major book,[3] and some treatments of it as a phenomenon of Western cultural life.[4] Like beauty, it is a somewhat sprawling concept and is probably best seen as "the name of several kinds of disease of the feelings."[5] At the very least, I suggest it involves three major traits or elements, closely bound up with each other. I shall treat each of these traits primarily as they are manifest in people

---

[2]Michael Tanner, "Sentimentality," *Proceedings of the Aristotelian Society* 77 (1976-1977): 127-47; Mary Midgley, "Brutality and Sentimentality," *Philosophy* 54 (1979): 385-89; Anthony Savile, *The Test of Time: An Essay in Philosophical Aesthetics* (Oxford: Oxford University Press, 1982), chap. 11; Mark Jefferson, "What Is Wrong with Sentimentality?" *Mind* 92 (1983): 519-29; Marcia Eaton, "Laughing at the Death of Little Nell: Sentimental Art and Sentimental People," *American Philosophical Quarterly* 26, no. 4 (1989): 269-82; Robert C. Solomon, "In Defense of Sentimentality," *Philosophy and Literature* 14 (1990): 304-23; "On Kitsch and Sentimentality," *The Journal of Aesthetics and Art Criticism* 49, no. 1 (1991): 1-14; Anthony Savile, "Sentimentality," in *Arguing About Art,* ed. Alex Neill and Aaron Ridley (New York: McGraw Hill, 1995), pp. 223-27; Joseph Kupfer, "The Sentimental Self," *Canadian Journal of Philosophy* 26, no. 4 (1996): 543-60; Deborah Knight, "Why We Enjoy Condemning Sentimentality: A Meta-Aesthetic Perspective," *The Journal of Aesthetics and Art Criticism* 57, no. 4 (1999): 411-20; Ira Newman, "The Alleged Unwholesomeness of Sentimentality," in *Arguing About Art,* ed. Alex Neill and Aaron Ridley (New York: McGraw Hill, 1995), pp. 320-22. A classic earlier treatment can be found in I. A. Richards, *Practical Criticism: A Study of Literary Judgement* (London: Kegan Paul, Trench & Trubner, 1929), chap. 6.

[3]Robert C. Solomon, *In Defense of Sentimentality* (Oxford: Oxford University Press, 2004). Solomon's concern is not with defending sentimentality as I am understanding it in this chapter, but what he calls the "tender" emotions—pity, sympathy, fondness, adoration, compassion. The "minimal definition" of sentimentality that controls his discussion is "an expression of and appeal to the tender emotions." He explains: "My central argument, here and throughout this book, is that no conception of ethics can be adequate unless it takes into account such emotions, not as mere 'inclinations' but as an essential part of the substance of ethics itself" (p. 9). According to Solomon the key weakness of standard attacks on sentimentality is a low view of emotion in general and of the tender emotions in particular.

This minimal construal of sentimentality is in many respects strange. I suspect that despite earlier uses of the word (when the term first appeared in the eighteenth century it was a term of commendation), most today would understand sentimentality negatively, as an emotional pathology, not merely something that (in a nonevaluative way) denotes a particular field of emotions. (Deborah Knight argues, *pace* Ira Newman, that there can be no such thing as a purely, descriptive nonevaluative sense of sentimentality, nor laudable instances of sentimentality; see "Why We Enjoy Condemning Sentimentality," pp. 414-15; cf. Newman, "The Alleged Unwholesomeness of Sentimentality.") As Knight rightly observes, "What Solomon wants to defend is not really sentimentality, but rather the sentiments, especially the gentle ones" ("Why We Enjoy Condemning Sentimentality," p. 417).

[4]See e.g., Digby Anderson and Peter Mullen, eds., *Faking It: The Sentimentalisation of Modern Society* (London: Penguin, 1998), and, in effect on the same theme, Stjepan G. Mestrovic, *Post-emotional Society* (London: SAGE, 1997).

[5]Tanner, "Sentimentality," p. 140.

(since sentimentality is a phenomenon properly applied in the first instance to persons), and only secondarily as they are evident in the arts, in artistic practices and artworks. The sentimentalist, I shall argue, (1) misrepresents reality through evading or trivializing evil, (2) is emotionally self-indulgent, and (3) avoids appropriate costly action. Let us take each in turn.

1. The sentimentalist *misrepresents reality* through *evading or trivializing evil.*[6] It involves a pretense, an attachment to a distorted set of beliefs; above all, "the fiction of innocence."[7] Unable to deal with the phenomena of evil, innocence is projected onto the world. So Anthony Savile speaks of sentimentality as the "false-coloring" of an object: we see things, including human nature, through rose-tinted spectacles.[8]

This disjunction from reality plays out in various ways. On the cultural level one of the most obvious examples is the Western doctrine of progress.[9] A heady mix of economic growth and confidence, technological achievement, medical advance, sometimes allied to various theories of biological development, progressive idealism and social Darwinianism, has for many generated a climate of thought that imagines a steady march of the human race toward freedom and justice, and that is characterized by a childlike belief in Western innocence and the fundamental rationality and goodness of humankind. I recall Professor Nicholas Lash once remarking that it was

---

[6]In my own view, unless we see something akin to the evasion or trivialization of evil as belonging to the center of sentimentality, we are unlikely to get very far in understanding its dynamics, insofar as we are concerned with how the word *sentimentality* is commonly used and understood. One of the striking features of the philosophical literature on sentimentality is that this is regularly either bypassed or marginalized (even allowing for an understandable hesitation about using a word as strong as *evil*). Mark Jefferson is one of the exceptions ("What Is Wrong with Sentimentality?"). He rightly criticizes Mary Midgley's contention that it is the misrepresentation of reality for the sake of indulging emotion that makes sentimentality morally objectionable, *regardless* of the emotion being exercised ("the central offence lies in self-deception, in distorting reality to get a pretext for indulging *any* feeling" [Midgley, "Brutality and Sentimentality," p. 386]). What matters, says Jefferson, is what *kind* of misrepresentation we are speaking about: "The qualities that sentimentality imposes on its objects are the qualities of innocence" (Jefferson, "What Is Wrong with Sentimentality?" p. 527). The editors of the somewhat controversial collection of essays *Faking It* are much blunter: "Most of all the sentimentalist is frightened by the idea that men *[sic]* have a natural capacity for evil. For to admit evil, and the will to evil, is to destroy his world which rests upon the supposition that utopia may be ushered in by the mere adoption of the right plan" (Digby Anderson and Peter Mullen, "The Idea of a Fake Society: Introduction and Summary," in *Faking It,* pp. 5-6).

[7]Jefferson, "What Is Wrong with Sentimentality?" p. 526.

[8]Savile, "Sentimentality," p. 225.

[9]See Peter Mullen, "All Feelings and No Doctrine: The Sentimentalisation of Religion," in *Faking It,* pp. 9-10.

hardly an exaggeration to say that Western modernism (as a worldview) could be defined by the twin belief that humanity's deepest problems not only *can* be solved but eventually *will* be. But faced with the horrors and terrors of history[10]—the vast quantities of pain, suffering and loss in the story of humankind (not least in modernity), and the fear of a future that cannot be wholly predicted and controlled—this misrepresentation of reality proves singularly ill-equipped. Intractable and starkly irrational evil, from Stalin's *gulag* to the rape of a twelve-week-old baby (reported on the national news as I was writing this), exposes the bankruptcy of all schemes that trade on the supposed immanent purity of human nature. Likewise, the resistance of "Mother Nature" to attempts to tame her, and her capacity to be hostile and cruel toward us, mock simplistic views of the world's harmony.

It is hardly surprising, then, to find that two common ways of reacting to evil or the will to evil (of whatever sort) are evasion and trivialization. Evasion involves selection; we restrict ourselves to the pleasing or undisturbing aspects of a situation, and disregard the rest.

> Western politicians knew perfectly well that al-Qaeda was a danger, but nobody took it too seriously until it was too late. Countries bordering the Indian Ocean knew about tsunamis, but hadn't bothered to install early warning systems. We all know that Third-World debt is a massive sore on the conscience of the world, but our politicians don't want to take it too seriously, because from our point of view the world is progressing reasonably well and we don't want to rock the economic boat—or to upset powerful interests.[11]

Sometimes, this evasion goes with an exaggeration of what is good or pleasing—as when we insist on seeing someone's kindness as far greater than it actually is, or on the social level, when we overstate the advantages of economic growth, or overplay the benefits of medical advance.

In the case of trivialization, the evil is acknowledged but in some manner deflated, rendered less angular or stark. The sentimentalist typically remarks, "They aren't that bad really" or "Things aren't that bad"—when they are. There is a drive toward simplicity, reducing the complexities and ambiguities that evil brings in its wake. There is a tendency toward premature harmony: in some forms of theodicy, for example, (justifying God in the face

---

[10]Richard Bauckham and Trevor A. Hart, *Hope Against Hope: Christian Eschatology at the Turn of the Millennium* (Grand Rapids: Eerdmans, 1999), p. 11.

[11]N. T. Wright, "God, 9/11, the Tsunami, and the New Problem of Evil," *Response,* Seattle Pacific University <www.spu.edu/depts/uc/response/summer2k5/features/evil.asp>.

of the existence of evil) the pains and losses of the world are presented as necessary darkness in order that the light of goodness may shine.

Almost any piece of art can be used to serve the evasion or trivializing of evil (certainly not "popular" art alone, as is often thought), and sometimes the art will have formal features or content that encourage this.[12] It is almost impossible not to mention greeting cards in this connection, especially those that treat the "last enemy," death, as a friend in disguise, merely a door into "the next room" (Scott Holland). This carries forward the tradition represented by the account of the death of Little Nell in Charles Dickens's *The Old Curiosity Shop,* a passage that epitomized Victorian sentimentality for many later critics.

> Dickens would have us accept a child who is not only uncomplaining [in the face of death], but whose only displayed emotions are increasing earnestness and gratitude. . . . Even had he succeeded in avoiding trite phrases and images, Dickens could not write in a way that would convince us that death or the dying are like this, for they are not. . . . At the very least, the onlookers suffer.[13]

In the same circle of ideas Robert Solomon cites a painting by Adolphe Bouguereau (1825-1905), a portrait of two pretty little girls in rosy pink and soft pastels, set against an expansive sky ("Childhood Idyll"). He comments:

> These girls don't do any of the nasty things that little children do. They don't whine. They don't tease the cat. They don't hit each other. They don't have any bruises. They aren't going to die. The art gives us a false portrait, a carefully edited portrait that limits our vision and restricts our sense of reality. . . . Above all, there is no discomfort, no ugliness.[14]

I need not dwell on this aspect of sentimentality now, but I can at least anticipate our later discussion by quoting words from the end of George Steiner's intellectual autobiography, *Errata.* Writing as one who struggles to believe in God, he finds he is engulfed by a sense of the evilness of evil, of some calamitous "break" with goodness:

> There are those who tear out the eyes of living children, who shoot children

---

[12]We ought to be hesitant about pointing to a piece of art and calling it "sentimental," since our interpretation and use of it *as* sentimental often depends hugely on matters of context—our state of mind and body, memories and associations, social and cultural conventions, and so forth. Nevertheless, we may justifiably speak of features of an artifact that lend themselves more readily to sentimental interpretation and use than others.

[13]Marcia Eaton, "Laughing at the Death of Little Nell," p. 276.

[14]Solomon, "On Kitsch and Sentimentality," p. 5.

in the eyes, who beat animals across their eyes. These facts overwhelm me with desolate loathing. . . . At the maddening centre of despair is the insistent instinct—again, I can put it no other way—of a broken contract. Of an appalling and specific cataclysm. In the futile scream of the child, in the mute agony of the tortured animal, sounds the "background noise" of a horror after creation. . . . Something—how helpless language can be—has gone hideously wrong. . . . I am possessed, as by a midnight clarity, by the intuition of the Fall. Only some such happening, irretrievable to reason, can make intelligible, though always near to unbearable, the actualities of our history on this wasted earth.[15]

2. Evading or trivializing evil does not, however, amount to sentimentality. Sentimentality is, after all, an emotional pathology. And so to the second trait: typically, the sentimentalist is *emotionally self-indulgent.* Emotion is exercised according to the misrepresentation of reality we have just described, and, at least in part, for the pleasure of exercising the emotion (whether through active deliberation or more passively).[16] Milan Kundera's much-cited definition of kitsch captures this well:

Kitsch causes two tears to flow in quick succession. The first tear says: how nice to see children running on the grass!

The second tear says: How nice to be moved, together with all mankind, by children running on the grass!

It is the second tear that makes kitsch kitsch.[17]

[15]George Steiner, *Errata: An Examined Life* (London: Phoenix, 1997), pp. 168-69.
[16]Hence Mary Midgley's claim that being sentimental is "misinterpreting the world in order to indulge our feelings" ("Brutality and Sentimentality," p. 521). Compare Karsten Harries: love is kitsch "if love has its center not in the beloved but within itself. Kitsch creates illusion for the sake of self-enjoyment" (*The Meaning of Modern Art* [Evanston, Ill.: Northwestern University Press, 1968], p. 80).
[17]Milan Kundera, *The Unbearable Lightness of Being* (New York: Harper & Row, 1984), p. 251. Kitsch is normally regarded as sentimental, but there is plenty of sentimental art which would not be labeled "kitsch" (some of Dickens, for example). Kitsch has a shorter history than sentimentality and would seem to be tied to certain socioeconomic conditions associated with the Industrial Revolution and modernization—e.g., mass production, technological progress, urbanization and the influx of peasant populations to the towns; and to romanticism—e.g., a stress on the dramatic, on pathos, immediate emotional appeal, and so forth. For discussion, see especially Thomas Kulka, *Kitsch and Art* (University Park: Pennsylvania State University Press, 1996). See also Hermann Broch, "Notes on the Problem of Kitsch," in *Kitsch: The World of Bad Taste,* ed. Gillo Dorfles (New York: Universe Books, 1968), pp. 49-76; Gillo Dorfles, *Kitsch: An Anthology of Bad Taste* (London: Studio Vista, 1968); Kathleen Higgins, "Sweet Kitsch," in *The Philosophy of the Visual Arts,* ed. Philip Alperson (Oxford: Oxford University Press, 1990), pp. 568-81; Solomon, "On Kitsch and Sentimentality"; Betty Spackman, *A Profound Weakness: Christians and Kitsch* (Carlisle: Piquant, 2005).

In other words, the sentimentalist appears to be moved by something or someone beyond themselves but is to a large extent, perhaps primarily, concerned with the satisfaction gained in exercising their emotion. (It is worth adding that part of this satisfaction comes from knowing the impression the emotion makes on others. We like others to realize that we are compassionate, tender and so forth. And even if others are not around, there can be something deeply gratifying about exercising feelings that most would admire.[18])

This explains why the sentimentalist cannot engage in depth with another's pain *as pain* (hence the strong link some see between sentimentality and cruelty)[19] or face up to another's negative features. We only need think of the friend who flatters us ceaselessly, regardless of our glaring faults, enjoying the pleasure it affords, or the obsessive counselor, often found in churches, waiting to descend on someone in crisis in order to feed their own emotional "need to be needed." Inasmuch as sentimentality is directed at other people, the other person becomes a means to an end—he or she is absorbed into the subjectivity of the sentimentalist. The sentimentalist loves and hates, grieves or pities not for the sake of the other but for the sake of enjoying love, hate, grief or pity.

In much discussion of sentimentality it is presumed that the emotions indulged in this way are "tender"—pity, sympathy, fondness and so on. But sentimentality can also implicate the "harsher" emotions—anger and rage, for example.[20] This might seem odd at first, given that the sentimentalist supposedly evades or trivializes evil. If we feel fury when we see an innocent mother in East Africa unable to feed her children because her country is torn apart with civil war—how can this be sentimental? The answer is: insofar as we are more concerned with indulging the anger than the plight of the woman and her family, and especially insofar as we take no action to alleviate her suffering (see the third point on p. 52). Indeed, sentimentalists show their true colors when they make it clear they do not want the object

---

[18]See Patrick West, *Conspicuous Compassion: Why Sometimes It Really Is Cruel to Be Kind* (London: Civitas, 2004). "Sentimental emotions are *artefacts:* they are designed to cast credit on the one who claims them. The sentimentalist is courting admiration and sympathy. That is why there is sentimental love, sentimental indignation, sentimental grief and sympathy; but not sentimental malice, spite, envy or depression, since these are feelings no-one admires" (Roger Scruton, *The Aesthetics of Music* [Oxford: Clarendon, 1997], p. 486).

[19]Tanner, "Sentimentality," pp. 143-44.

[20]See, e.g., Savile, *Test of Time*, pp. 223-27.

of anger to be removed (think of the committee member who *has* to have someone to oppose and who is strangely disappointed when people start getting on with each other).[21]

Again, art can easily be drawn into this process. To take only one example, there is a kind of art that—as the saying goes—seems to "wallow" in some negative emotional field and perhaps encourages us to do the same. Some might cite the grief of the last movement of Tchaikovsky's Sixth ("Pathetique") Symphony in this regard. Here, arguably, an emotional field is being rehearsed and churned over to the point it becomes more important than anything toward which it could ever be directed, perhaps even all-consuming. The same kind of thing can happen to almost any art. In a book about romantic love in contemporary North America, Laura Smit writes of the results of interviews she conducted as part of her research:

> Sometimes music [was] used not as a tool for moving on but rather as a tool for remaining in the pathos of the painful experience, for reliving the rejection, for keeping alive a fantasy that should have been allowed to die. One woman told of the pain she experienced during her senior year in high school when the boy she was in love with began to date her best friend. She listened to a particular CD over and over, and now, she says, "I really can't listen to it without feeling like it's the spring of graduation year."[22]

3. We may distinguish a third element in sentimentality: the sentimentalist *fails to take appropriate costly action.* Because her emotional engagement is not with reality X but a falsification of reality X and to a large extent for the pleasure of exercising the emotion, it cannot generate action that is appropriate to reality X. To echo Oscar Wilde, the sentimentalist wants emotion on the cheap, the pleasure of an active emotional life without the price.[23] In this light a number of characteristics associated with sentimental people quickly make sense. Sentimentalists typically resist any challenge to their

---

[21]Patrick West writes of the way crowds gather outside the courts that try alleged child murderers. "Two children had been murdered and people were at Peterborough, ostensibly, to express their anger at this crime. Yet it suspiciously appeared to be an excuse for a good, adrenaline-fuelled day out—a chance to prove one's 'human' credentials in the comfort of the crowd" (*Conspicuous Compassion*, p. 16).

[22]Laura A. Smit, *Loves Me, Loves Me Not: The Ethics of Unrequited Love* (Grand Rapids: Baker, 2005), p. 165.

[23]The sentimentalist "desires to have the luxury of an emotion without paying for it. . . . [T]hey always try to get their emotions on credit, and refuse to pay the bill when it comes in" (Letter to Lord Alfred Douglas, in *The Letters of Oscar Wilde*, ed. Rupert Hart-Davis [London: Rupert Hart-Davis Ltd, 1962], p. 501).

way of life.[24] They are much more often moved by strangers than by those close to them, since the former require no personal sacrifice.[25] They feel at home with ethical generalities (love, peace, justice, etc.) but struggle with the demands of awkward individuals. (Recall Linus: "I love mankind; it's people I can't stand.")[26] They are classically impatient; the cost of long-term commitment to someone in pain, for example, is just too great.[27] They display righteous indignation at a picture of a child dying of AIDS, but will do nothing about it. The sentimentalist will rely on routine banalities and clichés ("I'll always be there for you"; "you know you mean more to me than anyone else") since it takes too much time and effort to find just the right words for this or that particular person.

This also has its cultural forms. The Croatian sociologist Stjepan Mestrovic has described the postmodern condition as "postemotional."[28] Drawing on the works of David Riesman, Émile Durkheim, George Ritzer, George Orwell and others, he contends that emotions are the primary object of manipulation in postmodern culture. Emotion has increasingly been divorced from the intellect, judgment and thus from responsible *action:* "postemotional types," as he puts it,

> know that they can experience the full range of emotions in any field, domestic or international, and never be called upon to demonstrate the authenticity of their emotions in *commitment* to appropriate action. . . . Today, everyone knows that emotions carry no burden, no responsibility to act, and above all, that emotions of any sort are accessible to nearly everyone.[29]

Emotions are thus eviscerated of their power: "postemotionalism refers to the use of *dead,* abstracted emotions by the culture industry in a neo-Orwellian, mechanical, and petrified manner."[30] Mestrovic speaks about our society's love of staged "collective effervescence" (Durkheim), alluding to

---

[24]"In appreciating a sentimental ideal we are able to enjoy ourselves, just as we are, without challenge to our beliefs, values, or patterns of emotional response" (Kupfer, "Sentimental Self," pp. 546-47).

[25]Scruton, *Aesthetics of Music,* p. 486.

[26]"Sentimentality . . . steers us away from the twists and turns of particularity toward the bold line of generality" (Kupfer, "Sentimental Self," p. 549).

[27]Sentimentality is a "creed for people with no patience" (Anderson and Mullen, "Idea of a Fake Society," p. 10).

[28]Mestrovic, *Postemotional Society.*

[29]Ibid., p. 56.

[30]Ibid., p. 26.

such phenomena as the O. J. Simpson trial[31] (though "The Jerry Springer Show" might come more quickly to mind). Though Mestrovic's book appeared too early, the reaction to the death of Princess Diana is hard to avoid mentioning here: an upsurge of "conspicuous compassion" that led to very little in the way of positive, practical action.[32] In any case, Mestrovic believes that postemotionalism opens the way to manipulation by the unscrupulous on a vast scale, to a totalitarianism that is "so 'nice' and charming that it cannot lead to indignation or rebellion."[33]

Once again, it is not hard to see how the arts can be pulled in to these dynamics. (It is worth recalling the large part music and poetry played in the grieving over Diana.) The arts have been, and still are, widely used to offer a rich emotional experience that will screen out the darker dimensions of reality and thus prevent certain forms of action, turning the aesthetic into an anaesthetic, so to speak.[34] This may have its place in some contexts, but in others it can take cruel and heartless forms. Classic examples are William James's depiction of a wealthy matron shedding tears at the plight of characters on stage while her servants freeze outside; or Auschwitz commandant Rudolf Hoess weeping at the opera staged by condemned Jewish prisoners (needless to say, weeping at the characters portrayed, not the performers). Most macabre of all, perhaps, is the thought of the camp band at Auschwitz playing Schubert marches for the arriving truckloads of Jews, deceiving the newcomers into thinking they were entering some kind of pleasure camp.[35] Indeed, the links between the arts, sentimentality and totalitarianism can be very strong, something alluded to by Mestrovic and highlighted by many

---

[31]Ibid., pp. 5, 11, 56.

[32]West, *Conspicuous Compassion*, esp. chap. 2. The most notorious treatment of the Diana phenomenon as sentimental ("the elevation of feeling, image and spontaneity over reason, reality and restraint") is that by Anthony O'Hear ("Diana, Queen of Hearts," in *Faking It: The Sentimentalisation of Modern Society*, ed. Digby Anderson and Peter Mullen [London: Penguin, 1998], pp. 181-90). Some have argued that the outpouring of emotion at events like this may signal a genuine emotional distress at deeper levels; gestures such as lighting candles en masse could be read as reactions to a sense of powerlessness felt by many in the face of life's "tragic" dimensions (so David Kettle, *Beyond Tragic Spirituality* [Cambridge: Grove Books, 2005], pp. 8ff.). Perhaps, but I am not convinced that this significantly weakens the case of those who see such phenomena as a potent and concentrated expression of sentimentality.

[33]Mestrovic, *Postemotional Society*, p. 146.

[34]Knight, "Why We Enjoy Condemning Sentimentality," p. 417.

[35]Fania Fenelon and Marcelle Routier, *The Musicians of Auschwitz*, trans. Judith Landry (London: Joseph, 1977); Guido Fackler, " 'Des Lagers Stimme': Musik in Den Frühen Konzentrationslagern Des Ns-Regimes (1933-1936)" (doctoral diss., University of Freiburg, 1997); "Musik Im Konzentrationslager," *Informationen* 20, no. 41 (1997): 25-33.

others. To spotlight one example, during the rise of the Third Reich in the 1930s, one might imagine the radio waves being filled with rousing songs and upbeat patriotic marches. In fact, the vast majority of music broadcast was light music, typified by syrupy love songs akin to the cliché-ridden material that dulled people to the bleakness of the Weimar Republic—an ideal sugarcoating for the cruel propaganda broadcast with it.[36]

Sentimentality in Christian Worship

Enough has been said, I hope, to show that sentimentality, far from being a trifling matter, can constitute a "deep threat"[37] in culture at large and in the arts, and thus "deserves to be taken more seriously than it takes itself."[38]

It would be perilously easy for the church to distance itself from the currents we have been tracing, but Christians have been implicated in them as much as any others, and not slow to deploy the arts in the process.[39] It is likely that "Christian kitsch" will come to mind, especially in the visual arts. Betty Spackman has recently offered an impressive treatment of this phenomenon, showing how it involves economics, class and culture as much as any formal properties of the art itself. She stresses that kitsch is frequently the vehicle of deep and heartfelt faith (hence her title, *A Profound Weak-*

---

[36]Peter Wicke, "Sentimentality and High Pathos: Popular Music in Fascist Germany," *Popular Music* 5 (1985): 149-58 <www.tagg.org/others/pw3reich.html>. See also Saul Friedlander, *Reflections of Nazism: Essay on Kitsch and Death* (New York: Harper & Row, 1984). It might well be asked: Does not all art to some extent fictionalize reality, distance us from the "real" world to the detriment of costly involvement with it? In Nicholas Wolterstorff's words, we can easily begin to "prize the world of a work of art for its falsehood in various respects to what we believe actuality to be like. We want for a while to burrow into a world significantly different from our actual world. We want for a while to escape the drudgery and the pain, the boredom, perplexity, and disorder of real life" (*Art in Action: Toward a Christian Aesthetic* [Grand Rapids: Eerdmans, 1980], p. 147). The arts do indeed "frame" things artificially, and they do frequently encourage us to envision or imagine a world distinct from the actual world. However, this process does not necessarily mean we are thereby drawn irrevocably away from the truth of that actual world and from responsible action in it. Even in fiction, "*by way of* fictionally projecting his distinct world the fictioneer may make a claim, true or false as the case may be, about our actual world" (ibid., p. 125). Does not the best and most enduring "fantasy" art take us out of ourselves *in order* that we may "return" to a deeper appreciation of the reality in which we have our ordinary existence, and thus, where appropriate, to a deeper sense of ethical obligation?

[37]Kupfer, "Sentimental Self," p. 545.

[38]Tanner, "Sentimentality," p. 146.

[39]For a somewhat extreme attack on sentimentality in contemporary Christianity, see Mullen, "All Feelings and No Doctrine," chap. 6.

ness)—quick dismissals are out of place. Nonetheless, it is not hard to see links between much of the art she discusses and the strands of sentimentality we have marked out above.

But here I restrict myself to a few brief comments about another field, music in worship. Over the last thirty years or so in many churches we have witnessed a burgeoning of a certain kind of devotional song, often directed to the risen Jesus: a direct and unadorned expression of love, with music that is metrically regular, harmonically warm and reassuring, easily accessible and singable. It would be disingenuous to seek to exclude these songs from worship on the grounds of their aesthetic simplicity. The New Testament witnesses to the joy of an intimate union with Christ, and most Christian traditions have quite properly found room in their worship for such "plain" and heartfelt adoration. However, questions have to be asked if it is assumed that this kind of song exhausts the possibilities of "singing to Jesus," or if these sentiments are isolated from other dimensions of relating to God. Devotion to Jesus, after all, entails being changed into his likeness by the Spirit—a costly and painful process. It certainly involves discovering the embrace of Jesus' Father, Abba, but this is the Father we are called to obey as we are loved by him, the Father who judges us just because he loves us, and the Father who at salvation's critical hour was sensed as devastatingly distant by his only Son. If we ignore this wider trinitarian field we are too easily left with a Jesuology that has no room for Jesus as the incarnate Son of the Father, even less room for the wide range of the Spirit's ministries, and encourages us to tug Jesus into the vortex of our self-defined (emotional) need. Rowan Williams, while very sympathetic to much contemporary song writing, writes about the dangers of what he calls "sentimental solipsism," where the erotic metaphors of medieval and Counter Reformation piety reappear but without the theological checks and balances of those older traditions, where "Jesus as object of loving devotion can slip into Jesus as fantasy partner in a dream of emotional fulfilment."[40]

This should not be taken as a wholesale attack on this or that style of worship (in fact, most traditions have fallen into these traps at some stage). But our three strands of sentimentality are not that hard to see in this genre,

---

[40]Rowan Williams, "A History of Faith in Jesus," in *The Cambridge Companion to Jesus*, ed. Markus Bockmuehl (Cambridge: Cambridge University Press, 2001), p. 231. For a very fine, balanced treatment of these matters, see Robin Parry, *Worshipping Trinity: Coming Back to the Heart of Worship* (Carlisle: Paternoster, 2005).

whatever precise form it takes. In a quite proper concern for intimacy with God through Jesus, reality can be misrepresented (the first strand)—if sin is evaded and trivialized, God is shorn of his freedom and disruptive judgment and taken hostage to my emotional requirements. Most of us have attended services where we were invited to experience through music what Colin Gunton used to call "compulsory joy"—perhaps authentic for some on this or that occasion, but often disturbingly out of touch with what some have to endure in a world so obviously far from its final joy, the very world Christ came to redeem. Most have known services where music has been deployed as a narcotic, blurring the jagged memories of the day-by-day world, rather than as a means by which the Holy Spirit can engage those memories and begin to heal them. Emotional self-indulgence (the second strand) I have said enough about already. The failure to take appropriate costly action (the third strand) is sadly all too evident among those of us who sing most loudly. Comforting and immediately reassuring music may have its place, but something is amiss if this is the *only* function music is called upon to exercise. The widespread dependence on musical clichés in the church (especially those drawn from film music) should also give us pause for thought, even if there is a quite proper place for borrowing familiar idioms.[41] When Amos attacked music (Amos 5:23-24) it was because it was too "easy," blinding God's people to the downtrodden in their midst. We would do well to have Bonhoeffer's words (uttered in the midst of a racist regime) ringing in our ears: "only he who cries out for the Jews may sing Gregorian chants."[42]

Sentimentality and Beauty

But what of the relation between sentimentality and beauty? I began by observing that for many beauty is ineradicably associated with sentimentality. Why should this be? The reasons are many, but we can single out three. First, the pursuit of beauty is suspected as an offense against truth, a lie in the midst of a world so obviously *not* beautiful. Reality, in other words, is misrepresented by evading the truth about evil. The artist Thomas Kinkade may say "I

---

[41]Kathleen Higgins writes of the way kitsch typically depends on "icons" that guarantee a wholly predictable and instant response—elements or symbols that conjure up a cultural "archetype" of beliefs and desires ("Sweet Kitsch," p. 572). This is precisely how numerous chord changes and riffs function in much worship music.

[42]Dietrich Bonhoeffer, quoted in Eberhard Bethge, *Dietrich Bonhoeffer: A Biography* (Minneapolis: Fortress, 2000), p. 607.

like to portray a world without the Fall"[43] but we know such a world is a day-dream. The symphony with its closing fortissimo major chords, it is said, plays out the deceit of a harmonious reconciliation beyond life's conflicts.[44] We know enough now to be certain that the entire space-time continuum is heading for a bleak and empty future. Beauty with a capital B, in the arts as much as anywhere else, is an illusory consolation—our quest for it springs from a primal human urge for order in a world we cannot bear to admit is destined for futility. When attempted in art, it raises hopes where none should be had. Thus many will claim it is best to be done with beauty's beguiling deception, give up the pretense of a necessary link between beauty and truth, and allow art to awake us to a cosmos in turmoil with a hopeless future.

Second, the pursuit of beauty is suspected as an offense against goodness, in that it distracts us from our ethical obligations to others in need, and distracts those unjustly suffering from the wrongness of their plight. In other words, it is thought to misrepresent reality by encouraging an evasion of the evils that cry out for action. In the hands of the powerful and comfortable, the love of beauty is a luxury that screens out the world's victims, muffles the howl of those who know little or no beauty. Or, from the other side, beauty dulls the oppressed to the injustice of their predicament—an opiate of the people. "Sing your spirituals of heaven," the slave owners said, as they tightened the chains for the night. This suspicion of beauty has become a shrill cry in our time. Striving for beauty in art becomes nothing less than a moral crime, equivalent to being shown photos of 9/11 and remarking on what lovely weather it was that day. Artists, it is said, are best to be done with beauty's attendant immorality, deny its supposed ties with goodness and devote their energies to keeping society ethically vigilant.

These two suspicions we have touched on already. But there is a third and rather more subtle one: beauty is suspected as "harmonizing away" the evil-

---

[43]Thomas Kinkade, quoted in Gregory Woolfe, "Editorial Statement: The Painter of Lite™," *Image* 34 (2002): 5. Woolfe rightly says: "in refusing to see the world as it is, sentimentality reduces hope to nostalgia," i.e., the longing for a supposedly pre-fallen state (p. 6).

[44]It is significant that this cynicism is quickly read back into artists who may not have shared it themselves. A good example is the rush toward "ironic" interpretations of the last movement of Beethoven's ninth symphony (e.g., Nicholas Cook, Maynard Solomon). It is supposed that Beethoven could not possibly have been concerned with evoking a sense of joyful triumph after struggle, so we are offered strained readings of Beethoven's joy as supposedly interlaced with a profound hesitation before an "absent God." For a fine discussion see Anthony Monti, *A Natural Theology of the Arts: Imprint of the Spirit* (Aldershot, U.K.: Ashgate, 2003), pp. 148-51.

ness of evil (thus trivializing it). This has to do with the way beauty is conceptualized. There is a distrust of notions of beauty in which *balance, symmetry and equivalence* predominate and in some manner incorporate evil accordingly, so that evil's irrational, intrusive quality is suppressed. At worst, evil is included within a closed metaphysics of necessity. Put theologically, it might be suggested that God has eternally willed the history of sin and death as the necessary means of achieving his ends, that evil is an essential component in the unfolding of history's texture—in short, that beauty is not possible without evil.[45] The consequences for the doctrine of God can be stated very bluntly: God is either above good and evil (and thus essentially amoral) or to some degree God is evil himself, perhaps even wholly evil.

Here, all who warm to the metaphysics of German idealism, especially Hegel, or to theologies of creation relying on total systematic consistency need to be acutely wary of the dangers of constructing "aesthetic totality" theodicies. Even John Hick, who is often singled out for succumbing to this himself, highlights the weaknesses of "the aesthetic theme" in Augustine's theodicy,[46] a critique mounted much more carefully by Balthasar.[47] Anselm's justification of hell in *Cur Deus Homo* has been attacked along similar lines.[48]

---

[45]Some have argued that the movie *American Beauty* in effect illustrates "aesthetic totality" theodicy as a theistic response to the problem of evil (James S. Spiegel, "The Theological Aesthetic of *American Beauty*," *Journal of Religion and Popular Culture* <www.usask.ca/relst/jrpc/art4-americanbeauty.html>).

[46]John Hick, *Evil and the God of Love* (London: Collins, 1977), pp. 88-89. Hick acknowledges the limited usefulness of Augustine's aesthetic model for "natural evil," but has little time for it as applied to Augustine's view of moral evil and its devastating consequences.

[47]Hans Urs von Balthasar, *The Glory of the Lord. A Theological Aesthetics*, vol. 2, *Studies in Theological Style: Clerical Styles*, trans. Andrew Louth, Francis McDonagh, and Brian McNeil (Edinburgh: T & T Clark, 1984), pp. 26-129. Whether Balthasar himself is entirely free from "closed system" metaphysics is debatable; see n. 27 of chap. 1.

[48]Frank Burch Brown, "The Beauty of Hell: Anselm on God's Design," *Journal of Religion* 73 (1993): 329-56. See *Cur Deus Homo* 1:15: "And so, though man or evil angel refuse to submit to the divine will and appointment, yet he cannot escape it; for if he wishes to fly from a will that commands, he falls into the power of a will that punishes. And if you ask whither he goes, it is only under the permission of that will; and even this wayward choice or action of his becomes subservient, under infinite wisdom, to the order and beauty of the universe before spoken of. For when it is understood that God brings good out of many forms of evil, then the satisfaction for sin freely given, or if this be not given, the exaction of punishment, hold their own place and orderly beauty in the same universe. For if divine wisdom were not to insist upon things, when wickedness tries to disturb the right appointment, there would be, in the very universe which God ought to control, an unseemliness springing from the violation of the beauty of arrangement, and God would appear to be deficient in his management. And these two things are not only unfitting, but consequently impossible; so that satisfaction or punishment must needs follow every sin."

It is one thing to claim that God can and does bring good out of evil, that sin and death are constrained by divine providence to serve God's transcendent purpose; it is quite another to imagine that in the eschaton we will look back on some event of mindless cruelty in history and say: "Now, in the total scheme of things, I can see why that had to happen." The classic wrestling with these matters in modern times is to be found in Dostoyevsky's *The Brothers Karamazov*: what aesthetically harmonized final bliss, asks Ivan, could ever justify the torture and death of an eight-year-old child? "I don't want harmony. . . . [T]oo high a price has been placed on harmony. We cannot afford to pay so much for admission. . . . It's not God that I do not accept, Alyosha. I merely most respectfully return him the ticket."[49] Disentangling beauty from sentimentality is unlikely to be accomplished until it is recognized that evil (as with God's saving grace) cannot be accommodated within systems that seek to "make sense" of all things within closed cosmological and metaphysical systems.

Admittedly, there are gentler versions of this kind of aesthetic scheme that do not iron out evil's contingency, that do see it as an irrational intrusion, but that nevertheless construe God's salvation (in this life and the next) in terms of the logic or rationality of symmetrical perfection; atonement and salvation are essentially a matter of "balancing things out," restoring equilibrium. Insofar as they still allow for a genuine contingency in the created order, these definitely mark an advance on "closed system" theologies. However, those who are suspicious of beauty's charms press the question: What in the final "harmony" of the future could ever "match" or compensate for the kind of abysmal sin alluded to by Ivan? And even if one does speak of the possibility of hell, is this best imagined in terms of equivalence, perfectly balancing the good of heaven and thus contributing to the overall "beauty" of God's purposes?[50] The intuition here is that the metaphors of balance, however carefully articulated, are somehow inappropriate to the seriousness of the world's evil and thus to some extent still fall prey to sentimentality.

---

[49]Fyodor Dostoyevsky, *The Brothers Karamazov* (Harmondsworth, U.K.: Penguin, 1958), p. 287. Significantly, in another place Ivan challenges Alyosha on the question of necessity: "answer me; imagine it is you yourself who are erecting the edifice of human destiny with the aim of making men happy in the end, of giving them peace and contentment at last, but that to do that is *absolutely necessary,* and indeed quite inevitable, to torture to death only one tiny creature, the little girl who beat her breast with her little fist, and to found the edifice on her unavenged tears—would you consent to be the architect on those conditions? Tell me and do not lie!" Alyosha replies softly: "No, I wouldn't" (ibid., pp. 287-88, italics added).
[50]See Burch Brown, "Beauty of Hell."

The Countersentimentality of the Three Days of Easter

Are there then ways of construing beauty that avoid the pathologies of sentimentalism? Once again, everything hinges on how determined we are to allow God's reconciling self-revelation in Jesus Christ to form and transform all our prior conceptions of beauty; on whether we are prepared—as Balthasar would put it—to pursue a "theological aesthetics" (shaped by the unique beauty of God's self-disclosure) rather than an "aesthetic theology" (shaped by a priori conceptions of beauty).[51] In chapter one I outlined something of the contours of a theological account of beauty, oriented to the saving work of the Son and Spirit, and intrinsically related to the being of the triune God. This now needs to be filled out with particular attention to the Son's journey through crucifixion to resurrection. The dissociation of sentimentality and beauty is only possible inasmuch as we interpret both through the narrative of the Church's *triduum:* Good Friday, Holy Saturday and Easter Day. Only in this way will the true nature and seriousness of sentimentality be exposed, and only this way will we begin to understand how it may be countered, indeed, how it has *already* been countered in the dying and rising of Jesus Christ. In a nutshell, Christian sentimentalism arises from a premature grasp for Easter morning, a refusal to follow the three days of Easter as three days in an irreversible sequence of victory over evil. By the same token, a theological account of divine and created beauty can only be purged of sentimentality by appropriate attention to these three days, read as an integrated yet differentiated narrative.

We recall that sentimentality's emotional dynamics are built on a misrepresentation of reality through an evasion or trivialization of evil. A theological countersentimentality depends, I suggest, on meeting this with an appropriate construal of the relation between cross and resurrection. The issues here are enormous and much debated, but the core matter for our purposes can be opened up by turning to Alan Lewis's notion of a "stereophonic" reading of the three days of Easter.[52] According to Lewis, the story of Good Friday to Easter can be

> told and heard, believed and interpreted, *two different ways at once*—as a story whose ending is *known,* and as one whose ending is discovered only *as*

---

[51]Hans Urs von Balthasar, *The Glory of the Lord. A Theological Aesthetics,* vol. 1, *Seeing the Form,* trans. Erasmo Leivà-Merikakis (Edinburgh: T & T Clark, 1982), pp. 79-117.

[52]Alan E. Lewis, *Between Cross and Resurrection: A Theology of Holy Saturday* (Grand Rapids: Eerdmans, 2001), pp. 32ff.

it happens. The truth is victim when either reading is allowed to drown out the other; the truth emerges only when both readings are audible, the separate sound in each ear creating, as it were, a stereophonic unity.[53]

This is what the New Testament texts themselves offer. We are invited to view the crucifixion in the light of the blazing daybreak of Easter; Sunday morning vindicates the Jesus who was crucified, announcing that he was indeed God's chosen one, that the world's sin has been defeated in him. This is to view the cross from the outside, as it were, with the synoptic gaze we attain when we know the ending: Good Friday is seen to be a saving initiative, "Good." Yet along with this, we are also invited to read the story from the inside, from the perspective of those who live through the shadows of Friday and Saturday *without* knowing the ending, for whom the Friday is a catastrophic finale to the would-be Messiah's life, a day devoid of victory, a day of shredded hopes, drained of goodness. Hence the steady, day-by-day rehearsal of the passion story in many of our churches during Holy Week, when we play the events liturgically at their original speed.

Why are we given this "inside" story? For no other reason than to impress on us that the healing of the world is achieved in this way and no other. The one whom God vindicates on Easter morning is none other than one numbered with the lowest of low, naked, ignominious. The resurrection does not erase the memory of Friday: it confirms the cross as the specific locus where the weight of the world's evil is borne, and borne away. This is how God disarms the principalities and powers and triumphs over them (Col 2:15); this is how God's idiocy outstrips human wisdom (1 Cor 1); this is how "it is finished" (Jn 19:30). The scandal is captured with astonishing power in Rembrandt's etching "The Three Crosses" (1653), where the divine light-beam falling from above does nothing to alleviate the horror of Golgotha, but renders it as all the harsher. Easter does of course throw its light on the "renting" of Friday (to use Yeats's word), but not a soothing glow so much as a white light that exposes the rupture between Creator and creature, the depths to which the human creature has sunk and the depths to which God's love is prepared to reach.

---

[53]Ibid., p. 33. Hence Lewis's insistence that "the multiple meaning of the story will only emerge as we hold in tension what the cross says on its own, what the resurrection says on its own, and what each of them says when interpreted in the light of the other." Lewis goes on to recommend that the second day be seen as the vantage point from which this may be done, for it "serves both to keep the first and third days apart in their separate identities and to unite them in the indivisibility" (pp. 33-34).

Beauty, Sentimentality and the Arts

What then can we now say about beauty? And what might this mean for the arts?

As far as divine beauty is concerned, in chapter one I spoke of God's beauty as the beauty of ecstatic, outgoing love for the other. We can now stress that this outgoing love is nowhere more palpable, nowhere more acutely or sharply defined, than in the "way of the Son of God into the far country";[54] here the intratrinitarian *agape* "goes out" to that extremity of darkness into which our rebellion leads us, in order to win us back. This is emphatically *not* to say that the crucifixion as an event of torture and death is really beautiful and not ugly, if only we would change our perspective. That would be gross sentimentality (and, of course, opens the door to sadism or sadomasochism). But it is to say that in and through this particular torture, crucifixion and death, God's love is displayed at its most potent. The "form" of beauty here is the radiant, splendid form of God's self-giving love. As Cardinal Ratzinger (now Pope Benedict XVI) put it: "in his Face that is so disfigured, there appears the genuine, extreme beauty: the beauty of love that goes 'to the very end.' "[55] This is what Barth meant when he claimed that "God's beauty embraces death as well as life, fear as well as joy, what we might call the ugly as well as what we might call the beautiful."[56] He was not proposing that ugliness itself is in fact beautiful or that ugliness belongs in some way to God's own being, but that God's saving love has stretched out to redeem that which is ugly.[57] Compare Balthasar: "[God's beauty] embraces the most abysmal ugliness of sin and hell by virtue of the condescension of divine love, which has brought even sin and hell into that divine art for which there is no human analogue."[58] In other words, there can be nothing sentimental about God's beauty, because it has engaged with the worst

---

[54]Karl Barth, *Church Dogmatics* 4/1, trans. G. W. Bromiley and T. F. Torrance (Edinburgh: T & T Clark, 1974), pp. 157-210.

[55]Joseph Ratzinger, "The Feeling of Things, the Contemplation of Beauty," <www.second spring.co.uk/articles/benedict6.htm>.

[56]Karl Barth, *Church Dogmatics* 2/1, trans. G. W. Bromiley and T. F. Torrance (Edinburgh: T & T Clark, 1957), p. 665. Compare Augustine: "He hung therefore on the cross deformed, but his deformity is our beauty" (Sermon 27.6, in *Patrologia Latina,* ed. Jacques-Paul Migne, 40:89-90).

[57]The quote, I should note, is preceded by the words "In this self-declaration"—in other words, in God's self-revealing saving economy.

[58]Balthasar, *Glory of the Lord,* p. 124; see also his *The Glory of the Lord. A Theological Aesthetics,* vol. 7, *Theology: The New Covenant,* trans. Brian McNeil (Edinburgh: T & T Clark, 1991), pp. 202-35.

and shows itself most vigorously *as* it engages with the worst.[59]

Balthasar's words push us on to consider created beauty (the "divine art"). In chapter one I argued that Christ is to be seen as the ultimate measure of created beauty, since he is the one in whom creation has reached its eschatological goal. We can now stress that this was achieved only through divine beauty engaging directly with the world's wounded and deformed beauty; in the incarnate Son, crucified, risen and now exalted, we are given an anticipation of God's re-creation of the world's beauty. A constant "remembrance" *(anamnesis)* of the cross will prevent the pleasure that rightly attends beauty from sliding into sentimentality, for beauty at its richest has been forged through the starkness and desolation of Good Friday: indeed, as the Revelation to St. John reminds us, the risen Lamb on the throne bears the marks of suffering (Rev 5:6).

Now we can consider again the three suspicions of beauty I mentioned earlier and offer one or two glimpses of how the arts—insofar as *their* created beauty comes to terms with the beauty created and re-created in the crucified and risen Jesus Christ—might play a part in fostering a countersentimentality today.

There was, first, the suspicion that pursuing beauty fosters a lie, a denial of that heading-toward-death that marks all the world's phenomena. A Christ-centered response will likely be swift: the ultimate truth about the world is not to be found in this scenario but in the resurrection of the Son of God, whose beauty embodies God's promise for the final destiny of the cosmos. *Yet* we must now stress that the Son who is risen is the Son who was given up to the corrupting forces of sin and death afflicting creation, and in such a way that creation's beauty is exposed as fatally flawed and broken just *as* its corruptions are met and healed. Similarly, humankind is offered the possibility of being remade in the likeness of the beauty of the

---

[59]This is why we need Nietzsche, because he reminds us of the "ungainliness" of the gospel. "Nietzsche has bequeathed Christian thought a most beautiful gift, a needed anamnesis of itself—of its strangeness: . . . a God who goes about in the dust of exodus for love of a race intransigent in its particularity; who apparels himself in common human nature, in the form of a servant; who brings good news to those who suffer and victory to those who are as nothing; who dies like a slave and outcast without resistance; who penetrates to the very depths of hell in pursuit of those he loves; and who persists even after death not as a hero lifted up to Olympian glories, but in the company of peasants, breaking bread with them and offering them the solace of his wounds. In recalling theology to the ungainliness of the gospel, Nietzsche retrieved the gospel from the soporific complacency of modernity" (David Bentley Hart, *The Beauty of the Infinite: The Aesthetics of Christian Truth* [Grand Rapids: Eerdmans, 2003], pp. 126-27).

risen Son and to enact here and now that beauty in the power of the Spirit. *Yet* this very truth includes and depends on a direct engagement with and an exposure of the present pathos of the human condition.

Among the most impressive explorations of the world's beauty and pathos was a recent exhibition of works by fifteen North American visual artists, gathered together under the heading "A Broken Beauty" and presented in a book of that title. In the context of a countersentimental, "three days" faith, the project explored beauty in relation to the depiction of the human body, especially in the light of attitudes to the body in contemporary society. In this art, as Ted Prestcott puts it, "the bodies speak of a desire for a human image that can carry the weight of complex meanings, where beauty is not a mask and brokenness is not the only reality."[60]

The second suspicion of the quest for beauty was that it distracts us from our moral responsibilities to others in need and distracts the victims of injustice from the wrongness of their predicament. It should be clear by now that the quest for beauty, tempered through the three days of Easter, need not stifle action or deafen us to the cries of the world's wounded. It is worth recalling that justice concerns right relationships and that the same goes for beauty—the beauty God desires for the human community is the proper dynamic ordering of lives in relation to each other. Justice is beautiful.[61]

Some of the most striking Christian art of recent decades has encouraged, or has been used to promote an alertness to social injustice and the need for effective action. In this context I might mention John de Gruchy's profound theological examination of the arts (including Christian art) in apartheid and postapartheid South Africa,[62] or the British initiative "Soul in the City," in which thousands of young people in the summer months find that music-led worship leads directly into an energetic involvement in urban renewal.[63]

The third suspicion was of the tendency of concepts of beauty to "harmonize away" the evilness of evil, especially those dominated by notions of balance, symmetry and equivalence. Matters of considerable controversy

---

[60]Theodore L. Prestcott, "The Bodies Before Us," in *A Broken Beauty*, ed. Theodore L. Prestcott (Grand Rapids: Eerdmans, 2005), p. 24.

[61]It is worth recalling that the word *fair* can mean both beautiful and just! For a vigorous defense of beauty against the charge that it encourages injustice, see Elaine Scarry, *On Beauty and Being Just* (Princeton, N.J.: Princeton University Press, 2001).

[62]John W. de Gruchy, *Christianity, Art, and Transformation: Theological Aesthetics in the Struggle for Justice* (Cambridge: Cambridge University Press, 2001).

[63]"Soul in the City," *Faithworks* <www.faithworks.info/Standard.asp?id=4257>

swirl around us here, but for our purposes this much at least may be said. The raising of Jesus from the dead vindicates the crucified Christ, not crucifixion; it does not validate or legitimate a view of the world that imagines evil and suffering as necessary to its fulfilment. The three days of Easter do not tell us that the world's pain and agony are required for God to achieve his purposes (still less for God to be God), or that sin is a requisite part of the harmonious fabric of things, part of the world's chiaroscuro. God does not bargain with evil but shatters its power, overthrowing the principalities and powers; evil is a wholly contingent intrusion, an irrational interruption of original goodness. (This, incidentally, is where musical models of "resolution" in theology need handling with care, in that they could suggest that dissonance was composed into the cosmic symphony by the Composer.) By the same token we ought to be wary of schemes of salvation that suggest the divine strategy is, so to speak, primarily to balance things out (as in strictly retributive views of atonement and eschatological justice). The world is not so much balanced as *reconciled,* and reconciled with a God of infinite excess. Through the three days of Easter, evil, sin and death are defeated by a love that does not simply "match" what has been hurled at it from rebellious creatures, but infinitely *exceeds* anything and everything it "answers." The fulfilment toward which the resurrection points us, and which it anticipates, is not a mere restoration of a previous order, a return to the *status quo ante* of Eden; it is not only a recovery of what is lost but a *radical re-creation of all things.* Easter is—if I may put it this way—an aesthetic joke, vastly surplus to any "requirement" or "compensation," vastly outstripping any expectation and every predictable equilibrium, involving not merely the evening out but the transformation of creation's brokenness into something of infinitely expanding, superabundant beauty.

By the same token, do we not need to be wary of certain theologies, which out of an understandable concern to "take suffering seriously" actually sentimentalize it by robbing it of its irrationality, its interruptive offense and horror to God? I have in mind here certain forms of "suffering God" theology that in their zeal to affirm divine solidarity with the victims of suffering veer toward imprisoning God in the world's history and hence (albeit inadvertently) come close to eternalizing evil in God (thus, ironically, compromising God's freedom to save or redeem). That there is more than a hint of sentimentality at work here is confirmed by the emotional self-indulgence that can quickly creep in: an implicit assumption that God, in order to be worth believing in, *must* answer to our particular "need for" a suffering God.[64] I have in mind also certain British "tragic theologies," that out of a strong fear of metaphysical optimism, of anything that would trivialize evil, can come close to doing just that through appearing to presume a fundamental, perpetual order of violence and strife in creation, a scenario that arguably encourages something more akin to resignation before the magnitude of evil rather than a revulsion that stems from a confidence born of resurrection faith.[65]

To close, I cite just two pieces of art, both of which in their own way move against this tendency toward an overharmonized beauty. The first is by the Scottish Roman Catholic composer James MacMillan, who unashamedly relates music's particular powers of tension and resolution to the three days of Easter: "I seem to be going round and round in circles round the same three days in history. The fact is that if history had to be changed—if *we* had to be changed—then God had to interact with us in a severe way."[66] The contours of MacMillan's outlook find monumental expression in *The Triduum*—three orchestral works relating to the events and liturgies of Maundy Thursday, Good Friday and the Easter Vigil (respectively, *The World's Ransoming,* the *Cello Concerto* and *Symphony: Vigil*). In the *Cello Concerto,* the theme is Christ's crucifixion, the cello soloist shifting between the roles of protagonist, antagonist and commentator. In the first movement, vulgar dance-hall music evokes Christ's humiliation, and toward the end the players themselves shout the words of the Good Friday Latin plainsong "Crucem tuam adoremus, Domine." In "The Reproaches," MacMillan quotes "Dunblane Cathedral" (a Protestant hymn), a reference to the shooting of

---

[64]Certain varieties of process theology move strongly in these directions. The work of Jürgen Moltmann is sometimes cited in this connection also, though it should be stressed that he would distance himself sharply from some of the extremes to which his thought has been said to lead. For discussion, see John Thompson, *Modern Trinitarian Perspectives* (Oxford: Oxford University Press, 1994), chap. 3; Kenneth Surin, *Theology and the Problem of Evil* (Oxford: Blackwell, 1986), esp. chap. 4; Richard Bauckham, *The Theology of Jürgen Moltmann* (Edinburgh: T & T Clark, 1995); Paul D. Molnar, *Divine Freedom and the Doctrine of the Immanent Trinity* (London: T & T Clark, 2002), esp. chap. 7.

[65]Donald M. MacKinnon, "Atonement and Tragedy," in *The Borderlands of Theology: And Other Essays* (London: Lutterworth, 1968), pp. 97-104; Nicholas Lash, *Theology on the Way to Emmaus* (London: SCM, 1986), esp. pp. 194-96. See also Daniel W. Hardy, "Theology Through Philosophy," in *The Modern Theologians: An Introduction to Christian Theology in the Twentieth Century,* ed. David F. Ford (Oxford: Blackwell, 1997), pp. 252-85, 272-78. For a highly critical treatment, see Hart, *Beauty of the Infinite,* pp. 380-94.

[66]James MacMillan, quoted in Jolyon Mitchell, "Sound of Heart," *Third Way* 22, no. 5 (1999): 19.

sixteen children and their teacher by a lone gunman in Dunblane, Scotland, an atrocity that occurred as MacMillan worked on the piece. The movement climaxes with brutal percussion blows—nails driven mercilessly into Christ's hands and feet. In the Easter work, *Symphony: Vigil,* the music incorporates ecstatic, irregular dance, and its central movement, *Tuba insonet salutaris* ("Sound the trumpet of salvation"—from the *Exsultet,* sung at the Easter Vigil) is described by MacMillan thus:

> The brass quintet, which played unseen at the end of the first movement, now comes into the auditorium and the players position themselves at five different points, representing the trumpets of salvation. The aural perspective takes on new dimensions as music is heard from all angles, and the sounds are bright and startling.[67]

The "resolution" enacted in *Symphony: Vigil* neither effaces the harshness of the memories of the preceding days nor accords them any kind of ultimacy, but through a wide range of carefully controlled musical techniques, transfigures the dissonance into a novel and utterly beguiling beauty. Moreover, its beauty is anything but tidy; the forms overlap, material is scattered, dropped and picked up again, and we are given a concluding section with (in MacMillan's words) "luminous floating chords on high strings accompanying gently soaring trumpet calls and bright percussion."[68]

The second piece is a poem by Micheal O'Siadhail. After Auschwitz the oft-repeated cry goes up: "Never again." To heed such a cry entails keeping the memory alive; as the years pass, remembrance cannot be allowed to falter or fade. But part of what is needed also are ways of living that refuse to treat the diabolical forces that led to the *Shoa* as if they are to achieve finality. And that means knowing how to feast, how to play, how to laugh—how to celebrate the excessive, anarchic (but not chaotic) beauty of the love of God. Of course, this takes us to the very edge of sentimentality—to the verge of a flagrant evasion and trivialization of evil, an emotional self-indulgence that avoids responsible action, and to the verge of an empty "comedy" that does no more than celebrate life with wide-eyed naiveté. But if read through the three days of Easter, these pitfalls can be avoided. Part of any Christian response to evil will be cultivating patterns of life that will

---

[67]James MacMillan, "Composer's Notes," *Boosey & Hawkes,* August 1997 <www.boosey.com/pages/cr/catalogue/cat_detail.asp?musicid=771>

[68]Ibid. For further discussion of MacMillan, see Jeremy Begbie, *Resounding Truth: Christian Wisdom in the World of Music* (Grand Rapids: Baker, forthcoming), chap. 7.

not allow the powers of darkness a foothold, that come from knowing that in Jesus Christ a superfluity of love has already exceeded everything that could be thrown at it, that a resurrection life is available that in its overabundance will always surpass and outrun "the ruler of this world." Hence the defiance of Bonhoeffer who spoke of *hilaritas* as he faced his own execution; the clownlike defiance Georges Rouault had in mind when he said: "He who has forgotten how to laugh is only waiting to die"; the jazzlike defiance toward which O'Siadhail points us:

> That any poem after Auschwitz is obscene?
> Covenants of silence so broken between us
> Can we still promise or trust what we mean?
>
> Even in the dark of the earth, seeds will swell.
> All the interweavings and fullness of being,
> Nothing less may insure against our hell.
>
> A black sun only shines out of a vacuum.
> Cold narrowing and idols of blood and soil.
> And all the more now, we can't sing dumb!
>
> A conversation so rich it knows it never arrives
> Or forecloses; in a buzz and cross-ruff of polity
> The restless subversive ragtime of what thrives.
>
> Endless dialogues. The criss-cross of flourishings.
> Again and over again our complex yes.
> A raucous glory and the whole jazz of things.
>
> The sudden riff of surprise beyond our ken;
> Out of control, a music's brimming let-go.
> We feast to keep our promise of never again.[69]

---

[69]Micheal O'Siadhail, "Never," in *The Gossamer Wall* (Newcastle upon Tyne: Bloodaxe, 2002), p. 120.

3

CALL FORWARDING

Improvising the Response to the Call of Beauty

Bruce Ellis Benson

Hush! Hush! Somebody's calling my name
Hush! Hush! Somebody's calling my name
Hush! Hush! Somebody's calling my name
O my Lord, O my Lord, what shall I do?

But isn't this always the case? Somebody's calling my name. I hear the call and I'm faced with the question "What shall I do?" What *shall* I do? What shall *I* do? Who is this *I* who is being called? What happens to this "I" *in* being called? And who or what is calling me?

This pattern of call and response goes back at least as far as creation. God calls the world into being, and so the being of all that exists is a response to that call. But, of course, there is no *one* call, even in the creation narrative. Instead, there are multiple calls—calls upon calls—and thus responses upon responses, an intricate web that is ever being improvised with the result being a ceaseless reverberation of call and response. Yet what structures this relation of call and response? Further, how exactly does it relate to beauty?

In what follows I examine what I take to be reflections of God's beauty in creation. If all beauty originates from God, then all beauty found in the world is a reflected beauty. Rather than attempting to define beauty, to provide the "essence" of beauty or even to reflect on beautiful things per se, I will consider beauty in a roundabout way: by way of the call. Here I am following the call of Jean-Louis Chrétien as laid out in his book *The Call and the Response.*[1] There Chrétien reminds us just how central this structure of call and response is to creaturely existence, and how intimately connected to goodness and beauty it is. Here I unpack Chrétien's analysis of the call, likewise calling upon Hans Urs von Balthasar. Then I turn to how we might work out the call and response in black spirituals and jazz before reflecting on how they likewise provide an example of beauty. It is, I think, appropriate to consider music that originates from the margins of music, from those oppressed and considered the least. For Jesus—whom Paul terms the "icon" of God (2 Cor 4:4)—himself identifies with the hungry, the thirsty, the stranger, the naked and the prisoner, saying, "just as you did it to one of the least of these who are members of my family, you did it to me" (Mt 25:40). The beauty that is reflected by the marginalized is a broken beauty, one that reflects a God who not only takes a stand with those oppressed and broken but also becomes oppressed and broken himself. Yet that broken beauty likewise points to the eschatological beauty of the risen, reigning Lord.

Beauty *as* the Call

There is absolutely no sense of "beauty for beauty's sake" in Chrétien: as he says, "things and forms do not beckon us because they are beautiful in themselves, *for their own sake,* as it were. Rather, we call them beautiful precisely because they call us and recall us."[2] Here we have a surprising reversal. Chrétien is clear regarding the relation of call, beauty and goodness. But it is the *order* of them that he puts into question. "Beautiful, *kalon,* is what comes from a call, *kalein,*" he says.[3] So the call is what constitutes the beautiful rather than the other way around. Things are beautiful precisely because they call out to us. Or we might put this the other way around: God's call precedes the pronouncement of beauty. In creating the world God calls various things into being. "Let there be light," says God, and only *after* calling it into being does he then reflect on its goodness (Gen 1:3-4). In this sense, *kaleō* is more primordial than *kalon.* Or, as Chrétien puts it, "The word 'beautiful' is not primary, but responds and corresponds to the first call, which is the call sent by thought construed as a power to call and to name."[4]

---

[1]Jean-Louis Chrétien, *The Call and the Response*, trans. Anne A. Davenport (New York: Fordham University Press, 2004).
[2]Ibid., p. 3, italics added.
[3]Ibid., p. 7.
[4]Ibid.

Yet the creation of light lacks the dimension of a *human* call. Light may "respond" by illuminating, but a person called by God responds both by a readiness to hear and a readiness to act. In this regard it is remarkable how similar the responses of Moses and Samuel are to God's call. God calls out from the burning bush, "Moses, Moses," and Moses responds, "Here I am" (Ex 3:4). This "here I am" is to say, "I am at your disposal." And the formula that Eli gives to Samuel is, "Speak, LORD, for your servant is listening" (1 Sam 3:9). What takes place in these exchanges is a crucial reversal. Emmanuel Levinas puts it as follows: "here I am *(me voici)!* The accusative here is remarkable: here I am, under your eyes, at your service, your obedient servant."[5] In other words the subject is now truly *subject* to the Other, the one who calls, and so stands in the accusative case. Similarly, Balthasar, influenced by the famed writer on acting Konstantin Stanislavsky, speaks of a *disponibilité* in which "the whole human system is available."[6]

Yet how does beauty call and what is its attraction? While the Hebraic priority of the voice has often been contrasted with the Hellenic priority of sight, the "call" can come in either form or another form altogether. Relating his enlightenment from Diotima in the *Symposium,* Socrates speaks of moving from an *eros* for the body to an *eros* for the soul to an *eros* for beauty itself.[7] Ultimately, this *eros* for—or, we might well say, call *to*—beauty is disconnected from both sight and sound. So it would seem that the call may be delivered through sight or sound, or even something else. However, Chrétien points out that, even in the *Symposium,* "vision, at every step, produces speech in response [e.g., the very speech that Socrates is making at the banquet]" and so concludes that "visible beauty calls for spoken beauty."[8] What exactly, though, is beauty's allure? In commenting on Plato, the Neo-Platonist philosopher Proclus makes the insightful etymological observation that beauty calls *(kalein)* "because it enchants and charms *(kelein)*."[9] Chrétien concludes that the charm beauty exerts results in "voice,

---

[5]Emmanuel Levinas, "God and Philosophy," in *Basic Philosophical Writings,* ed. Adriaan T. Peperzak, Simon Critchley and Robert Bernasconi (Bloomington: Indiana University Press, 1996), p. 146.

[6]Hans Urs von Balthasar, *Theo-Drama: Theological Dramatic Theory:* vol. 1, *Prologomena,* trans. Graham Harrison (San Francisco: Ignatius, 1988), p. 288. Here Balthasar references Konstantin Stanislavsky, *Das Geheimnis des schauspielerischen Erfolges* (Zurich: Scientia, n.d.), p. 168.

[7]Plato *Symposium* 210a-e.

[8]Chrétien, *Call and the Response,* p. 11.

[9]Proclus, *Sur le premier Alcibiade de Platon,* ed. and trans. A. Segonds (Paris: Belles Lettres, 1986), 2:361, cited in Chrétien, *Call and the Response,* p. 12.

speech, and music."[10] Of course, Chrétien is overstating his case. No doubt beauty *often* results in speech and music, but it can likewise move us to paint or sculpt.

Yet Proclus does more than define beauty in terms of enchantment and charm, for he likewise connects this enchantment with God. In his *Platonic Theology,* he writes, "beauty converts all things to itself, sets them in motion, causes them to be possessed by the divine, and *recalls them to itself through the intermediary of love.*"[11] We find this same connection of beauty and God in Dionysius—or Pseudo-Dionysius—again by way of the call: "Beauty 'calls' all things to itself (whence it is called 'beauty')," writes Dionysius, who makes it clear that "Beauty" here is another name for God (in his text titled *The Divine Names).*[12]

So beauty enchants and this enchantment comes from God. But once moved, how do we forward the call? The answer to that question can best be found in analyzing the initial call itself. And here I turn to Balthasar. For, although the language of call and response is not central to Balthasar's thought to the degree that it is in Chrétien, his description of how beauty charms us is remarkably in line with Chrétien. Yet Balthasar adds at least three elements (and no doubt many more) that help clarify the call. All three of these elements can be found in the following passage from the *Theological Aesthetics:*

> The form as it appears to us is beautiful only because the delight that it arouses in us is founded upon the fact that, in it, the truth and goodness of the depths of reality itself are manifested and bestowed, and this manifestation and bestowal reveal themselves to us as being something infinitely and inexhaustibly valuable and fascinating.[13]

Let me enumerate these elements. First, whereas secular liberalism/ modernism (particularly as exemplified by Immanuel Kant) had disconnected the traditional transcendentals of the good, the true and the beautiful,

---

[10]Chrétien, *Call and the Response,* p. 12.

[11]Proclus *The Platonic Theology,* trans. Thomas Taylor (El Paso: Selene, 1988), p. 77. Here I am following the quote as translated by Anne A. Davenport in Chrétien, *Call and the Response,* pp. 9-10 (italics added).

[12]Pseudo-Dionysius, *The Divine Names* 701c-d, in *The Complete Works,* trans. Colin Luibheid and Paul Rorem (New York: Paulist, 1987). The English translation uses "bids" in place of "calls." But since the verb is *kaloun* in the Greek text, then "calls" seems a more accurate translation.

[13]Hans Urs von Balthasar, *The Glory of the Lord: A Theological Aesthetics,* vol. 1, *Seeing the Form,* trans. Erasmo Leiva-Merikakis (San Francisco: Ignatius, 1982), p. 118.

Balthasar reconnects them and makes them not merely logical operators (as in the thought of Duns Scotus) but truly part of the created order.[14] Second, and closely related, in Balthasar "the beauty of the world" and "theological beauty" are once again connected, as they were in Thomas Aquinas.[15] This reconnection is why Balthasar insists that his is a "theological aesthetics" rather than an "aesthetic theology." But this means that God's call to us is very much connected to the beauty of the earth, even while surpassing and pointing beyond that earthly beauty. Third, the possibility of the call is due to what Balthasar calls a "double and reciprocal *ekstasis*—God's 'venturing forth' to man and man's to God."[16] Balthasar goes so far as to speak of the "elevation of man to participate in [God's] glory."[17]

On both Chrétien's and Balthasar's accounts of the call, then, participation is central. But how do we participate in the call? In one sense that participation is possible because God both transcends the world and yet is reflected by it. One can—on this point—agree with John Milbank, who writes that "participation can be extended also to language, history and culture: the whole realm of human culture" precisely because "human making participates in a God who is infinite poetic utterance."[18] While it seems to me that Milbank here unduly limits participation to *poiesis* (i.e., artistic making)— and I would want to broaden it to include *phronesis* (i.e., practical wisdom)—the context for these reflections, music, certainly makes *poiesis* an appropriate way in which to participate in the divine beauty. Of course, there are different ways of thinking *poiesis*. The notion of artistic "creation" has been a guiding one in the arts. No doubt, artists *are* "creators" of a sort. Unfortunately, the term *creation*—at least in the modern period—has come to have rather individualistic connotations and an unhealthy tinge of ex nihilo. Given that the call always precedes us—and is what makes it possible for us to call in response—a significantly better notion would be that of "improvisation," which (as one dictionary would have it) is simply to "fabricate out of what is conveniently on hand."[19] Improvisation is, I think, a helpful

[14]On this point, as well as the one that follows, I am indebted to Oliver Davies's "The Theological Aesthetics," in *The Cambridge Companion to Hans Urs von Balthasar,* ed. Edward T. Oakes and David Moss (Cambridge: Cambridge University Press, 2004), pp. 131-42.
[15]Balthasar, *Glory of the Lord,* 1:80.
[16]Ibid., 1:126.
[17]Ibid., 1:125.
[18]John Milbank, *Being Reconciled: Ontology and Pardon* (London: Routledge, 2003), p. ix.
[19]"Improvise," in *Merriam-Webster's Collegiate Dictionary,* 11th ed. (Springfield, Mass.: Merriam-Webster, 2003).

way of conceptualizing the call and the response, and a far healthier—not to mention more accurate—way of thinking about what artists do.

Here I am building upon my previous work on improvisation. In my book *The Improvisation of Musical Dialogue,* I have argued that improvisation is a key moment in all of music making.[20] Although it is most evident in explicit improvisatory performance practices—such as jazz and baroque music—there I contend that it is likewise present in all musical discourses, even in classical music. My way of thinking about music making, then, is that composers, performers and even audience members are part of an improvisatory practice. Composers "improvise" on the conventions of their music genre (not to mention the work of previous composers); performers improvise certain elements of their performances (more or less, depending on prevailing conventions); and listeners are part of the improvisatory practice by how they listen.

Improvising the Response

In this section I turn to black spirituals and jazz—musical practices that are strongly improvisatory—to illuminate what takes place in the call and the response. As will become clear, my principal points are that (1) the call always *precedes* me; (2) in responding, I do not speak entirely on my own behalf but on my behalf and the behalf of others; and (3) the improvised response is always a repetition and an improvisation.

The first characteristic, then, is that the call always precedes me. It is not just that the response is to a prior call; it is that even the call in these songs echoes a prior call. That call can be spelled out in terms of the previous performance of these pieces. But it can likewise be traced back to earlier calls. For these songs are, in effect, echoes of echoes—going back to the call from God at the beginning of the world or, in the case of spirituals, to Jesus' call to his disciples. Jesus says to Peter and Andrew: "Follow me, and I will make you fish for people" (Mt 4:19). That call is, in turn, broadened by the Great Commission, in which the disciples—and, by extension, *we*—are called to "Go therefore and make disciples of all nations" (Mt 28:19). Here we become explicit messengers of God's call to the world. We do not call in our

---

[20]See, e.g., Bruce Ellis Benson, *The Improvisation of Musical Dialogue: A Phenomenology of Music* (Cambridge: Cambridge University Press, 2003), and "The Improvisation of Hermeneutics: Jazz Lessons for Interpreters," in *Hermeneutics at the Crossroads,* ed. Kevin Vanhoozer, James K. A. Smith and Bruce Ellis Benson (Bloomington: Indiana University Press, 2006), pp. 193-210.

name but "in the name of the Father and of the Son and of the Holy Spirit" (Mt 28:19). This is why Chrétien speaks of it being "always too late for there to be an origin," for the origin of the present call far precedes it.[21] Thus responding to the call is both a responding to a present call—one here and now—and to the calls that have preceded it. Scripture echoes this kind of echoing of calls: so, for example, when Jesus calls for repentance, he is echoing God's multiple calls to Israel through Moses and the prophets.

We do not *first* call; rather, we call because we have already been called. To improvise in jazz, then, is to respond to a call, to join in something that is always already in progress. One becomes an improviser by becoming part of the discourse of jazz. While it would take considerably deeper analysis than we have time for here to explain what is involved in becoming a jazz musician and learning how to improvise, I can briefly summarize what happens as follows. Speaking with Pierre Bourdieu, we might say that one must cultivate a habitus, a way of being that is both nurtured by and results in what Bourdieu terms "regulated improvisations."[22] They are "regulated" precisely by the constraints that make jazz "jazz"—and not something else. One becomes habituated into this habitus by *listening,* and learning to listen is the precondition for all future improvisation—especially when one improvises with others. So we can say that each improvisation is like a response to improvisations of the past. To become an improviser, one must have an intimate knowledge of past improvisations and the possibility conditions for those improvisations (i.e., the conventions of improvising). To be able to improvise means one is steeped in the tradition and knows how to respond to the call of other improvisers. Although we tend to think of jazz improvisation in terms of spontaneity, that quality of improvisation—while undoubtedly present—is usually greatly exaggerated. It is also remarkably paradoxical. Not only are many "improvisations" often heavily "scripted" but also spontaneity is only possible when one is well prepared. It takes a great deal of work to be spontaneous. It also takes a significant knowledge of improvisations of the past, for they provide the guidelines for improvisations of the present and future. Consider what Wynton Marsalis says in response to a question of how he achieved his remarkable level of success:

I would listen to records, I would buy all these etude books. Any money I

---

[21]Chrétien, *Call and the Response,* p. 5.

[22]Pierre Bourdieu, *Outline of a Theory of Practice,* trans. Richard Nice (Cambridge: Cambridge University Press, 1977), p. 78.

would make on little pop gigs I would buy trumpets or books with it. I would get all the etude books, I would go to different teachers, I would call people, and really seek the knowledge. I would go to music camp in the summer time. Practice, listen to the recordings of Adolph Herseth [the principal trumpet in the CSO for many years], or Clifford Brown, trying to learn the records.[23]

Further, "being spontaneous" is not something one simply wills. Keith Johnstone notes that it is the "decision not to try and control the future" that allows for spontaneity.[24] The implication here is that one opens oneself up to the future to allow something to happen. But, of course, that is only possible by being fully prepared and that requires a thorough grounding in the tradition. In jazz, knowing the past is what makes the future possible.

Of course, in realizing the debt to and dependency on the past, the jazz musician is aware that any response to the call is made possible by a *gift.* The call is a gift to me, something that comes—like life itself—ultimately unbidden and simply disseminated. Rowan Williams reminds us that art "always approaches the condition of being both recognition and transmission of the gift, gratuity or excess."[25] There is, of course, a long tradition (both inside and outside of the Christian tradition) in which the ability to paint or sculpt or improvise has been seen as a gift, something simply bestowed on one that calls for responsibility on the part of the receiver to cultivate, nurture and exercise.[26] In this sense both the ability and the products arising from that ability are gifts. And such gifts are hardly given simply to Christians or to the religious faithful. Indeed, they are sometimes—perhaps often—given to people who neither appreciate them nor are thankful for them, and may not even exercise them. Yet if one takes his or her gift character seriously, then one senses a kind of responsibility for exercising artistic gifts. Although it is theatrical rather than jazz improvisers who speak in these terms, the call is like an "offer" that can be either "accepted" or

---

[23]Wynton Marsalis, "Music's Jazz Maestro," *Academy of Achievement,* January 8, 1991 <www.achievement.org/autodoc/page/mar0int-4>.

[24]Keith Johnstone, *Impro: Improvisation and the Theatre* (New York: Theatre Arts Books, 1979), p. 32, italic added.

[25]Rowan Williams, *Grace and Necessity: Reflections on Art and Love* (Harrisburg, Penn.: Morehouse, 2005), p. 163.

[26]Just as an example, I note that at the Iridium Jazz Club (NYC) website one finds the following regarding the famed jazz guitarist Les Paul: "Les Paul says his greatest God-given gifts are perfect pitch, a love for music with the ability to learn it quickly, and the curiosity and persistence of an inventor who wants to know 'how things tick' " ("Les Paul," *Iridium* <www.iridium jazzclub.com/les.shtml>).

"blocked."[27] To "accept" the call is to respond in kind, to say yes to what is being offered and thus develop the call.

Second, my response is never mine alone. To be sure, I speak for myself, yet also for others and in their name. To improvise is always to speak to others, with others (even when one improvises alone) and in the name of others. Given that the call precedes me, I do not begin the discourse, nor do I bring it to a conclusion. For instance, if I'm playing one of the perennial standards of jazz, I do so along with so many others—whether those playing alongside me or those playing the tune in some other corner of the world, or all of those who have played it before. Jazz musicians typically have a sense of what the author of Hebrews calls a "great . . . cloud of witnesses" (Heb 12:1). Moreover, when I play a tune, I am never simply improvising on that tune alone. I am improvising on the tradition formed by the improvisations on that tune—what literary theorists call its "reception history." Whereas, in regard to literature, Harold Bloom has spoken of "the *anxiety* of influence"—which is the desire to be new, fresh and original—jazz musicians would rather speak of "the *joy* of influence."[28] Bloom's talk of "anxiety" stems from the romantic paradigm of art, with its drive to be "original." The primary artistic goal in the modern, romantic paradigm is to carve out a place for oneself by overcoming the influence of previous artists. One wants to become (to use Bloom's language) a "strong poet" who stands out as unique and thus distances oneself from the tradition.

But jazz provides an entirely different model for the artist. It is one far more along the lines of that in T. S. Eliot's "Tradition and the Individual Talent,"[29] and one that aptly reinforces the kind of model of artistic participation Balthasar has in mind. As a jazz improviser, one becomes part of a community of improvisers. As improviser, one works with material that already exists rather than creating ex nihilo. As improviser, one is aware of being wholly indebted to the past. As improviser, one speaks in the name of others. Although Chrétien almost certainly did not have jazz in mind, he opens *The Call and the Response* with a quotation from Joseph Joubert that captures these aspects per-

---

[27]"I call anything that an actor does an 'offer.' Each offer can either be accepted, or blocked. . . . A block is anything that prevents the action from developing" (Johnstone, *Impro*, p. 97).

[28]Harold Bloom, *The Anxiety of Influence* (New York: Oxford University Press, 1973); and John P. Murphy, "Jazz Improvisation: The Joy of Influence," *The Black Perspective in Music* 18, nos. 1 and 2 (1990): 7-19.

[29]T. S. Eliot, "Tradition and the Individual Talent," in *The Norton Anthology of English Literature*, ed. M. H. Abrams et al., 3rd ed. (New York: W. W. Norton, 1975), pp. 2553-60.

fectly: "In order for a voice to be beautiful, it must have in it many voices together."[30] My voice is always composed of many voices and so is never simply "my own." Chrétien goes on to say that "every voice . . . bears many voices within itself."[31] In a beautiful article titled "The Other in Myself," Rudolf Bernet writes, "Only somebody who must hold a lecture discovers that he or she is continually paraphrasing other authors and speaks as well in the name of colleagues and friends."[32] Interestingly enough, it so happened that the last time I spoke at the Wheaton Theology Conference there was a student visiting from the University of Leuven—where I did my doctoral work—who was just then taking a course with Professor Bernet, who was my doctoral adviser. After my address she commented, "Listening to you was like being in class with Bernet." Which I took as a compliment! So indeed we professors are constantly improvising on what our professors taught us, and they on their professors. What emerges in this improvisation upon improvisation is an ever-evolving hybridity in which identity and ownership are often stretched to their limits. Is an improvisation "mine" if it is so indebted to other improvisers? Further, even my identity as an improviser is interconnected with those of other improvisers. I may still have an identity, but it is hardly fixed or simple.

This question of identity naturally leads to my third point, which is that my response is always both a repetition and an innovation. Chrétien writes of the strange logic of improvisation (even though he is hardly thinking explicitly of improvisation, let alone jazz): "Our response can only repeat. It starts by repeating. Yet it does repeat by restating."[33] Chrétien goes on to explain this enigmatic claim by saying that there is kind of space that is opened up *in ourselves* that gives us a voice so that we are able to pass on the call without mere repetition. We hear the call and we translate it into an idiom of our own. Yet how should we think this mélange of sameness and difference, a repetition that is not merely a repetition but also a development?

A particularly influential way of thinking about this identity and difference is Henry Louis Gates Jr.'s notion of "signifyin(g)."[34] It is interesting—

---

[30]Chrétien, *Call and the Response,* p. 1.

[31]Ibid.

[32]Rudolf Bernet, "The Other in Myself," in *Tradition and Renewal: The Centennial of Louvain's Institute of Philosophy* (Leuven: Leuven University Press, 1992), 1:85.

[33]Chrétien, *Call and the Response,* p. 25.

[34]Henry Louis Gates Jr., *The Signifying Monkey: A Theory of African-American Literary Criticism* (New York: Oxford University Press, 1988), p. 46. Here I simply assume that "signifyin(g)" can have a positive function, though I discuss this question in detail in my forthcoming article "The Fundamental Heteronomy of Jazz," *Revue internationale de philosophie.*

and quite instructive for my point here—that Gates admits that he is in effect improvising on Derrida's notion of *"différance."*[35] Gates says that "all texts Signify upon other texts," but we could modify that by simply saying that "all improvisations improvise upon other improvisations."[36] On Gates's view, there are two ways in which one "signifies." Given that Gates is providing an account of how Africans and African-Americans relate to white culture, one of those ways of "signifyin(g)" is repetition with "a compelling sense of difference based on the black vernacular."[37] Yet signifyin(g) can also take the form of "homage," in which one performs the music of another—or improvises upon the improvisations of another—as (and here I quote Gates) "a gesture of admiration and respect."[38] Murphy provides a fine example of such homage by analyzing a solo of Joe Henderson that utilizes a theme from Charlie Parker's improvisation on "Buzzy."

> It is the "Buzzy" theme that tenor-saxophonist Joe Henderson chooses to transform during his improvisations on two performances of a 12-bar blues in F. The first transformation is heard on his "If." . . . One might argue that the appearance of Parker's motive at the end of Henderson's third chorus is a coincidence, but the fact that Henderson moves on to construct the entire next chorus on a restatement of the motive in its original form, followed by two transformations, shows it to be a conscious manipulation of Parker's idea.[39]

Here we have a blend of repetition and transformation, but one clearly designed to pay a kind of homage to Charlie Parker. Or to take a different example, Paul Berliner provides a fascinating genealogy of a particular jazz lick from 1946 to 1992. It starts with Billy Eckstine and Miles Davis and makes its way through Bud Powell, Clifford Brown, Dave Young, Paul Chambers, Red Garland, Ella Fitzgerald, Cannonball Adderley, The Manhattan Transfer, John Scofield, Benny Green and Christian McBride.[40]

Anyone familiar with jazz realizes that these names cover a rather long and wide sweep in its life. So a given lick can constantly be transformed while having enough "sameness" to have a continued identity. Yet each of

---

[35]For more on the notion of *différance,* see Jacques Derrida, *"Différance,"* in *Margins of Philosophy,* trans. Alan Bass (Chicago: University of Chicago Press, 1982), pp. 3-27.
[36]Gates, *Signifying Monkey,* p. xxiv.
[37]Ibid., p. xxii.
[38]Ibid., pp. xxvii, 63.
[39]Murphy, "Jazz Improvisation," p. 10.
[40]Paul Berliner, *Thinking in Jazz: The Infinite Art of Improvisation* (Chicago: University of Chicago Press, 1994), pp. 576-78.

these voices adds something along the way. An example like this provides us with a way of conceptualizing differing voices all improvising in their own respective ways on the same basic line. And this in turn helps us think about how the call of beauty can go forth in so many different ways and be continually transformed.

Beauty and the Call

It may seem that in the last section we left beauty in order to focus on improvisation. Yet beauty has been present all along. Since beauty is precisely the call and its enchantment, then beauty is part of improvisation. But in this section I wish to consider the implications of linking beauty, the call and improvisation for the practicing artist.

If we can rightly say that our artistic creation is a participation in God's *poiesis* (which I believe we can), then our calls are rightly seen as continuation of God's calls. Of course, I have argued that the beautiful must be taken not merely as a logical operator but as a transcendental that is connected to goodness and truth. With that in mind, all art that reflects beauty, goodness and truth is beautiful, good and true. However, this connection of beauty with goodness and truth does not simplify but instead makes the situation complex. For what is the status of beauty in the midst of a fallen world, in which all is not necessarily beautiful, good or true? And what is the artist to *do* in such a world?

The artist is certainly faced with a difficult situation. The world is still—in many ways—as God pronounced it: "good." Yet it is so full of that which is "not good" as well. Traditionally, artists have particularly focused on that which is beautiful in the world, whether the human figure or the natural landscape or pleasing harmonies. It has been only more recently (and *recent* here is defined in terms of the long history of Western art) that artists have turned their attention to subjects that are not traditionally thought to be beautiful. While there is no question that some art created today is shocking just to be shocking and vile just to be vile, it is likewise the case that artists who, say, paint that which is not beautiful in some traditional sense do so out of a deep commitment to truth. So, for example, Dmitri Schostakovich's symphonies are not necessarily "pretty," but they are faithful witnesses (the thirteenth, for instance) to the horrors of his time. Here we might be tempted to say that such music puts greater emphasis on the true rather than the beautiful. It is not that the beautiful has simply been neglected; rather, we witness a sense of the beautiful that is not Kant's harmonious free play of the faculties but what Bruce Herman has called a "broken beauty."[41] To quote Herman, "We long for completeness and health and perfection; yet more often than not we encounter fragmentation, weakness, and at best a tragicomic dignity."[42]

What unites Christian artists whose work is part of the current exhibition "A Broken Beauty" is that they depict *both* "suffering and hope," *both* "human brokenness and human beauty."[43] And here we can make a strong connection to both black spirituals and black improvisers. So many of the spirituals speak of both "suffering and hope" with a recognition that they are currently captives but that freedom looms on the horizon. So we have "Swing Low, Sweet Chariot" that is "comin' for to carry me home." Or "Steal Away," which ends with the line: "I ain't got long to stay here." There is clearly an eschatological hope in these spirituals, both for the more immediate eschaton of escape from slavery and of the ultimate eschaton of being "home." Likewise, black jazz improvisers have seen their music as a way to "overwrite, resist, and confound both conventional musical practices and the orthodox social structures those practices reflect."[44] Many black improvisers have seen their work as undermining repressive, white social structures. And, indeed, it was partly due to the respect that black improvisers slowly gained that blacks in general gained dignity. Houston A. Baker says of the blues that they transformed the "economics of slavery" into a "resonant, improvisational, expressive dignity."[45] We could likewise say that jazz has helped transform the "economics of oppression" into a similar sort of dignity.

Is it the logic of God's reversal in which the lowly are lifted up that explains why jazz is seen today as arguably the greatest American contribution to music? Or is it that suffering often produces art of poignant beauty? I'm not sure. In any case, both the spirituals and jazz have this sense of suffering

---

[41]Immanuel Kant, *Critique of Judgment*, trans. Werner S. Pluhar (Indianapolis: Hackett, 1987), p. 62.

[42]Bruce Herman, foreword in *A Broken Beauty*, ed. Theodore L. Prescott (Grand Rapids: Eerdmans, 2005), p. vii.

[43]Timothy Verdon, "Broken Beauty, Shattered Heart," in *A Broken Beauty*, ed. Theodore L. Prescott (Grand Rapids: Eerdmans, 2005), p. 25. (The exhibit has been at the Laguna Art Museum in Laguna Beach and the Joseph D. Carrier Gallery in Toronto.)

[44]Daniel Fischlin and Ajay Heble, "The Other Side of Nowhere: Jazz, Improvisation, and Communities in Dialogue," in *The Other Side of Nowhere: Jazz, Improvisation, and Communities in Dialogue*, ed. Daniel Fischlin and Ajay Heble (Middletown, Conn.: Wesleyan University Press, 2004), p. 2.

[45]Houston A. Baker Jr., *Blues, Ideology, and Afro-American Literature: A Vernacular Theory* (Chicago: University of Chicago Press, 1984), p. 13.

tempered by hope. Duke Ellington knew what it was like to be treated as a second-class citizen, but he was able to look to the day when such was no longer the case. In the meantime, he gave us some of the most beautiful—even if also haunting—music. It is this music that enchants, that calls to us to listen. Hear the words of his tune "Come Sunday":

Lord, dear Lord above,
God almighty, God of love,
Please look down and
see my people through.

I believe God is now,
was then and always will be.
With God's blessing we can
make it through eternity.[46]

Don't these words enchant? Don't they call to us and to God? And aren't they echoes of the call of a God who promises to protect and deliver his people?

As fallen, earthly vessels, we receive God's call and improvise a response that goes back to God and forward out to all of creation. It is indeed incumbent upon us—in light of the Great Commission—to spread that call. And art—whether aural or visual—is a powerful way of speaking God's call. The beauty that results is undoubtedly imperfect and broken. It should come as no surprise that our art reflects the brokenness of ourselves, our souls and bodies. Moreover, we are called by God himself to heed the voices that come from the margins, from those whose reality is in many cases far more broken than ours but likewise whose voices are sometimes much more forthright and honest. And here we must connect *poiesis* to *phronesis;* for the art that we make as a response to God's call ought to be in service of a *phronesis*—that is, a practical acting in the world—that pays heed to the marginalized of the world. Art, as Nicholas Wolterstorff long ago reminded us, must be connected with *action*.[47] Through art, we are reminded of the broken beauty that surrounds us and we are summoned to act.

Yet art can also serve as an icon that points us to the glorious beauty of God's kingdom to come. We stand on this side of the Jordan, able only to catch a glimpse of God's beauty but knowing that one day we shall see "face to face" (1 Cor 13:12)

---

[46]Duke Ellington, "Come Sunday" (Tempo Music, 1943).
[47]Nicholas Wolterstorff, *Art in Action* (Grand Rapids: Eerdmans, 1980).

PART TWO

Visual Arts

Recognizing True Beauty

After the Fall

4

THE CASE FOR A BROKEN BEAUTY

An Art Historical Viewpoint
E. John Walford

In this paper, I will make the case for a "broken beauty" from an art historical viewpoint, and against the backdrop of the historical assumptions about beauty, truth and goodness as manifest in idealist art in the Classical tradition.

In both the theory and practice of Western visual art, Greek concepts of the interrelatedness of beauty, truth and goodness have lurked not far below the surface.[1] It is hardly surprising that with the Christianization of the Roman Empire, such Greek notions of beauty, truth and goodness were recast into terms that appeared to fit well with Christian faith and practice.[2]

Given the traumatic nature of modern experience and the widespread rejection of both Christian and humanistic thought, perhaps it is a little more

---

[1]The book title *The Beauty of God* brings together the concepts beauty, God, theology and the arts. None of these are neutral terms, but when they are brought together, certain tacit—and provocative—assumptions come into play. To juxtapose the terms *art* and *beauty* within contemporary artistic discourse is itself provocative. To link God to the arts is, for some Christians, a dubious enterprise, and within the art world there are few who care to see art and theology considered in relation to one another. In the title lies an underlying assumption that in forging works of beauty artists create some sort of epiphany of God, or that the role of artists is to create beauty that points to truth. These are questionable assumptions, especially when considering contemporary art. What sort of "beauty" and what kind of "truth" are implied?

[2]The Neo-Platonic approach stressed ideal form as superior to earthly matter; the Aristotelian approach stressed the order within earthly matter. This has found expression in both idealizing Neo-Platonic terms and also in Aristotelian ones, as in the writings of Thomas Aquinas. The latter version is more prevalent in our time, as in the work of such Neo-Thomists as Jacques Maritain and others, who promote notions of earthly beauty—as embodied in a sense of perfection, proportion, order, harmony and clarity—that point to its transcendent source.

surprising that a Christianized version of these Greek concepts has endured
to the present; witness the foundational reference, in this conference, to "the
excellency and beauty of God," as articulated by Jonathan Edwards.

Time does not permit detailed review of Neo-Platonist or Aristotelian
concepts of beauty, or consideration of their merits and shortcomings.
Rather, after brief theological reflections, my intent is to explore an alterna-

**Figure 4.1. Rembrandt, *Self-Portrait as St. Paul*, 1661, oil on canvas; Rijksmuseum,
Amsterdam. Photo: © Rijksmuseum, Amsterdam.**

tive model—that of a "broken beauty"—as seen in Rembrandt's *Self-Portrait as St. Paul* (fig. 4.1), for its fittingness to convey a Christian vision of life, understood within a framework of belief in creation, fall and the redemption of humanity. I offer an art historical perspective on the nature and merits of a "broken—or disfigured—beauty," by considering both historical and contemporary examples of works that are true to the human condition, also in acknowledging suffering, while preserving hope.

Theological Grounds for a "Broken Beauty"

In the theoretical discourse of the Dutch Reformed tradition in the last half-century or so, one finds both affirmation and questioning of the Christianized Neo-Platonic heritage that calls for the artist to create beauty in pursuit of truth and goodness.

For instance, Abraham Kuyper, statesman, scholar and founder of the Free University, Amsterdam, in his Stone Lectures on Calvinism (Princeton, 1898), claimed that "art has the mystical task of reminding us in its production of the beautiful that was lost and of anticipating its perfect coming luster."[3] The implication is that the artist should therefore avoid addressing the brokenness of creation as we experience it, but rather conjure an ideal beauty that evokes what was lost at the Fall, yet is to come when Christ returns. Many Christian artists still do, indeed, attempt something of that kind. But often such works fail to engage the viewer because they are devoid of the substance and grit of life as we know it.[4]

On a theoretical level, aesthetician Calvin Seerveld, in his book *Rainbows for the Fallen World,* takes strong issue with what he calls "the grand old theory of Beauty," and offers as an alternative defining attribute for art the quality of "allusiveness." By this he means, as I understand it, the capacity of a work, through the nature of its forms, to function as a multilayered, metaphorical set of suggestion-rich allusions to reality.[5] He therefore rejects Kuyper's allegiance to the grand old theory of Beauty—with a capital *B.*

---

[3]Abraham Kuyper, "Calvinism and Art," in *Lectures on Calvinism* (1898; reprint, Grand Rapids: Eerdmans, 1961), p. 155, quoted in Calvin Seerveld, *Rainbows for the Fallen World* (Downsview, Ont.: Toronto Tuppence, 1980), pp. 121-22.

[4]For a review of the concept of beauty as an intonation of the divine, especially as found in a twentieth-century Neo-Thomist writer such as Jacques Maritain, see Gordon Fuglie, "Beauty Lost, Beauty Found: One Hundred Years of Attitudes," in *A Broken Beauty,* ed. Theodore Prescott (Grand Rapids: Eerdmans, 2005), pp. 59-76.

[5]Seerveld, *Rainbows for the Fallen World,* pp. 125-35.

Another in this Dutch Reformed tradition, my mentor, the late Hans Rookmaaker, an art historian who worked at the Free University, Amsterdam, was
anything but a Neo-Platonist, and he eschewed any notions of ideal beauty.
But, unlike Seerveld, he continued to find use in the term *beauty*. He conceived of beauty in a different light than that of traditional aesthetics, down-
playing traditional notions of beauty of form and emphasizing rather that
"beauty and truth are closely related."[6] Thus, as he observed, there can be
beauty in the truth of an artist's portrayal of the demonic as demonic or of
despair as real despair, just as that which is ugly but loved is beautiful because of the love shown toward it—as, he suggests, in Albrecht Dürer's
drawing of his old, ugly mother.[7] What he would have made of Quentin Metsys's satirical but doubtfully historical *The Ugly Duchess*[8] history does not
record.

As Rookmaaker rightly points out, plenty of works of art have as their
subject what is horrible and ugly, representing human depravity, suffering,
sin, crime, pride and all that is evil and ugly. Yet these works can be "beautiful" in the sense that they are truthful. He thereby separates beauty from
what is sweet or sentimental, and from beauty of form alone, associating
beauty rather with the truth of the work. He goes on to say that truth in art
"does not mean doing accurate copies, but that the artist's insight is rich and
full" since, "Truth has to do with the fullness of reality, its scope and meaning." In this sense, he adds, "fairy tales can be true, if they show human action and behavior in keeping with human character—within the framework
of fairy tale reality."[9] Rookmaaker thus advocates art that is true to the human condition.

Following in this same vein, I want to ask: Does art more fittingly seek to
represent God or the human condition, or, indeed, the point of intersection
between the two? The idealist tradition implies God; the realist tradition, the
human condition, or such points of intersection. It seems ironic to me that
Jonathan Edwards, a Protestant, should indirectly presuppose the former,
not the latter, given the historic skepticism of Protestants concerning the capacity of art to evoke God. Edwards's position, it would seem, like Kuyper's,
would press beauty into the service of pointing beyond the human condi-

---

[6]H. R. Rookmaaker, *Modern Art and the Death of a Culture* (Downers Grove, Ill.: InterVarsity
Press, 1970), p. 234.
[7]Ibid., pp. 234-35.
[8]Quentin Metsys, *The Ugly Duchess,* The National Gallery, London (c. 1525-1530)
[9]Rookmaaker, *Modern Art,* pp. 237-38.

tion to a beauty once lost and eventually to be regained.

More recently, Jeremy Begbie introduced the concept of a beauty based on the redemptive work of Christ, thus beauty in the transformation of the disfigured, which held immediate resonance for me, as an art historian.[10] While rejecting the concept that art be "qualified by the aspiration towards beauty," Begbie considers it still "proper to speak of beauty as a *desirable* feature in art"—so long as we adopt a very broad understanding of beauty. Even beyond that, though, he goes on to ask,

> might not the creation and redemption of the world in Christ yield a richer and deeper concept of beauty than many traditional philosophical theories presuppose? Beauty . . . has all too often been abstracted from time and temporal movement, and been turned into a static, timeless quality. Suppose, however, we refuse to divorce it from the transformation of the disorder of creation in the history of Jesus Christ. Suppose we begin there? Does this not open up a more dynamic, and more theological paradigm of beauty?

Begbie finds support for his proposal in the writings of Karl Barth and Hans Urs von Balthasar. He cites from Barth's writings:

> *God's beauty* embraces death as well as life, fear as well as joy, what we might call the ugly as well as what we might call the beautiful. It reveals itself and wills to be known on the road from the one to the other, *in the turning from the self-humiliation of God for the benefit of man to the exaltation of man by God and to God*.

Begbie then observes how similar this is in conception to the thought of Hans Urs von Balthasar, who, as Begbie notes, "urges that we see God's creation out of nothing and his saving economy as together the exemplar of true beauty." Thus, notes Begbie, Balthasar asks, "should we not . . . consider this art of God's to be precisely the transcendent archetype of all worldly and human beauty?" Begbie concludes that "the most fruitful model of beauty for the artist will be found . . . (not in some formula) . . . but by directing our attention first of all to the redeeming economy of God which culminates in Jesus Christ," which would "equip us with a concept of beauty much more distinctly Christian" than Platonic ones.[11] Before we attempt to measure such a concept against the practice of contemporary Christian art-

---

[10]Jeremy Begbie, *Voicing Creation's Praise: Towards a Theology of the Arts* (Edinburgh: T & T Clark, 1991), pp. 224-25.
[11]Ibid.

ists, we need also to consider the situation within the contemporary art world, of which such artists must also take account.

What Is Art's Most Fitting Role?

We may also put the issue this way: What is art's most fitting role? To represent the ideal as a means to conjure the divine? Or treat the real as a means to illuminate the human condition? Or are artists—especially Christian artists—more effective in focusing on the place where these two intersect? In answering this question a comparison of Rembrandt and idealist artists such as Nicholas Poussin may shed some light on the issue.

In 2006 the art world celebrated the four hundredth anniversary of Rembrandt's birth. Wouldn't he be pleased to know that his works have been valued this long! As we consider his *Self-Portrait as St. Paul* (1661), we can ask ourselves why. In a recent article in *The New York Review of Books*, noted art critic Robert Hughes touched the heart of the matter, and so I am going to quote him at length. He writes:

> There are some great artists whose achievements we admire, so to speak, from the outside. They do not excite the sense of empathy: not, at least, in any personal way. You may admire Piero della Francesca, or Raphael, or Poussin. You may find yourself transported by the calm, columnar beauty of Piero's *Madonna del Parto,* or by the heroic and somewhat abstract grandeur of the figures who populate Poussin's *Institution of the Seven Sacraments,* or by the overwhelming kingliness of Titian's portrait of Charles V. . . . But what you are not likely to feel is a sense of community with these magnificent products of human thought and imagination. . . . We admire their difference, and their distance, from us.

"But then," continues Hughes, "there are artists whose work is not like this. They are the ones who acknowledge human imperfection and mortality."[12]

Of course, Rembrandt, as seen for example in his *Self-Portrait as St. Paul,* was one of those who "acknowledge human imperfection and mortality." What then of the others Hughes mentions? Each, in his way, offers an idealized vision of life. As Michelangelo, sculptor of the serene *Pietà* (1498-1500) and the supreme master of such art, wrote in one of his poems, "Every beauty that is seen here recalls, more than other things, that fount of pity,

---

[12]Robert Hughes, "The God of Realism," *The New York Review of Books* 53, no. 6 (2006): 6.

whence we all come, to feeling people; nor do we have other earnest, nor other fruit of heaven upon this earth; and he who loves you with faith ascends to God, and sees death as sweet."[13]

Behind Michelangelo's words—as well as his art—lies a Christianized, Neo-Platonic view of beauty and art that recurs in later academic art theory. According to this theory the commendable artist is one who eschews representation of the particularity of the broken, fallen world, and instead strives to represent the imagined ideal. By contrast, Rembrandt and many others reject that notion, depicting instead, as Hughes indicates, "human imperfection and mortality."

A Comparison of the Holy Family as Treated by Rembrandt and Poussin

By way of comparison, consider these two mid-seventeenth-century images of the holy family, one by Nicholas Poussin, his *The Holy Family on the Steps* (1648) (fig. 4.3) and one by Rembrandt, his *The Holy Family* (1640) (fig. 4.2). While Poussin presents the viewer with idealized figures in a harmoniously balanced and orderly setting, Rembrandt renders the image of the family in terms of the household of a Dutch working family. From the academic point of view, as informed by its then notion of beauty, Rembrandt's work falls far short. But does it? Short of what: Ideal beauty? Truth? Invocations of goodness? As Rembrandt scholar Jakob Rosenberg observed many years ago, in Rembrandt's work spiritual truth—with roots in the Bible—trumps a classicist sense of beauty based on fully controlled order. Though since debunked as a mythic construction of a profound Rembrandt, Rosenberg argued that "since for Rembrandt the essence of truth about man and nature lies in the ultimate relationship of everything created to the Creator, he [Rembrandt] accepts all things, beautiful or not; their mere existence makes them worthwhile, as issuing from God." This, according to Rosenberg, also explains the formal qualities of Rembrandt's art. He writes:

> Forms, in his compositions, are not allowed to become too definite or to have finality, since this would break their contact with the life process. If Rembrandt's chiaroscuro has any deeper purpose, it is this: to suggest, to keep alive these mysterious relationships, so true yet so impenetrable for the purely

[13]Michelangelo, "Veggio nel tuo bel visto, Signor mio . . . ," *The Penguin Book of Italian Verse* (Harmondsworth, U.K.: Penguin, 1965), p. 165.

Figure 4.2. Rembrandt, *The Holy Family* (sometimes called *The Carpenter's Shop*), 1640, oil on panel; Musée du Louvre, Paris, France. Photo: Erich Lessing/Art Resource, NY.

rational approach, so strongly felt by the artist's intuitive and religious mind, yet closed to the view of the aesthete and the Classicist who insist upon beauty and a fully controlled order.

"Thus," concludes Rosenberg, "one of the oldest problems of Christian civilization was recognized again as a fundamental issue and answered with a new consistency and in a new form."[14]

Poussin's work (see fig. 4.3), by contrast, is a paradigm of academic classicism, which is why Hughes invokes his name in opposition to Rembrandt. Consider, though, some of the implications of academic practice. One of the best-known works of Poussin takes as its subject rape. True, his *Rape of the Sabine Women* (1635)[15] can be read as a political allegory that "might makes right" and justifies conquest by reference to a founding myth of the Roman Empire. Nevertheless, the violence and cruelty of war, pillage and rape are idealized through the heroic bodies and grand, rhetorical gestures of the main protagonists, to which the futile and sorrowing gestures of the woman act merely as a dramatic counterpoint. Is such idealized beauty of form as Poussin conjures fitting to such a subject, and does it point to truth, inspire goodness or carry within its magnificent forms an intonation of the divine?[16]

We must leave aside the type of appeal and significance that lies within the classical ideal of beauty. We will give our attention, instead, to an alternative approach to art and beauty as found in the Netherlandish tradition.[17]

An Alternative Approach to Art and Beauty

The Netherlandish school of art had long run counter to the Neo-Platonic

---

[14]Jakob Rosenberg, *Rembrandt: Life and Work,* 2nd ed. (London: Phaidon, 1964), excerpt reproduced in "Jacob Rosenberg: Rembrandt in his Century," in Harold Spencer, *Readings in Art History,* 3rd ed. (New York: Charles Scribner's Sons), 2:208-09. Gary Schwartz, in his monograph *Rembrandt: His Life, His Paintings* (Harmondsworth: Viking, 1985), pp. 358-65, esp. pp. 363-64, debunks Rosenberg's view of a profound Rembrandt, and that of others writing in like vein, as mere myth, claiming that a reading of the documents shows up Rembrandt, in his dealings with others, as of "a nasty disposition and an untrustworthy character . . . lacking in intellectual sophistication, or possessing a perverse simplicity,"—in short, "boorish and recalcitrant" rather than "a sensitive human being with spiritual depth" (p. 363). Of course, it is possible that Rembrandt, like his art, was both coarse and spiritually insightful, since, as Scripture attests, we bear these gifts in earthen vessels.

[15]Poussin, *Rape of the Sabine Women* (1635), The Metropolitan Museum of Art, New York.

[16]Recognizing the problem of representing violence and such in art, the eighteenth-century academician Sir Joshua Reynolds said that "if you mean to preserve the most perfect beauty . . . you cannot express the passions, all of which produce distortion and deformity." He went on to acknowledge that "Art has its boundaries, though imagination has none," and thus art is not "able to execute the conceptions of a romantic imagination" (Sir Joshua Reynolds, "Discourse V," in *Discourses on Art,* ed. Robert R. Wark [San Marino, Calif.: Huntington Library, 1959], p. 72).

[17]For this alternate Netherlandish tradition, see further Lisa J. DeBoer, "A Comic Vision? Northern Renaissance Art and the Human Figure," in *A Broken Beauty,* ed. Theodore Prescott (Grand Rapids: Eerdmans, 2005), pp. 43-57.

Figure 4.3. Nicholas Poussin, *The Holy Family on the Steps,* **1648, oil on canvas; The Cleveland Museum of Art, Leonard C. Hanna, Jr., Fund 1981.18. Photo: © The Cleveland Museum of Art.**

tradition of adherence to an idealized form of beauty, preferring to represent humanity in its fallen state, satirizing human folly and giving form to the struggle between flesh and spirit to which Paul gives such articulate expression in Romans: "I can will what is right, but I cannot do it. . . . Wretched man that I am. . . . [W]ith my mind I am a slave to the law of God, but with my flesh I am a slave to the law of sin." (Rom 7:18, 24-25).

Quentin Metsys's 1514 painting of *The Moneylender and His Wife*[18] gives us a hint of this in the distracted attention of a woman at her devotions, drawn by the sin of avarice to refocus her thought instead on the pile of coins being counted by her husband. In this context the weigh scales seen in the painting also carry a double meaning: weighing coins in the present and weighing souls in the hereafter. Through this double-entendre the painter also begs the question: where will you lay up your treasure—on earth or in heaven?

Later, in the Netherlands in the early seventeenth century, one finds the

[18]Quentin Metsys, *The Moneylender and His Wife* (1514), Musée du Louvre, Paris.

historical assumptions about ideal beauty challenged and rejected on grounds that there is no need to represent an idealized Arcadia, since the beauty and wonder of God is manifest even in the most humble sand dune that holds back the mighty sea from swamping the low-lying Dutch polders or the wind-swept grain fields, as seen in Jacob van Ruisdael's *Wheat Fields* (fig. 4.4), indeed also in the anatomy of a louse. Such thinking was grounded in the Netherlands Confession of Faith, which stated, in this respect, that "(the world) is before our eyes as a beautiful book, in which all

Figure 4.4. Jacob van Ruisdael, *Wheat Fields,* ca. 1670, oil on canvas; The Metropolitan Museum of Art, New York. Photo: © The Metropolitan Museum of Art.

created things, great and small, are like letters, which give us the invisible things of God to behold, namely His eternal power and divinity." Dutch poets, from Spiegel, early in the seventeenth century, to Poot, one hundred years later, describe their responses to landscape as a progression from visual sensation to deeper contemplation, nature providing a ladder by which our thoughts climb to God. At the same time, the Netherlands Confession and Catechism, taught in all Dutch schools, reminded readers to see in the

Figure 4.5. Claude Lorraine, *Landscape with Dancing Figures* (sometimes known as *The Marriage of Isaac and Rebekah* or *The Mill*), 1648, oil on canvas; Galleria Doria Pamphili, Rome. Photo: © Alinari/Art Resource, NY.

corruption of all earthly matter a reminder of the fallen state of man.[19]

Consequentially, the Dutch—to the dismay of the academies of Europe—painted just that: the sand dunes and vaporous landscape of water and polders as well as insects, seashells, glass, pewter, peeled lemons, feathers and flowers. Furthermore, in painting these elements they often also made allusion to the fragility of life and the corruption of all earthly matter, something academic idealists consciously avoided.

---

[19]These same poets even condemn those who do not contemplate the beauty of nature with a spiritual eye, and are willfully blind to its deeper significance. Although these writers drew heavily from classical literary models, that they had their own country in mind when making such observations is evidenced by their references to polders, sand dunes, water-logged fields and "living tubs of butter" (cattle). Thus Constantijn Huygens, an early admirer of Dutch realist landscape and marine painters, marveled at the way in which sand dunes, piled up by storm and water, formed a barrier to the sea, exclaiming: "The Lord's goodness is manifest on the top of every dune" (see E. John Walford, *Jacob van Ruisdael and the Perception of Landscape* [New Haven, Conn.: Yale University Press, 1991], pp. 20-26, and chap. 2, nn. 25-55, esp. nn. 25, 27, 38).

Consider the contrast of outcomes to which such thinking leads: To take two seventeenth-century landscapists, compare the work of Claude Lorraine, a French artist working in Rome for mostly aristocratic patrons, with that of the Dutch artist, Salomon van Ruysdael (uncle of the aforementioned Jacob), painting for middle-class Dutch burghers. Consider, first, Claude's idealized river panorama, *Landscape with Dancing Figures* (fig. 4.5). The trees are lush, unharmed by time or storm, the scene is tranquil and the space expansive, drawing the eye into an ever-more dreamy

Figure 4.6. Salomon van Ruysdael, *Farm in the Dunes,* 1626 (28?), oil on panel; Fitzwilliam Museum, Cambridge. Photo: © Fitzwilliam Museum, The University of Cambridge, reproduced with permission.

distance. Humanity finds itself in harmony with nature, untroubled by toil or care.

By contrast, the Dutch artist, Salomon van Ruysdael, in this modest work *Farm in the Dunes* (fig. 4.6) depicts a man resting beside a battered cottage, with decaying thatch, at the side of a sandy road, in a wind-swept dune landscape. The artist presents the viewer with an image of man's unstable dwelling set amid a world of sand, straw, cloud and wind. What could be more ephemeral? Even when the same artist painted a calm river landscape, as in his *River View near Deventer* (1645),[20] how different are his river and its setting, from that of Claude's! The world evoked by Salomon van Ruysdael may lack the grandeur and idealism of Claude's, yet is it not more true? Much as Robert Hughes comments on how we relate to Rembrandt, in contrast to Poussin, doesn't the same argument hold for these two landscapes?[21]

It was, perhaps, in pursuit of truth rather than traditional notions of beauty that Caravaggio broke with the conventions of his time and place, early seventeenth-century Italy, to paint some of the most direct, unvarnished representations of the gospel that the West had seen. Such is Caravaggio's *Entombment of Christ* (1602-1604),[22] in which the Virgin Mary could be any grieving mother, and Mary Magdalene a girl of the street, while Joseph of Arimathea has been given the sun-baked face of a peasant. Caravaggio's image broke with all decorum but, in so doing, made the grief of Christ's followers palpable and deeply moving. In turn the viewer is drawn into their emotion and their world, thus bringing Christ that much nearer. It was from such works that Rembrandt took his cue, as a current exhibition in Amsterdam makes clear.[23]

I have taken Rembrandt, as the leading exponent of the Dutch school of painting, as my model for a "Broken Beauty," and Salomon van Ruysdael and Jacob van Ruisdael, two Dutch landscapists, as exemplifying the virtues of an unvarnished beauty seen in our immediate, broken world.

We will move now to the present, and to the status of beauty in the current art world, which provides the immediate context within which contemporary Christian artists have to function.

The Modern and Postmodern Revolt Against Beauty

In the practice of modern, postmodern and contemporary art, it is no secret

---

[20]Salomon van Ruysdael, *River View near Deventer* (1645), Rijksmuseum, Amsterdam. In his *River Landscape* (1645), the church, house and vegetation virtually float between expanses of water and sky, a serene and familiar environment, yet with a precarious grip on the surface of the earth.

[21]Furthermore, by the same measure, we may ask which serves as a more fitting vessel to turn our thoughts toward the Creator? Does ideal beauty really serve as a Christianized Neo-Platonism supposes? Even if, to some measure, it does, shouldn't our theology of art more fittingly grow out of a gospel of redemption? And aren't artists better placed to represent the human condition and the world around us, than imagine that they can manipulate an idealized beauty to conjure truth?

[22]Caravaggio, *Entombment of Christ* (1602-1604), Pinacoteca, Vatican Museums, Rome.

[23]"Rembrandt-Caravaggio" (Amsterdam: Rijksmuseum-Vincent van Gogh Museum, 2006). See <www.rijksmuseum.nl/tentoonstellingen/rembrandt-caravaggio/?lang=en>.

that beauty has been perceived within the art world as profoundly problematic. Given modernist skepticism of both Christian and humanist assumptions, an undercurrent of angst, and the hovering threat of nihilism, artists find few grounds for beauty, traditionally conceived. Thus, when in 1919 Marcel Duchamp added a moustache to a reproduction of Leonardo da Vinci's *Mona Lisa* and exhibited it as art, a little more than subversive whimsy was at play. In our own time, Damien Hirst has launched a successful career exhibiting dead or dissected animals—from a notorious tiger shark to sheep or pigs preserved in formaldehyde—such as *This Little Piggy Went to Market, This Little Piggy Stayed at Home* (1996), which have been taken as "an examination of the processes of life and death," and as embodying "the ironies, falsehoods and desires that we mobilize to negotiate our own alienation and mortality."[24] In such works beauty, shock and cruelty meet head on.

Noted photographer Cindy Sherman, who has spent a couple of decades addressing issues of female identity, in the 1990s turned toward the grotesque and disturbed, as in her work, *Untitled #250,* which presents the female figure in a violent, horrific and grossly violated manner. When asked about this aspect of her work, she replied, "The world is so drawn toward beauty that I became interested in things that are normally considered grotesque or ugly, seeing them as more fascinating and beautiful. It seems boring to me to pursue the typical idea of beauty, because that is the easiest or the most obvious way to see the world. It's more challenging to look at the other side."[25]

Writing in *The Journal of Aesthetics and Art Criticism* in 1999, Peg Zeglin Brand sees artists such as Hirst and Sherman as operating with what aestheticians today see as a reconceptualized version of the sublime: Beauty infiltrated by the dangerous, transgressive, bizarre, grotesque and the horrible.[26]

---

[24]Norman Rosenthal et al., *Sensation: Young British Artists from the Saatchi Collection* (London: Thames & Hudson/Royal Academy of the Arts, 1997), pp. 22, 33-34. See also <www.art chive.com/artchive>. His best known work of this kind is *The Physical Impossibility of Death in the Mind of Someone Living* (1991), which is of the encased tiger shark.

[25]Cindy Sherman, as reported by Noiko Fuku, "A Woman of Parts," *Art in America* 85 (1997): 80, as quoted by Peg Zeglin Brand, "Beauty Matters," *The Journal of Aesthetics and Art Criticism* 57, no. 1 (1999): 7. For Sherman, see <www.cindysherman.com/art.shtml>, also the image source *Untitled #250.*

[26]Peg Zeglin Brand, "Beauty Matters," *The Journal of Aesthetics and Art Criticism* 57, no. 1 (1999): 7.

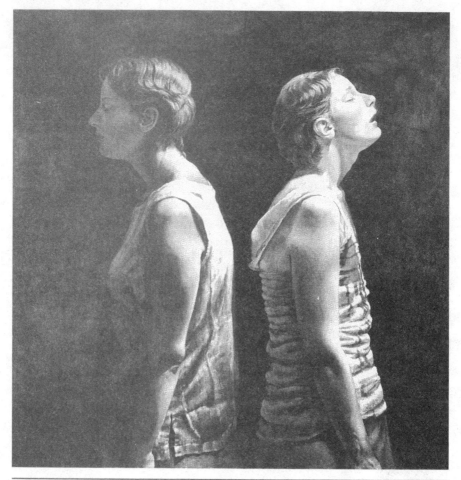

Figure 4.7. Melissa Weinman, *St. Agatha's Grief,* 1996, oil on canvas; collection of the artist. Photo: Susan Dirk; reproduction permission of the artist, Melissa Weinman.

Contemporary Christian Artists and the Practice of a "Broken Beauty"

It is in the face of such practice that contemporary Christian artists, such as Melissa Weinman, as seen in *St. Agatha's Grief* (fig. 4.7), have to forge their path, knowing that beauty, in any common usage of the word, will be dismissed as obvious, easy and boring, to cite Cindy Sherman.[27] Yet to explore

---

[27]A significant challenge for contemporary Christian artists is that for at least two and a half centuries, few artists have produced powerful works of biblical narrative. Furthermore, for the

the transgressive, bizarre and grotesque would not only have their fellow believers up in arms, but neither would it likely attract them.

On the other hand, as David Hooker acknowledges in his curator's statement for the small exhibit [accompanying the conference behind this book] "Wrestling with Beauty," "Beauty is back, but illusive. Artists find themselves questioning the nature of beauty. If beauty exists, whose beauty is it, whose ideal forms its basis, and how does that affect content and meaning? Is it possible to have beauty on a sliding scale?"

I have already mentioned that Jeremy Begbie introduced the concept of a beauty based on the redemptive work of Christ, thus beauty in the transformation of the disfigured. It is encouraging to see a number of the most thoughtful contemporary Christian artists working in a parallel vein, though not necessarily aware of Begbie's writings.

The work of some fifteen current Christian artists has been brought together for a 2005-2006 traveling exhibition, "A Broken Beauty," and its accompanying publication. Viewing their works, one finds repeatedly a form of beauty forged out of the transformation of the disfigured.

Among those artists, Edward Knippers has long stood out for the scale, drama and expressionistic bravura of his works, as well as for the fact that his work—almost all on biblical themes—treats the human figure nude, as in his piece *Ash Wednesday* (2003), exhibited at the CIVA (Christians in the Visual Arts) Show, at Gordon College, Wenham, Massachusetts, June 2003.[28] Some will debate the wisdom or indeed the efficacy of his approach, but the work is undeniably powerful and moving. His works are never sweet or pretty, but forcefully beautiful in their mix of violence, pain and occasional glimpses of love and compassion. Their raw violence is Knippers's way to

---

past century, to treat biblical subjects was virtual taboo. Yet for a Christian artist, biblical narrative and Christian tradition offer a model and framework in which to cast—by analogy—contemporary experience, and his or her understanding of its ultimate significance. Thus a number of artists, such as Weinman—searching for ways to connect with other artists in their faith tradition—have turned to Christian iconography from earlier periods of history, and attempted to adapt it to their own time and circumstances. Such is the context for *St. Agatha's Grief*, included in the 2005-2006 "Broken Beauty" traveling exhibition and its accompanying publication: Theodore Prescott, ed., *A Broken Beauty* (Grand Rapids: Eerdmans, 2005), p. 108, fig. 17. The legendary St. Agatha, who suffered mutilation rather than yield her virtue to a lustful ruler, serves here both as paradigm for her modern counterpart and as encouragement to those who undergo the consequences of breast cancer. In this double image, part of her persona stands in darkness, tormented, while her counterpart, wounded, turns to the light, in search of healing.

[28]For Knippers, the nude is his way to avoid setting this great human drama within any specific time frame or geographic context, in order to evoke its universal validity.

underscore that grace enters a brutal world, and that grace has to take on that yoke in order to conquer it.

The work *Annunciation* (fig. 4.8), from the series "Elegy for Witness" (2002), by Bruce Herman graces the cover of *A Broken Beauty*, attesting both to Herman's vision for this enterprise as well as his acknowledged mastery of its artistic embodiment. In this particular work he uses a traditional, Chris-

Figure 4.8. Bruce Herman, *Annunciation* (from the series "Elegy for Witness"), 2002; © Bruce Herman, 2002; oils, alkyd resin, silver leaf on clay-prepared wood panels; diptych, 76" x 98"; collection of Mr. and Mrs. William R. Cross. Photo: John Walford, reproduced by permission of the artist.

tian diptych format, fitting to the subject of the *Annunciation*. He uses gold and silver leaf for its association with the sacred in late Medieval Italian altarpieces, working on top of that with the more contemporary medium of oil and alkyd resin. The mix of media itself functions as a metaphor for the point of intersection of the divine and the human implicit to the subject. Mary, as in the work of Knippers, is depicted nude, her pose a mix of Greek funerary sculpture and an informal, everyday pose. As with Knippers, Herman thereby attempts to place her outside of any particular context, perhaps an image of womanhood in general. The color, texture and execution of the painting have great allure to the eye, yet Mary's body is a broken beauty, arms truncated at points that echo those of the famous Greek sculpture the *Venus de Milo* and the pigment of her skin evidencing much layering and scraping, thus subverting any idealized—or sensual—impact that a nude might otherwise give off. With these various means Herman suggests that we—like Mary—meet God in our broken state and, like Mary in her stillness, we are at our best as recipients of grace, a grace that comes to us from above.

Catherine Prescott, though not featured in the "Broken Beauty" exhibition, takes a different path than both Knippers and Herman, as a portrait painter. Consider Prescott's *I Drink Your Whiskey and Your Sorrow: The Poet Scott Cairns* (fig. 4.9). Taking neither sacred themes nor elevated subjects, Prescott takes her subjects in all the complex and concrete particularity of their lives.[29] Her gift—rare at that—is to find in any given individuals both their dignity, as humans created in the image of God, and their dislocation, as frail mortals. We cannot look into the faces of her subjects without seeing parts of ourselves, and they look back at us as if with mutual understanding. Isn't this very much what Robert Hughes finds in Rembrandt's sitters, and why we like them? Both artists—whatever the differences in the level of their talent—acknowledge in their subjects this mixture of human frailty and divine grace. That, it seems to me, is part of what it means for an artist to work out of a vision of life that finds its center in the person and work of Christ.[30]

Christian artists have found different ways to engage biblical and Christian tradition. Another strategy is seen in the works of Joel Sheesley, as for example in his large work *Knowledge Tree* (fig. 4.10). Taking his lead, in part, from the writings of biblical theologian Walter Brueggemann, Sheesley

---

[29]Given the historic association of portraiture with status and vanity, and the need to please—indeed flatter—a commissioning patron, hers is a challenging task. Prescott knows better than to yield to such pressures, and she also knows all too well the depths of human frailty and deceit.

[30]How does this come through in Prescott's portraits? She struggles to find a correlation between the painted image and the substance of the person before her, not just the outer appearance, but something of the inner being, as intoned through posture, inflection of the head, hand and body gestures, eye glance, and more subtle elements: the fall of light, the weight of shadow, color, the texture of paint, the feel of space, and setting. See further David Morgan, *Prescott and Prescott: Image and Substance,* exhibition booklet (Brauer Museum of Art, Valparaiso University, 2005). See also Kate Daniels, "Painting Poems: The Psychological Portraits of Catherine Prescott," *Image: A Journal of the Arts and Religion* 36 (2002): 31-39. Thanks also to Catherine Prescott for supplying digital images of her work.

Figure 4.9. Catherine Prescott, *I Drink Your Whiskey and Your Sorrow: The Poet Scott Cairns,* 2004, oil on canvas; collection of the artist. Photo: Courtesy of the artist, and reproduced by permission.

has often taken as his subject life outside Eden and inside suburbia. From Brueggemann, Sheesley took the idea of viewing typical human, everyday situations and behaviors as contemporary variants of biblical narratives. By way of pictorial strategy, he has also drawn from the Northern satirical tradition, with its realism and its surprise reversals, by which one small detail casts a different light on everything else.[31]

In the case of Sheesley's *Knowledge Tree,* at first we see an ordinary apple tree, rendered in lush, photo-realist detail. But the title hints at more. On

Figure 4.10. Joel Sheesley, *Knowledge Tree,* **2005, oil on canvas, 48" x 72"; collection of Mr. and Mrs. E. John Walford. Photo: John Walford, reproduction, by permission of the artist, Joel Sheesley.**

closer inspection we see that the trunk of the tree is somewhat aberrant in form, with unnatural bulges and crevices that give it an anthropomorphic quality. This can be read on many levels, not least suggestive of the absent figures of Adam and Eve reaching for the tree of knowledge of good and evil. As for the apples on this tree, their luscious red forms jump out at us, waiting to be plucked. Isn't that the nature of temptation? It is not that which tempts that is inherently evil; rather, it is not ours for the taking. Such a paint-

---

[31]Such is Sheesley's *After Paradise* (2002), in Prescott, *A Broken Beauty,* pp. 84-85, and fig. 4.

ing not only puts us in the shoes of Adam and Eve; it also shows us just how much of them is in us. With its captivating color and form, it lures and tempts us, and why should we resist? Surely, because, if we look yet closer at the painting, one single leaf, at the center of our gaze, has turned yellow,

Figure 4.11. David Wittig, *Elemento VII,* 2004, C-print, 40" x 20"; Collection Fondazione Cesare Pavese, Santo Stefano Belbo, Piedmont, Italy. Photo: Courtesy of the artist, and reproduced by permission.

will wither and die, just as temptation takes us down a path that leads not to life, but death.[32] Yet the life-affirming beauty of the painted tree points us back to life.

It seems fitting to end with a work by one of the upcoming generation of Christian artists, photographer David Wittig's *Elemento VII* (fig. 4.11), which is part of a solo exhibition of his work in Italy, that opened in May 2006.[33]

---

[32]Sheesley's *Knowledge Tree* (2005) was exhibited in his one-man show, Gescheidle Gallery, Chicago, 2005. My colleagues in the art department at Wheaton, Sheesley among them, have been thinking through the theme of the figure in the landscape, something which has rubbed off on some of our students. It seems fitting, therefore, in pointing to the establishment of a new tradition in Christian art, to note also a work by one of our 2006 graduating students, Elicia Castle, in a series she titled "On Fragility" (2006). These haunting works, which comprise her senior show, are made in a fragile medium, addressing a painful passage of life. The figures and landscape, based on photographs from a family vacation, are seen through the backs of scraped-down mirrors that partially reveal and partially obscure the images. The scale is large—about six by twelve feet—and the impact of the black, grey and tan color sober. No one figure connects with another, each is lost in his or her own thought, and none are cheered by the sight of sea, sand and palm trees that come with an exotic Caribbean vacation. It is certainly a work made somewhere on the path outside Eden, and one can but pray that God's Spirit will stir in the minds of those cast down heads, leading them further on the path toward redemption. But the image itself extends no such sure hope, except—as measured by the standard of contemporary art—in the degree of dignity conferred on each individual within the scene.

[33]Franco Vaccaneo, E. John Walford and Maria Walford-Dellù, *Alchimia degli elementi: Sui sentieri di Cesare Pavese: Immagini fotografiche di David Wittig* (Roma: Pieraldo, 2006), pp. 40-65, especially pp. 53-56, 59 and, as illustrated in color, pp. 104-5.

As well as its juxtaposition of two sorts of order—nature and culture—part of its appeal, both aesthetically and conceptually, lies in the contrast of the freshness of the vine leaves with the corroded texture and colors of the rusty old barrel.

Conclusion

All forms of beauty touch our desire for wholeness, yet a broken beauty offers something different. A broken beauty is not only true to the human condition, but it can embody the essence of the gospel of redemption, or, at very least, manifest its fruits. Neo-Platonic notions of beauty convey a longing for an unspoiled Garden of Eden or a concept of idealized perfection. Neo-Thomist notions of beauty—as embodied in a sense of perfection, order and harmony within the created order—may point to the transcendent. But a broken beauty can be a redemptive beauty, which acknowledges suffering while preserving hope. Without entering into the realm of the horrific and grotesque in the manner of those postmodernist artists who find in beauty only boredom, for the Christian artist the incarnation of Christ provides a basis to engage with integrity both beauty and ugliness, pleasure and pain.[34]

---

[34]As my friend, the wise and distinguished painter Bruce Herman, wrote in the preface to *A Broken Beauty* (2005), featuring the work of current Christian artists, we all have a story to tell. Within the Christian tradition, he continues, many have "sought to bear witness to the surprising beauty found in moments of suffering or loss or brokenness. Unlike the potential hubris of a more purist aesthetic, *A Broken Beauty* strives to show the mystery and mess of a *story* that is far from over—one that is ever more complex and problematic, yet moving toward a sense of resolution." This story, he adds, is "like the Bible, itself a tragicomic story that begins with a cosmic problem and ends in a wedding feast." Vincent van Gogh, seen in his *Self-Portrait with Bandaged Ear and Pipe* (1889) (private collection) was one whose art bears witness to such surprising beauty found amid suffering, as seen throughout his work. I too have my story—as each of us does—and have sought, in my own limited—and playful—way, to lend it visual form.

5

WOUNDS AND BEAUTY

Bruce Herman

Most history seems to carry on its back vestiges of paradise. At some point in more or less remote times things were better, almost golden. A deep concordance lay between man and the natural setting. The myth of the Fall runs stronger than any particular religion. There is hardly a civilization, perhaps hardly an individual consciousness, that does not carry inwardly an answer to intimations of a sense of distant catastrophe. Somewhere a wrong turn was taken in that "dark and sacred wood," after which man has had to labor, socially, psychologically, against the natural grain of being.[1]

Nostalgia for a golden age, for childhood—not simply of the individual but for that of the world—appears to be universal. Harmony and perfection always seem clearer in the rearview mirror, and we all feel a certain sense of exile in the more severe landscape and colder light of adulthood. The Genesis story and its motif of paradise lost is the archetype for much literature, and a great deal of poetry and art is dedicated to the recovery or enshrining of the paradisal, or an imagined, innocence. Popular versions of this motif abound, and the financial empire enjoyed by Thomas Kinkade, the so-called *Painter of Light,* is a dramatic testimony to just how powerful the desire to escape reality can be. Kinkade gives us fedora-wearing men and 1950s-style homemaker women in heels walking dewy lamp-lit streets that are lined with classic automobiles and other symbols of American individualism. All this is bathed in the golden twilight of yesteryear, a veritable Bedford Falls painted by an artist as ambitious and rich as Mr. Potter—the cor-

---

[1]George Steiner, "The Great Ennui," in *In Bluebeard's Castle* (New Haven: Yale University Press, 1972). "The Great Ennui" is originally from the T. S. Eliot Memorial Lectures, Yale University, March 1971.

rupt banker in Frank Capra's film *It's a Wonderful Life*. This nostalgia for the American dream is not confined to places and things but also affects our aesthetic understandings generally.

Our sense of the beautiful often participates in this backward glance, and for over two hundred years the European and American cultural standard of perfect human beauty has been the female figure just-past-pubescence—an evanescent moment in a woman's life, and one that requires ever more effort to preserve or extend. Most of our cosmetic culture aims at this ideal, and the rise of eating disorders alongside the billion-dollar industries of fashion, diet fads, plastic surgery and facial cosmetics all mirror the Kinkade kitsch-art phenomenon, providing a corollary in human body culture.

Beauty is everywhere colonized by the Romantic longing for perpetual youth.

Christians as well as their good pagan neighbors seem easily seduced by commercial interests that prey on this nostalgic aesthetic. Is there a viable alternative to this rather pathetic human tendency, and is there a truer, more redemptive visage of the beautiful? In this essay I will interpose the possibility of a clear-eyed *adult* aesthetic that bears the marks of Christ's resurrected body—marks that memorialize suffering but move beyond it to redemption, healing and eternity. The ascended Christ stills bears earthly wounds, and his new body can be treated as a starting point for a new aesthetic—a broken beauty if you will—and as a means of working through and beyond pain to a perfection that need not participate in idealization, in the unattainable standards of our celebrity and youth-obsessed culture.

The question is the same for beauty as for goodness and truth: how are we to understand a good God in a broken world—how are we to receive or encounter divine beauty in an ugly or disfigured human society? Much more theology has been written to reconcile truth with history; ethicists, theologians and philosophers have written reams trying to come to grips with the implications of goodness in the midst of the universal moral failure that we experience in adulthood. But beauty seems to be a Cinderella of sorts—left out of the party as her sisters, goodness and truth, enjoy the attentions of the great minds of Christian tradition. My hunch is that, as Hans Urs Von Balthasar has said, "beauty requires at least as much courage and decision as do truth and goodness." He goes on to say, "We can be sure that whoever sneers at her name as if she were the ornament of a bourgeois past—whether he admits it or not—can no longer pray and soon will no longer be able to love."[2]

Is there a theoretical basis for receptivity to a nonnostalgic, mature aesthetic of the human form? What I hope to discuss in this essay is the idea that beauty cannot be encountered in its fullness apart from acknowledgement of suffering, aging, contingency and need. Moreover, my deepest hunch is that beauty is only really known in a reciprocal relation—that is, when two or more participate in beauty and its ritual celebration. Marriage, and not the unrequited longing of adolescence, is the model I would like to employ in order to explore broken beauty.

The yearning of adolescence is the reigning model of erotic desire—and hence of beauty—in Western tradition since before the Romantic era. Illustrations of this tendency to enshrine the "crush" that a boy has for the perfect girl are found everywhere in our literary and artistic traditions (which may say as much about the predominantly male artists and their relative degree of emotional maturity as it says about Western civilization). But as Freud and many others since have said, constraint and eros are locked in an inexorable dance. And this dance or conflict is constitutive of civilization.

Erotic yearning and its battle with constraint are the particular subtext, if not the theme, of much of the Western literary and artistic tradition post-1750. A good example of this is the imagery found in a familiar poem by John Keats, *Ode on a Grecian Urn*. For those of us raised in the tradition of English literature, Keats's poem has the feel of a proverb. "Beauty is truth, truth beauty,— that is all / Ye know on earth, and all ye need to know." Yet, like most proverbs, its actual import may be masked by overfamiliarity. In fact, I'd wager that at least half of my readers could easily have quoted this famous line from the poem without necessarily remembering the overall mood Keats achieves. When my fifth-grade teacher, Mrs. Clarke, introduced our class to the *Ode,* she offered an innocent enough interpretation of it (which as good fifth-graders we accepted without question). The teacher assumed, like most, that Keats was expressing melancholy over death and longing for immortality—a familiar enough interpretation of Romanticism in general, and largely accurate, no doubt. However, whether Keats intended it or not, I believe he was also serving as a medium for another, slightly more veiled sentiment germane to our topic. The final lines from the poem will serve to illustrate my idea:

---

[2]Hans Urs Von Balthasar, *The Glory of the Lord: A Theological Aesthetics,* vol. 1, *Seeing the Form* (San Francisco: Ignatius, 1982).

O Attic shape! fair attitude! with brede
Of marble men and maidens overwrought,
With forest branches and the trodden weed;
Thou, silent form! dost tease us out of thought
As doth eternity: Cold Pastoral!
When old age shall this generation waste,
Thou shalt remain, in midst of other woe
Than ours, a friend to man, to whom thou say'st,
"Beauty is truth, truth beauty,—that is all
Ye know on earth, and all ye need to know."

The beauty that Keats praises is one which haunts a perfect longing: un-requited and unrequite-able love; a beauty that is perfectly constellated by another line earlier in the poem, "Heard melodies are sweet, but those un-heard / Are sweeter." In this tradition the perfect yearning descends from the pattern of courtly love left to us by the troubadours and the largely male intelligentsia who seemed to have thought a perfect love was the one just out of reach. A wife is a necessity for domestic chores and progeny, but a pure porcelain lover is the Muse and true emblem of beauty and immortal-ity. Keats is at pains in the poem to paint for us an icon of true beauty: the timelessness of a love and a worship that will never grow old (or be con-summated) because both are etched *in media res* forever on the sides of a Grecian memorial vase. As a Christian and as a painter of the human figure who seeks genuine beauty, I differ with Keats and his romantic comrades. Nostalgia and yearning will never be adequate for me—as my golden age lies not behind me but before me in the uncharted future. Moreover, for bib-lical believers, marriage must be the paradigm of divine love—not simply the locus of convenience and procreation. This side of eternity, marital love may be a wounded love, but it is nevertheless real—and the beauty that this love enshrines is real beauty, perhaps even the only beauty we know or need to know on earth.

This broken or wounded beauty is such because it flows from a deep and committed love that, by God's grace, ultimately defies time and sin, and in time yields the fruit of true intimacy and union. The love found in a good marriage is subject to the ravages of time and sin precisely because it *is* real and involves real persons who struggle and sin, seek forgiveness, and hope-fully find reconciliation. Trying to disentangle beauty from love and intimacy is work I must leave to my philosopher colleagues—and this work is undoubtedly important for clarity's sake. But as a painter I cannot disentangle my art from my life (and therefore my marriage) and so I will proceed from this place of entanglement. Plainly stated, my idea is that beauty is inextricably intertwined with eros, and that the best expression of both (beauty and eros) is seen in the face of an earthly beloved—not an idealized and unattainable one. The problem that immediately besets us in this discussion is that our own tradition of the beautiful flows from pagan assumptions about love, knowledge and the ideal beauty.

The Greco-Roman inheritance does grant us great benefits—perhaps even especially in the realm of the arts. And clearly the patrimony of the Mediterranean has given us much by way of lovely literature, music, architecture and painting. The early church realized this and preserved that cultural deposit faithfully despite the fact that the hands which formed those artifacts were stained with martyrs' blood. But I think the underlying cultural assumptions about women and slaves and marriage that undergirded the Greco-Roman world were not without consequence to the set of understandings we are examining here. Let me explain.

First, the Platonic concept of the beautiful seems to strain at a kind of transcendence that diminishes the value of domestic reality—or for that matter, anything realize-able, gritty or "inconvenient," as Shakespeare might have put it. Without trying to explicate this fully, I'll just say that incarnate love seems to embarrass those who strive for a gnostic sort of perfection. And the courtly love tradition, which enshrines unrequited eros, is a species of this very thing, the longing for a face that doesn't really exist—a Helen or a Beatrice—not an earthly woman. When erotic desire is placed outside of the covenantal bond of lifelong commitment and daily-ness, its goal is unreachable because genuine intimacy is impossible to know apart from trust (which itself cannot be known apart from life-long fidelity). Moreover, our sense of human beauty always flows from erotic desire (yet not necessarily from desire for sex). Keats's *Ode* is a further ramification of that unbound desire that manifests as a yearning for what he calls "eternity"—but which by a Christian reckoning is more a kind of Egyptian immortality than the eternity we expect to inhabit.

Pagan understandings of beauty and desire seem always to have as their locus the perfect geometry of "unheard melodies" (as Keats put it)—an idealized notion of human perfectibility as over against the present reality, marred as that is by contingency and need. It is as though our good pagan ancestors are saying, "The ultimate reality *must* be better than this! Death, disease, bad breath and bad teeth"—all results of a fallen world. Their hankering for a prelapsarian golden age is understandable enough. Most of us have had at least a few childhood hours that seemed perfect and pain-free—our own golden age. And our Hebrew predecessors seem to have had a sense of the same thing reflected in their desire to return to Egypt. As Steiner says, this seems to be the perennial beginning of every account of history: things were better in an imagined childhood of the human race before we fell from grace. This longing is the subtext of fairy tales, myth and much religious narrative. The key difference, as I see it, between the biblical religious vision and the rest is that the pathos of paradise lost is never allowed ascendancy. We are moving out from Eden toward the City of God, not "back to the Garden" as the 1960s Woodstock anthem envisioned it. In the biblical vision nostalgia is never given a foothold because the best is yet to come.

The pervasive nostalgia for adolescence and its bittersweet yearning in Romanticism yields a vision that ultimately locates beauty outside of human attainability—and that is why the metaphor of marriage instead of courtly love has relevance to our discussion of beauty. First, because marriage, and not romantic love, is the image offered us in biblical revelation; and second, because marriage is potentially a crucible of virtue—and in Christian thought, goodness and beauty cannot be separated. Once again, as Balthasar says:

> We no longer dare to believe in beauty and we make of it a mere appearance in order the more easily to dispose of it. Our situation today shows that beauty demands for itself at least as much courage and decision as do truth and goodness, and she will not allow herself to be separated and banned from her two sisters without taking them along with herself in an act of mysterious vengeance. We can be sure that whoever sneers at her name as if she were the ornament of a bourgeois past—whether he admits it or not—can no longer pray and soon will no longer be able to love.[3]

Truth and goodness: Where are these foundational realities located in human experience if not in covenantal relationship? I am aware that marriage is not available to all persons, but some form of covenantal love is. And that, I feel, is what Jesus refers to when he calls himself the Bridegroom and names the church his bride. Throughout the Old Testament the image of a

---

[3]Ibid.

divine marriage between God and God's people is elaborated. And that marriage is subject to all the flaws and failures of any earthly marriage we know
about—infidelity, duplicity, lovelessness, vanity and so on. In fact, the entire
Old Testament could be read as a failed marriage and the New Testament
as the ultimate hope of its restoration. The divine union has indeed been
broken and with it all genuine experience of untrammeled beauty is lost.
But that broken marriage is also spoken of as expecting healing and having
a redemption point in history—in and through the consummation of the
Bridegroom and his redeemed bride—in Christ and the church.

I will state my case concretely: redeemed marriage, and not courtly love,
is the best image of human beauty we have. I would go further and say that
the divine invitation, voiced throughout biblical history, that we come into
"marriage" with God—this invitation is a glimpse of genuine beauty in its
ultimate realization. Moreover, the erotic imagery of bridegroom and bride
is pivotal to a robust grasp of this true beauty. This is the same imagery employed in the Song of Songs, which has often been a rich source of literary,
musical and artistic inspiration in Christian tradition. The marriage described
in the Song involves the transfiguration of an earthly erotic love into something hinting at the divine beloved. As you may recall, Shulamith[4] awakens
from love's sleep a transformed wife and queen, now admired by the court-
iers who once threatened her. They say to her:

We have a little sister,
and she has no breasts.
What shall we do for our sister,
on the day when she is spoken for?
If she is a wall,
we will build upon her a battlement of silver;
but if she is a door,
we will enclose her with boards of cedar.

Shulamith responds to this concern or obsession with virginity:

I was a wall,
and my breasts were like towers;
then I was in his eyes
as one who brings peace. (Song 8:8-10)

Shulamith is reminding these older brothers that premarital sexual purity—

[4]Shulamith is the "black and beautiful" (Song 1:5) princess in the Song of Songs.

the Hebrew variation of Keats's perpetual virgin—is not for its own sake or for perpetual aesthetic delectation, but for the sake of giving oneself away in marriage.[5]

To imagine a transfigured marriage—an earthly eros redeemed by charity and longsuffering—differs significantly from a beauty that attaches to images of idealized perpetual youth (like that depicted on the side of Keats's funerary urn). The face of an earthly beloved transfigured by lifelong committed fidelity is likely someday to be full of wrinkles and loss of muscle tone. But trust me, as a seasoned artist and one who has been married for over thirty years to the same woman, that aging face will be a beautiful face. Second, the heart of a good marriage is mutuality—give and take. What is given and what is taken is nothing less than *everything*—and this is an icon of divine union. As my former pastor, Gordon Paul Hugenberger, once quipped, "The problem with most modern marriages is that the couples are unclear on the concept. Marriage is not a 50-50 proposition—it is 100 percent-100 percent." In other words, the beauty glimpsed in a wholeheartedly sacrificial relationship is, or should be, the norm.

Furthermore, beauty that flows from the covenant enacted on the cross offers additional counterintuitive meanings in this context. As the apostle says, the cross is "a stumbling block to Jews and foolishness to Gentiles" (1 Cor 1:23). Perhaps we could be allowed to substitute the term *intelligentsia* for Gentiles, and *self-righteous religious* for Jews, in order to update Paul's message and disentangle it from modern-day ethnic misunderstandings. The cross remains a symbol of futility, barbarity and ignominy to those who cannot see its beauty—but it is the true locus of beauty if we understand a mysterious consummation of eros as happening precisely when a bridegroom lays down his life for his bride. This is when erotic love bears its best fruit in *caritas*.

Psychologists commonly claim that for women, erotic desire is most often aroused by generosity, considerateness and protection—not just male abdominal muscles or hormones (despite what the popular TV show *Sex and the City* seems to sell). We Christian men could take heed if this is the case. Christ's self-donating love is the supreme image of this generosity and considerateness. Beyond this, I think that the cross reveals other lessons about beauty. The broken body of Christ (in the Eucharist) is the basis for the cov-

---

[5]Thanks are due for this idea to Dr. Dan Russ, the director of the Center for Christian Studies at Gordon College, Wenham, Massachusetts.

enantal community. And just as in a good marriage, where mutual sacrifice builds loyalty and trust and undergirds erotic desire, the Christian community finds its own beauty and love in another form of reciprocity and mutuality.

David Ford, in his book *Self and Salvation: Being Transformed,* speaks of the human self being redeemed in and through community in the act of *facing one another.* This "facing" takes the form of the *hospitable self;* the *self without idols;* the *worshiping self;* the *singing self* and finally the *Eucharistic self*—the self-donating Christ-self. The gist of his book has bearing on my thesis, namely, that the foundation of committed, covenantal relationship—self and other, self and God—is the true icon of heaven. Plainly stated, one might say that beauty, which finds its final form in heaven, *is* relational, harmonic. This beauty is indeed in the eye of the beholder, but it is also in the face of the beloved—inevitably a wounded beloved and a marred face here on earth, due to sin and the broken symmetry of human love. Yet beauty's very woundedness is the occasion of redemption. That is why the apostle speaks of "God's foolishness" as wiser than human wisdom (1 Cor 1:25). By choosing the broken, weak, despised and foolish face over the idealized face of beauty, Christ (who in Is 53 is prophesied as a wounded, disfigured Messiah) overturns the tables of the Greco-Roman model of physical perfection along with its gods, themselves extensions of this all-too-human notion of bodily perfection.

Thus a new form of beauty is inaugurated when Jesus ascends into heaven bearing the marks of earthly pain. After the resurrection he displays these wounds to Thomas in order to assure the man of his reality. Thanks to honest Thomas, we have a testimony to this new beauty. These marks on transfigured hands and side are our hope for our own transfiguration in the midst of a wounded life. As a painter of the human form and story, I take great comfort and inspiration from all this. Like my hero Rembrandt, I am less drawn to Arcadian youths sporting immortal muscles on a porcelain vase than I am to a slightly lumpy (but *real!*) female body that radiates the authentic light of time-tested love.

A couple of disclaimers before I conclude: one, I do not believe that I have said anything new or revolutionary. I do not mean to diminish the very real role of what is pretty in the beautiful; neither do I intend to place all of beauty under the rubric of suffering or the sublime. I merely want to show that beauty's complexity includes surprising turns—perhaps most surprisingly in the cross as well as in the crucible of marital love. Moreover, I want to say that facing true beauty means facing the otherness of God, the reality of sin and depravity, and realizing that simply "transcending" is not a real answer to the problem of pain and evil. Redemptive beauty is found, surprisingly, in the face of the aged as much as in the face of a perfect child or female figure—and that surprise comes only by steadfast engagement with the other over many years of committed love.

In conclusion, then, I wish to make another brief comment on the Romantic vision of beauty. Keats and his intellectual grandchildren seem to think that beauty alone is salvific—hence the later permutations of that vision in Matthew Arnold and a host of other thinkers who promoted belief in a so-called disinterested art of pure aesthetic contemplation. As a painter of people (and one can never truly be dispassionate about people), I've grown tired of this idea. In a word, I find it false and insubstantial. As our friend Nick Wolterstorff has insisted, art must find its humble place in the life of the community.[6] The cult of the lone genius, the hero of high Romanticism, is the only religion wherein the better you practice it, the fewer converts you make. The shrinking coterie of the art world demonstrates this truth and reveals the falsity of the claim that art can save. This high-minded view of art not only fails to account for the barbarity and cruelty exercised by those Nazis who were connoisseurs of art and music, but it also has an even more surprising consequence: when art is expected to usher in a utopian salvation it is diminished in its own capacity to fulfill its legitimate calling. Much of the literature, music and art that were spawned in the Romantic era is now thought to be sentimental trash, its shelf-life being exceedingly short. Our own era may suffer a similar fate.

Be that as it may, the phenomenon of highly cultivated aesthetic taste coexisting with vicious racism and injustice in the same person or society would appear to present an insuperable problem for theologians or artists hoping to see deep connections between the good, the true, and the beautiful. My thesis can be recapitulated in this context as follows: Only eyes trained by gazing continually toward the cross—only eyes cleansed by that second innocence, childlike habitual charity—can see true beauty, true goodness.

When Jesus said, "Unless you become as a little child you cannot see the kingdom of God," he clearly meant the opposite of the cloying nostal-

---

[6]Nicholas Wolterstorff, *Art in Action: Toward a Christian Aesthetic* (Grand Rapids: Eerdmans, 1980).

gia that would counter a world of pain with an escapist fantasy world of yesteryear. On the contrary, Jesus was pointing forward, toward the only completed aesthetic—*caritas*—which alone allows us to glimpse the lineaments of heaven.

The best is yet to come.

"Like Shining from Shook Foil"

Art, Film and the Sacred

Roy Anker

The title "Like Shining from Shook Foil" is taken from the most famous of all Gerard Manley Hopkins's poems, "God's Grandeur." "The world is charged with the grandeur of God. / It will flame out, like shining from shook foil," and though humankind has heedlessly obscured that radiance, the dazzle abides still, "never spent," because, as the last lines announce, "the Holy Ghost over the bent / World broods with warm breast and with ah! bright wings." Hopkins emphasizes in extreme images of flame and shining that the physical world is, or at least once was, bright unto brilliance, displaying, at least from time to time, a dazzling iridescence shot through with an intensity of splendor that bespeaks the presence of a loving, beauty-bent Creator who puts on the whole spangling show for the sheer heaven of it. The Christian tradition—from the Genesis creation to John Calvin, yes, even the dour Calvin, to Hopkins, T. S. Eliot and Annie Dillard—is replete with this sense that a gorgeous created nature is somehow, mysteriously, a manifestation of God's own fierce shining. For our part as human creatures set within this arena, a state of astonished delight and gratitude at the beauty of it all, of "beholdment," is right and fitting and proper, a blessed thing.

What is of primary interest here is not so much Hopkins's natural theology as the possibility that there might in fact be something such as "shook foil," meaning a human instrumentality or artifice that might capture or approximate the gorgeousness that nature and people at times display. That art—indeed, like much of Hopkins's own poetry—might actually do some-

thing of this sort, evoking the splendor of the holy One, or stunning us with
wonder and gratitude for its presence is these days within the context of
much modern art practice and criticism a very hard sell. To refer to anything
at all as partaking of what we call beauty or metaphysics comprises a far-
fetched sort of speculation that is likely, at least in the academy, to get one
hauled away in a padded wagon. Indeed, modernism and whatever has followed it have proven downright skittish in approaching notions of either
beauty or the sacred. Perhaps Darwin's "nature red in tooth and claw" has
once and for all de-divinized the natural world. Or perhaps Freud's opening
of the floodgates of the unconscious has simply provided a more interesting
terrain for imagination. Or, perhaps it is that Marx's descendants have per-
manently criminalized aesthetic pleasure. Out has gone beauty, and in has
come the sublime, an aesthetic of fright and fear that seems more apt for the
ceaseless genocidal tumult of modernity in which Western culture has so violently flayed both humankind and mother earth.

There is, however, a certain obduracy to the notion of beauty; it won't go
away, no matter how we anesthetize and rationalize its pressure. For one,
the word *beauty* is whispered again in odd places. For instance, James El-
kins, who teaches at the Art Institute of Chicago, has wrestled aloud over
dimensions of aesthetic response; his titles pretty much speak for themselves: *Pictures and Tears: A History of People Who Have Cried in Front of
Paintings* (2001) and, in a sequel of sorts, *On the Strange Place of Religion
in Contemporary Art* (2004), which elaborates on the paucity of the sacred
art in the twentieth century and the dearth of critics capable of talking about
any kind of sacred anything.

In another recent book, and even more brave, *On Beauty and Being Just*
(1999), Elaine Scarry of Harvard sets out to dismantle prevalent notions that
somehow art and enjoyment of beauty are morally illegitimate. Scarry takes
on those who complain that beauty diverts attention from the suffering of
the world or that the human gaze invariably violates by expropriation any
and everything for selfish ends. For Scarry these reflexes have worked to
sever art from once commonplace notions of beauty and aesthetic delight.
Scarry goes on to argue that for all sorts of moral reasons "what should be
argued is not the banishing of beauty but beauty's immediate return."[1] Scarry
contends that the experience of beauty imparts a sort of generalized rever-

---

[1]Elaine Scarry, *On Beauty and Being Just* (Princeton, N.J.: Princeton University Press, 1999), p.
75.

ence, though she never uses that term, for a Being in general that nurtures moral regard. It is right and fitting then that we, in her verb, *gape* or, for that matter, behold, weep, laugh and, to push her point to a religious threshold, though Scarry does not, kneel or at the least mutter quiet alleluias and amens, which is to enter the precincts of the sacred.[2] In any case, what is afoot seems a long way from the sterilization of art into pure form and detached emotional indifference.

If the notion of beauty and the legitimacy of even an appetite for it have been banished in the post-WWII art world, there's one visual arena whose endless eye candy, meaning the visually delectable in general, positively dazzles hordes of folks who take it in for the plain fun of it. And once in a while in the movies, stories and images beckon talk of beauty and the abiding power of art to move us in depths and paths that are, for lack of a better term, sacred or holy. And that happens not just with the independent fare loved by film snoots but smack in the middle of some of the popular films of our time. Here beauty breaks open and a kind of holy work is achieved, and such is the alchemy of art on the one hand and grace or shining or whatever on the other. That might seem a rather large rhetorical leap by one who's consumed too much of la-la land, but for a little time, at least, let us try it out.

The question, then, is what might film, cinema, "da movies" have to do with notions of beauty and the sacred. In many ways Hopkins's image of foil seems a remarkably apt parallel to—indeed, almost an anticipation of—the physical mechanism of film projection: a reflective screen designed to mirror back for the purposes of viewing patterns of light previously imbedded on an absorptive medium, the film stock or, increasingly these days, in digital code. Despite the aptness of Hopkins's simile, the question of whether film can indeed "shake" so as to bring audiences to recognize some sort of "shining" remains, and lots of folks have different answers to that. Presuming the answer is yes, we then ask the question of means: Just how much of the right kind of "shaking" does it take to generate this thing called "shining"? Indeed the "how" question is the big one, and not at all a new one.

These sorts of questions are greatly complicated by the nature of the medium. Film is predominantly a narrative visual art wherein whatever beauty or shining emerges results from a delicate intertwining of both story and vi-

---

[2]Ibid., p. 29.

sual representation: some film images stand on their own because of something or another about the image, and others assume meaning because of the stories that give them meaning. We'll look at a few of those in just a bit. Having said that, though, we must concede initially that when it comes to simple beauty or something akin to shining, there arises a problem that is perhaps intrinsic to the medium, and that is its own stubborn physicality. From its very earliest days, audiences have always been dazzled by the medium's replicative realism; indeed, about one hundred years ago in shoebox theaters in Europe and America the very first viewers of film saw simple documentary clips of waves crashing and ducked to avoid spray. The appeal of cinema's fidelity to the ordinary perceptible physical world—realism, in short—still compels. If anything, audience insistence on plausible-looking worlds of material surface and immediacy is all the more extreme (just try showing old film or bad prints to students), and we now deploy armies of computers to generate real-looking depictions of fantastic kingdoms like Narnia, Middle-earth or life inside a computer matrix. Now more than ever, perhaps, it simply must look real. That audience demand does not leave a lot of room for personal visual expressiveness or much of anything else.

And there's the rub, to be sure, too much of a good thing perhaps. The problem can be put like this: film is so fixed, mired in its own intractable physicality, visually and narratively, that it has trouble leaping beyond itself, beyond the inert, mundane empirical world it depicts: how does the medium conjure beauty, spirit or the sacred from the seeming dross of the material, though that might admittedly pose a false dichotomy? How do we take matter and make it arresting, and better still, in questions of spirit, how do we make the invisible visible? That this sort of thing does happen in film, at least from time to time, is beyond dispute. But where does beauty come from and reside? In film criticism generally, while there is much appreciation for technical ingenuity, the word *beauty* is rarely employed, save perhaps occasionally to describe the effectiveness of a particular cinematic device. In this case, beauty lies in some aspect of production or technical facility.

To go after this question of shining and shook foil, I want to survey briefly three ways filmmakers have tried to render in various guises the reality and also the nature of the divine. And indeed, it seems pretty much a cultural-theological given in the West that when the divine shows up, beauty displays as one of its signal traits: beauty beyond beauty, beauty beyond words, and that, to be sure, is where the movies come in since, as we all know, a picture is worth a thousand words or, better yet, simply goes where words cannot. Beauty is in fact one of the pivotal indications of the veridicality of divine disclosure. And it is no surprise either that each of these stylistic modes deploys notions of beauty as the declarative center of its narrative discourse and that each of these aesthetic strategies contains its own unique metaphysic.

The Holy Epic

First, there's been the "usual approach" to beauty and the sacred: hierophany by the numbers, excess, bigness, whatever. This route has pushed cinema's enormous capacity for verisimilitude, and the logic goes something like this: if we can just make slices of life or, for example, of the Bible, look real and pretty enough, and big enough, usually with a cast of thousands, handsome heroes, and impressive settings, that will (1) give the divine its due, and (2) attract and sanctify the masses (and, not coincidentally, the box office; strange how providence works). With religious material, this strategy presumes that biblical literalism literally transposed bigger than life to the screen—life times two or five in living color cinemascope—must inexorably do holy work, and this for a long time was the manner of Hollywood's raid on the sacred. Big is beauty is majesty is God. The key ingredient here has been invocation by spectacle and sentiment. These films had their heyday when Hollywood was fast expanding its technical reach with full color, widescreen, 3-D and Cinerama. Size and vividness seemed what film was best suited for, and this gave rise to films of epic length, scope and portentousness, general overall hugeness. The goal here seemed not so much to be beauty but giganticism. A couple of examples suffice: Cecil B. De Mille's 1956 *The Ten Commandments* with its cast of thousands spread through all three hours and forty minutes of blustering Chuck Heston as the big M, and golly, who could not like that, a megaproduction that rivaled God's own seven days' worth back whenever. In 1965 George Stevens, the fellow who made the classic western *Shane,* did his devout Catholic best with his life of Jesus, *The Greatest Story Ever Told,* which ran almost four very long hours of a blonde, long-haired and very Swedish Max von Sydow as Jesus preaching in American Swede amid the grandeur of John Ford's Monument Valley. And on it went, and still does. With Mel Gibson's aesthetics of pain in *The Passion of the Christ* we return to the same strategy: if we just whack the fellow bloody enough realistically (and prettily) enough long enough, we'll be moved.

All of this brings to mind, frankly, though perhaps somewhat harshly, the prophets of Baal who haul out all the liturgical stops to light that fire, an invocation by extremity and desperation, to say the least (1 Kings 18). The problem is that all these gestures do little to illumine the character of the divine, except to say that God is big: big miracles, big suffering, maybe even majestic, though not particularly endearing except when we come to gentle Jesus, gooed up though he is. Big Daddy and Sweet Jesus.

Transcendental Style in Film

On the other hand, at pretty much the same time, across the Atlantic, a number of different filmmakers charted an opposite path to the divine—not with a surfeit of cinematic bigness but with a stark minimalism, less is more, even a kind of antispectacle cinema that intentionally subverted prevalent filmmaking habits and audience expectations, at least those in North America. If the Hollywood holy blockbuster represents the prophets of Baal trying to rouse the divine, this school is Elijah doing just the opposite but with greater success. Beginning in the 1950s, Swedish writer-director Ingmar Bergman, son of a prominent Lutheran minister, simply changed the topic, demonstrating in such films as *The Virgin Spring, The Seventh Seal* and *Winter Light,* that it was indeed possible to tell plausible, haunting stories of furious religious wrestle amid, for example, the hard primitive life of the Middle Ages. And sometimes God did show up, depending on how, needless to say, one reads some of Bergman's calculated ambiguities. What we saw in Bergman's early cinema, and this is important to remember, is people grappling with an elusive, hidden transcendent. For the most part, at least in these early films, Bergman hewed to the conventions of cinematic realism, albeit of a stripped-down kind of gothic woodcut starkness, a mode he discarded as he left his religious belief behind and his films became ever more psychological.

The one who charted a path of holy minimalism was French writer-director Robert Bresson. It is Bresson who fashioned in his slim body of work what writer-director-critic Paul Schrader has famously named, in the title of his 1972 book, "transcendental style in film." Bresson eschewed established cinematic practice, instead fashioning a genuinely subversive style that brings audiences cognitively, experientially, to encounter, purely and directly, the Transcendent itself. This differs significantly, on the one hand, from Bergman's once-removed, secondhand approach of watching characters thrash about in their hair-shirts of humanity as they search for the divine. And it goes directly counter to Hollywood practice of making God lavishly conspicuous and pretty. The words most often used to describe Bresson's cinematic style are *severe* and *austere,* though I prefer the less judgmental term of *sparse,* about which I will say more later. In general it means that Bresson withheld from his viewers the usual conventions and satisfactions of film viewing until the last frames when he laid it on thick in order to deliver something he deemed far more substantial—a revelatory religious moment in which, in great mystery, God shows up.

A case in point and the easiest access into Bresson is to examine what he did with acting in classic pictures like *The Diary of a Country Priest, The Pickpocket* and *Au Hasard Balthazar.* Bresson typically used nonprofessional actors with the purpose of effacing personality from his films. In addition, he told his actors to play their roles flat, delivering uninflected readings and immobile faces. Moreover, he shot them at middle distance, forgoing close-ups and other cinematic ploys that cultivate emotional intimacy with characters. And last, he cast mundane faces, emphasizing the unexceptional and the ordinary—no Hestons or von Sydows here. Bresson extended this plainness to the rest of the film story: little film music and nothing visually picturesque. His obsession was to flatten both screen and story. In *Balthasar,* for example, he used a single 50 mm lens for the whole picture. The purpose of all of this was to detach audiences from emotional connection, not to have viewers care so much about characters' feelings and fates, so certain other "recognitions" might happen: seeing the soul instead of personality, sensing not plot but divine presence, and finally, grasping the iconic beauty of grace when it comes clear in the film's close.

Typically Bresson in his last frames leaps from minimalism to a dramatic, musical and visual lushness, relatively speaking, in order to confront the viewer with, in Schrader's words, "the Wholly Other he would normally avoid." Events and images request the viewers' "participation and approval. . . . [The ending] is a 'miracle' which must be accepted or rejected."[3] The chief aspect of these last frames is the presentation of a visual icon that challenges the viewer to embrace a new perception of the world: in *The Trial of Joan of Arc,* the last shot is of the empty, smoke-shrouded stake on which Joan of Arc burned, an echo, for sure, of the empty tomb. And the closing

---

[3]Paul Schrader, *Transcendental Style in Film* (New York: De Capo, 1988), p. 81.

sequence in *The Diary of a Country Priest* consists of a voiceover reading a
letter that describes the dying hours of a very flawed young priest, a man
who is neither very competent nor certain in his belief, on the whole para-
noid and faltering. We start with a still of the letter (fig. 6.1) from which

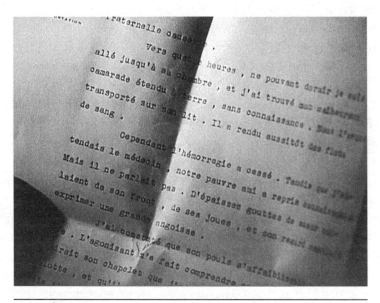

Figure 6.1.

slowly emerges an image of the cross (fig. 6.2) and the letter then dissolves
entirely, leaving only the cross (fig. 6.3), as the voice continues to read for
another seventy seconds or so, an eternity of screen time, until the priest's
and the film's last words, "All is grace."

The closing tableaus in these Bresson films, including as well *Au Hasard
Balthasar,* challenge the viewer to existential choice, arguing thus: no, the
world is not flat, hollow and impersonal like the one put up there on the
screen for the length of the whole of the film, but surprise, the world is like
this as contained in this last image, albeit a portrait shrouded in mystery. The
pervasive sparse flatness of the story is disrupted at last with sudden, even
shocking clarity, or so the theory has it. In all these films, viewers grapple
with the existential residue of the characters' lives, and that is put within a
clear frame of transcendent reference. With his narrative style Bresson hauls
viewers themselves psychospiritually into the gap where the divine discloses

Figure 6.2.

Figure 6.3.

to the viewer in ways that are not necessarily clear even to characters in the film. Bresson displays, in effect, what God looks like and how God does God's thing, which Bresson's theo-aesthetic labels "transformative." This is, to be sure, not a modest goal.

Needless to say, elements of Bresson's style effectively ramify in all sorts of film that even so much as dally with the religious. An obvious case in point is the stylistic lineage of the notion of the wordless iconic disclosures that erupt at the end, often replete with amply declarative music, that retro-actively clarify and complete all that has very often very cryptically gone on heretofore. At the very end, then, thanks to this fixed closing image, as the image comes to function iconically within the context of the narrative, we finally "get it," understanding where this whole long story was heading all along. This fruition is apt, a revelatory moment that can only be displayed but not verbalized never so nearly as well. These disclosures, in any case, recalling Hopkins, constitute the moment of "shining" when the divine in-vades an opaque world or, to put the matter alternatively, depending on one's theology, the world itself becomes translucent, at least in terms of meaning and Presence. And within these many contexts, the grace that comes arrives steeped in beauty, and it is beauty that makes the grace pal-pable, lambent and trenchant. Ah, so that is what this is all about! Because of the sparse means used to tell the story, all that flatness, this final disclo-sure, replete with close-ups, emotion and music, overwhelms and envelops. Or that's the theory behind the sudden bestowal of cinematic richness, what I call "lush" means, as opposed to sparse means of the story telling.

And of course, Bresson has been enormously influential; Schrader himself did a straight-on remake of *The Pickpocket* in his 1980 *American Gigolo* and then again in 1992 with *Light Sleeper.* Here is Bresson's ending (fig. 6.4), and next to it is Schrader's (fig. 6.5), and they share essentially the same last line: it has taken me so long to come to you, in Schrader's rendition. And Bresson lays on a burst of music; Schrader in *American Gigolo* goes so far as to make his burst of music an organ and very churchly at that.

A whole host of very well-known films borrow this device, though they deploy the rest of Bresson's aesthetic unevenly, if at all. One film of notably sparse means, Bruce Beresford's *Tender Mercies* (1983), tells the story of a washed-up alcoholic country and western singer, and it's pretty Bressonian throughout in its minimal dialogue, empty, nonpicturesque setting. Com-pare these shots, the first of Mack Sledge, played by Robert Duvall, dwarfed

Figure 6.4.

Figure 6.5.

by the huge empty expanse of Texas sky (fig. 6.6), and the second of the country priest making his way to the home of a parishioner (fig. 6.7). Both are lost, solitary men, and all the viewer needs is one glimpse of this sort of framing in the setting to tell that tale.

Figure 6.6.

Figure 6.7.

And finally the ending of *Tender Mercies* consists simply of a long word-less sequence of stepfather and stepson, two lost boys who've found rest with each other, throwing a football back and forth in quiet joy, home at last, which is the country motel on the horizon in the background (see fig. 6.8). The original score had a huge orchestral burst over this long, wordless closing sequence, something hugely different from the soppy lyrics of the

Figure 6.8.

music in the later DVD edition. Apparently Bresson did get to Texas after all.

Or consider these, films that deliver this unfathomably rich, reflexive "wordless payoff," as one critic calls it, and you'll recognize these soon enough, and if the images have succeeded, they should instantly reignite much of the psycho-emotive-spiritual impact of the films, moving from the somewhat unknown to the well known:

1. In Lawrence Kasdan's 1992 film *Grand Canyon,* a random, disparate group of people and classes come together for this meditation on the mystery of life, which proves far from being a Darwinian nightmare conjured early in the film (see fig. 6.9). This is set in LA after all, which proves none-theless to be "not all bad." The film set the path for two later, more powerful films, P. T. Anderson's *Magnolia* and Paul Haggis's *Crash*. Think of the frogstorm in the first and snow falling in the second.

Figure 6.9.

2. And then there's this film about a young banker wrongly convicted of murdering his wife. After decades in prison he escapes immediately after he realizes, appropriately enough, that his emotional coldness was at least indirectly responsible for his wife's murder. His route out of the prison is through five-hundred yards of sanitary sewer that spills into a creek, into which he spills to be washed clean by the rain and light of a thunderstorm (see fig. 6.10). Suddenly, the title of the film, *The Shawshank Redemption* (1994), becomes clear.

Figure 6.10.

Figure 6.11.

3. Or this man (see fig. 6.11), an eighteenth-century marauder, a Paulista, who enslaves the indigenous Guarani and kills his own brother over a woman and takes on an arduous penance only to receive unexpected pardon from the very indigenous people he has pillaged into slavery.

4. Or this (see fig. 6.12), a remarkable unexpected end to what is in most ways formulaic Hollywood melodrama. In 1935 in Waxahachie, Texas, the young local sheriff is accidentally shot to death by a teenaged black man who

Figure 6.12.

Figure 6.13.

is then subsequently tortured and murdered by the clan. That's in the first fifteen minutes, and much brokenness goes on between that and the end. A long last scene takes place during holy communion in a small church, a communion like no other insofar as it becomes increasingly surreal and ends with, in this last shot of the film, the two dead of the film, the killer and the killed, bestowing the peace of God on one another. It drove the religiously tone-deaf American critical establishment nuts (*Places in the Heart* [1984]).

5. And last, just for fun, there's this one (see fig. 6.13), and here we know just who this mysterious visitor is after all, and Spielberg himself belatedly came to know half-way through shooting when it dawned on his Catholic school screenwriter, Kathleen Kennedy, just whose story they were telling (*E.T. the Extra-Terrestrial* [1982]).

And so it goes, happily, for this structuring has allowed the visual potential of cinema, in all of its iconic depths, to shout loudly and affectingly. However, and it is a big however, as justly celebrated as Bresson is, there is a problem with this "style" and that lies in the transcendental theo-metaphysics implicit in it. The style presumes that God in the normal course of living is everywhere sealed off from this world, "hidden," distant, the realm of daily life being opaque and empty—save for those supernaturalist moments when the divine intrudes in epiphanic recognition, if not for the character then for the viewer. This, in short, propounds a dualistic metaphysic, in Bresson's case influenced very likely by an ascetic Jansenism. In this case, to put the matter rather simply, the dualistic sense of a world of starkly separated matter and spirit at least shapes if not altogether dictates story and style: solitary figures grope their way through an immense, featureless and usually hostile world. The material world is deemphasized, is made dross, opaque, spiritless, empty, so the spiritual can break through decisively, unambiguously. The climatic event poses a hard either-or question to the audience. Sparse means imply a sparse divine.

Beyond Transcendental Style

So persuasive has been Schrader's analysis of Bresson and two others, Ozu and Dreyer, that his notion of transcendental style has more or less become the norm for defining genuinely religious film, despite Schrader's comment that there are other possibilities. This is challenged by the subsequent emergence of a third and maybe even fourth transcendental style that is now and again showing up in wildly disparate films, and I want to look briefly at two films that illustrate what I mean. They differ hugely from Bresson because, bluntly put, the theology behind them differs hugely. Rather, these presume, reverting back to Hopkins, the abiding luminous presence of the Spirit of God, that broods still over the bent world, imbuing it with "dearest freshness, deep-down things." Here the divine is wonderfully near and present, if only we had the eyes to see. Indeed, it is difficult to know what to label these styles; perhaps immanentalist rather than transcendental or, in a term hauled over from literary studies, metafictive.

They are distinguished consequently by their use of the whole storehouse of cinematic means, what I call lushness, using fully, even exultantly, the capacities of the medium to haul viewers into characters' experiential depths. If Bresson stayed on the outside, avoiding intimacy, these go inside and out to let us know what characters see and feel, and they are dense with close-ups, expressive acting, gymnastic cameras, shining and shadows, bold palette, and musical flourish to the extent that sometimes music itself becomes a character.

The first is that very controversial 1999 film *American Beauty,* written by Alan Ball and directed by Sam Mendes. Smack in the middle of the film comes a meditation that informs all of what has gone before and all of what will follow. A young, troubled character by the name of Ricky Fitts, who goes about videotaping just about everything, explains to his plain-Jane girlfriend "the most beautiful thing I've ever seen." What Ricky sees stands in stark contrast to the vision of every other character in the film. The first hint of this comes as they walk home from high school; note the setting (see fig. 6.14), cathedral-like, even quietly majestic, surely not something one would see in the indifferent natural world of Bresson.

The gist: God is there if one looks hard enough—the coda for the film, sprinkled throughout, is "look closer." We still don't have very good words to describe this.

And then this, up in Ricky's room. Ricky and Jane watch his tape of a white bag blowing in the wind against a red wall, which in itself does not tell us much, but Ricky sees, and we see too, and we see and hear Ricky seeing, transfixed and luminous (see fig. 6.15). His words as he watches the bag: "I realized that here was this entire life behind things, and this incredibly benevolent force that wanted me to know there was no reason to be afraid. Ever. . . . Sometimes there's so much beauty in the world I feel like I can't take it . . . and my heart is going to burst."[4]

To quote from a wonderful book I'd recommend—my own, in fact, *Catching Light* (2004):

> Ricky has seen through both matter and all the cultural dross of his time to grasp the radiant splendor of the created world, and what he sees is enough, for him, to warrant constant attention and praise. Ultimately, what sustains and shows through the beauty of it all, as he says, is God. . . . In Ricky, and at the

Figure 6.14.

---

[4]Alan Ball, *American Beauty: The Shooting Script* (New York: Newmarket, 1999), p. 60.

Figure 6.15.

core of *American Beauty* as a whole, lies the rudimentary assertion that what counts most in human life is pure, astonished amazement at the fact that anything at all should exist and, greater still, that anything and everything should display such beauty.[5]

And then a second film, *Three Colors: Blue,* by Polish writer-director Kryztof Kieslowski, who at the time of his early death in 1996 at only fifty-three, was recognized by many as the world's most accomplished film-maker. In *Three Colors: Blue* (1993), largely a wordless film, one installment of a trilogy on the colors of the French flag, Julie, played by French-Canadian actress Juliette Binoche, has lost her young daughter and hus-band, an internationally known composer, in an auto accident. In a tidal wave of grief Julie has chosen to shut herself off from life and feeling sim-ply in order to survive. Suicide she can't manage, but on the other hand a return to full life is, in the immense pain life randomly imposes on some, unthinkable. Except that something, something, will not leave her alone, despite her best efforts to shut down. It is color, sound and event, the or-dinary stuff of life, the divine welling up and through the fabric of life all over the place.

In a long sequence ten minutes into the story, a recuperating Julie sits alone on a chaise lounge when out of nowhere erupts an emphatic arresting fragment from the "Symphony for Unification of Europe," a commission on

[5]Roy M. Anker, *Catching Light: Looking for God in the Movies* (Grand Rapids: Eerdmans, 2005), pp. 356-57.

Figure 6.16.

which her husband, and she too maybe, were working at the time of the accident. And as the staging indicates, this is no pleasant nostalgia but a fierce approach, even visitation, by something beyond Julie herself that threatens to hound and devour the new widow, refusing to let her alone, and it happens over and over again in the film, seven times in all. The ferocity with which this musical-mystical presence besets Julie is seen not only in the raptness of her concentration as she listens but also in the manner in which Kieslowski floods the screen with shades and waves of blue that go so far as to fade to full blackness (see fig. 6.16).

Unbidden and unwanted, it envelops her now and repeatedly through the film, insistently summoning her back to the fullness of life and love. And there is a choral text too, as becomes clear in the course of the film, though North American audiences were unaccountably not provided subtitles for its Greek, and the text is 1 Corinthians 13 in all of its splendor. Kieslowski here uses cinema's enormous abundant means to display the ferocity, fullness and readiness with which the divine comes to particular people. And it is there as well in Julie's love of color, specifically blue, her favorite color, and ultimately as Kieslowski melds music to color, the music becomes the sound of the color of love, divine love. Here in everything from camera style to editing we see a lush deployment of the means of cinema to depict the Transcendent as near and abundant.

Possibility

All of this lushness of vision and cinematic means pushes hard the sugges-tion that there is a Love that has fashioned a world of shining to make us gape and delight. And films are endlessly inventive in discovering and dis-playing the curious ways in which the divine shows up in human affairs, of which the films themselves may be one instance.

What I find heartening here is the capacity of the lush resources of cin-ema to revalidate the significance of sensory experience, to restore to us through the sensorium to a universe shaped and infused by divine love, flaming and shining for delight and doxology. And one path to this doxo-logical universe lies through art, itself beauty, and indeed shook foil.

PART THREE

Texts and Culture

Bearing Witness to Redemption

7

"Silver Catching Midday Sun"

Poetry and the Beauty of God

Jill Peláez Baumgaertner

Until we know the name of something, it hardly exists at all for us. Once we learn the name, we suddenly find it everywhere. Think of Helen Keller and Anne Sullivan, her teacher, on a summer morning in 1887. Keller's sudden acquisition of language was brilliant—a split second when the lights went on for her, when objects began to have an identity associated with words. In fact, she learned language and suddenly understood beauty: "Words," she wrote, "made the world blossom for me. . . . [T]he living word awakened my soul, gave it light, hope, joy, set it free." What is most interesting is the connection Keller also made between knowing how to name the world and acquiring a moral sensibility. Helen learned the name for water—she experienced its beauty—and suddenly with the word she had an identity as a moral being feeling repentance and sorrow.

These are Helen's words:

We walked down the path to the well house, attracted by the fragrance of the honeysuckle with which it was covered. Someone was drawing water and my teacher placed my hand under the spout. As the cool stream gushed over one hand, she spelled into the other the word *water*, first slowly then rapidly. I stood still, my whole attention fixed upon the motion of her fingers. Suddenly I felt a misty consciousness as of something forgotten—a thrill of returning thought; and somehow the mystery of language was revealed to me. I knew then that "w-a-t-e-r" meant the wonderful cool something that was flowing over my hand. That living word awakened my soul, gave it light, hope, joy, set it free! There were barriers still, it is true, but barriers that could in time be swept away.

I left the well-house eager to learn. Everything had a name, and each name gave birth to a new thought. As we returned to the house every object which I touched seemed to quiver with life. That was because I saw everything with the strange, new sight that had come to me. On entering the door I remembered the doll I had broken. [She had earlier destroyed the doll in a fit of temper.] I felt my way to the hearth and picked up the pieces. I tried vainly to put them together. Then my eyes filled with tears; for I realized what I had done, and for the first time I felt repentance and sorrow.

I learned a great many new words that day. I do not remember what they all were; but I do know that *mother, father, sister, teacher* were among them— words that were to make the world blossom for me, "Like Aaron's rod with flowers." It would have been difficult to find a happier child than I was as I lay in my crib at the close of that eventful day and lived over the joys it had brought me, and for the first time longed for a new day to come.[1]

In other words: we cannot experience creation fully and in fact we cannot respond as moral beings if we do not have the language that names creation and our experiences in it. To take this several steps further—the big questions: Who am I? Why am I here? Where is God and what does he have to do with me? are essential questions that without language, without the act of naming, we would not be able to *think,* much less even ask. As much as I hate to admit it, my dog does not have language, and as a result I am quite sure that my dog does not wonder about God. (In fact, my dog thinks that I am God.) As a Christian and as a poet I am constantly concerned with how language and our sense of identity as people of the Word coalesce, how they work together for our essential purpose to glorify God in all our endeavors. But I am also interested in how, in some contemporary poetry, language and identity never quite dissolve into each other, never get around to grabbing each other's electrons to create a new compound, but instead remain in a kind of colloidal suspension.

In December of 1993 in Toronto at the annual convention of the Modern Language Association, I attended the Presidential Forum titled "Amo, Amas, Amat . . . Literature." The president of MLA had invited four scholars to speak, each of whom was well-known for his or her aggressive voice in one of the current, predominant areas of literary theory. Jonathan Culler, knight errant

---

[1]Helen Keller, *The Story of My Life* (New York: Bantam, 1990), pp. 16-17.

first of structuralism and later of deconstructionist theory, sat at the table facing the grand ballroom filled with MLA members. "Amo, Amas, Amat . . . Literature." Would he actually claim to love literature, he whose theory went about deconstructing it? When he rose to speak, I was reminded of O. E. Parker from Flannery O'Connor's short story "Parker's Back." Parker is mystified by his attraction to the very plain and bony Sarah Ruth. He is, to quote from the first paragraph, "embarrassed and ashamed of himself." And so was Jonathan Culler, who prefaced his remarks with disclaimers. He was going to talk about a piece of literature he had memorized during his college years. He was embarrassed, he said, that he was attracted to a poem with such a sentimental topic, the resurrection. But he had memorized the poem years before, and it had been in his head ever since, for some mystifying reason.

He then proceeded to quote from memory a poem by the Victorian Catholic poet Gerard Manley Hopkins, "The Leaden Echo and the Golden Echo"—a poem about the difference between the transitory and the transcendent, and ultimately about the resurrection of the dead. It was clear that the Hound of Heaven was at work in the most unlikely place—the soul of a deconstructionist—at MLA. One felt in listening to Culler that the only parts of his faith that were still alive were his doubt and his memory of something long ago and far away, something almost romantic in its impossibilities. But it was language that had its hold on him—language that had pushed its roots deep into his spirit—the language of poetry which had, in fact, so long ago given him an identity, had named him, as unlikely as it seemed, had named him, like a character in *Pilgrim's Progress,* Hopeful. He couldn't explain it. But there it was, a constant revelation to him of God's mercy and love, although his intellectual self fought it vigorously.

This language was poetry—poetry that speaks as no other language can. It does what no other art form can do. It compresses experience; it intensifies language; it uses words to say the unsayable. Imagine what the world would be without it. Imagine what Jonathan Culler's spiritual life, as meager as it already appears, would be without it. Poetry cracks open our everyday lives, the mundane worlds in which we spend so much unconscious time, and it releases the extraordinary, bringing us to a different level of attentiveness.

And of course one of the reasons poetry has such power is that it relies on our senses—which means it relies on part of what makes us particular human creatures with individual identities. Poetry awakens first our senses and *then* our feelings and thoughts.

But poems do more than describe sounds or scenes. They actually *become* the sounds or scenes. You read a poem about the resurrection and you know a bit of what it feels like to have restored and renewed flesh.

In order to have this effect, poetic language must "upset the ordinary" in some way. Now here's the rub: consider the predicament of so much religious language these days. It certainly does not upset the ordinary. It is cliché-ridden; it resorts to formula phrases. It is so familiar that it is invisible. It has great potential but it doesn't realize it. And many, in frustrated response, have dangerously concluded that the fault lies in the theology, not in the language. Paul Mariani writes:

> The trouble is that we live in a time when anything one says, from the banal to the sublime, is in danger of degenerating into a kind of white music. . . . But is that not where the artist comes in: as the reinventer, the remaker, of the language? . . . For the poet who would attempt to create or recreate a viable religious language for his time it is necessary to remember that it is the *language* and *not* the underlying reality that needs to be reconstituted. It is words—if St. John's verbal pun on the verbal can be made to work again for us—that need to be realigned again with the Word.[2]

So the poet who is working with religious subject matter has a big job—nothing less than revitalizing the language so that it expresses truth, which it cannot do in hackneyed forms that are, essentially, dishonest: masking truth, glossing over it, never piercing to the core of an experience, never unmasking its paradoxes and ambiguities.

I was recently asked in an interview to define the kind of poetry I look for as poetry editor of a Christian publication. I look for deep engagement with the core human questions: What does it mean to be human? Who is God? How can we make sense of suffering? Why does God sometimes seem so silent? I do not want pat, easy answers. I also do not want abstract philosophical responses. I am looking for poems that intensely engage the senses. This is what sacramental language does. Paul Mariani points to the scene in the film *The Mission* where contact is made with what had appeared to be savage indigenous peoples—a tribe that had crucified earlier Jesuit missionaries. Contact is finally made "not by preaching *at them* but by playing [a] flute *for them*." Mariani continues: "Think of this scene as a par-

---

[2]Paul Mariani, *God and the Imagination* (Athens: University of Georgia Press, 2002), pp. 230-31.

able of the artist's entry into a world that does not yet understand what is meant by a sacramental vision of the world. And yet, because music is universal, the skillful writing of a fiction—a poem, a novel—will at least give the religious writer entry into that world."[3]

What it finally boils down to is that Christian poets must bring the spirit into flesh just as the incarnation is Spirit becoming flesh. And this is what poets can do for theologians. In fact, theologians need poetry just as much as Christ needed to speak in parables. Mariani writes: "Mustard seeds, birds' nests, swept rooms, buried treasure, lit lamps, lilies, lost pennies. What similes, what metaphors, what words, after all, does one use to find the Kingdom of Heaven if not the things of this world?"[4] Such is the sacramental vision, which Christ himself possessed.

The beauty of God is our theme. And who better to give us glimpses of that beauty than the poets? The thing is—the glimpses of the transcendent that visit us in our everyday lives can be few and far between: "Silver catching midday sun," as one poet puts it. Consider the way Eliot describes these flashes and glimmers (from "Burnt Norton" in *Four Quartets*):

Sudden in a shaft of sunlight
Even while the dust moves
There rises the hidden laughter
Of children in the foliage
Quick now, here, now, always—
Ridiculous the waste sad time
Stretching before and after.[5]

The laugher of children in a sudden shaft of sunlight—hidden but heard and felt, a glimpse of something more than the mundane—a momentary transformation of the ordinary into the extraordinary, and then the falling back into "the waste sad time / Stretching before and after."

Or consider Richard Wilbur's "Love Calls Us to the Things of This World," in which that moment between sleeping and waking offers its own glimpse of the transcendent. The speaker is awakened by the "cry of pulleys" as a neighbor pulls on those tenement clotheslines stretched high in the air from building to building. Before he is fully conscious, a full citizen of the workaday world, while he is still drifting out of sleep, he looks out the window

[3]Ibid., pp. 241-42.
[4]Ibid., p. 244.
[5]T. S. Eliot, *The Complete Poems and Plays* (London: Faber & Faber, 1969), p. 176.

and concludes that "the morning air is all awash with angels."

> Some are in bed-sheets, some are in blouses,
> Some are in smocks: but truly there they are.
> Now they are rising together in calm swells
> Of halcyon feeling, filling whatever they wear
> With the deep joy of their impersonal breathing;
>
> Now they are flying in place, conveying
> The terrible speed of their omnipresence, moving
> And staying like white water; and now of a sudden
> They swoon down into so rapt a quiet
> That nobody seems to be there.

Wanting to rest in that vision of laundry turned to angels, the speaker is reluctant to fully awaken. He says, "The soul shrinks / From all that it is about to remember, / From the punctual rape of every blessed day." There is that return to normalcy, to the world without the glimpse of the extraordinary. For Eliot it was "the waste sad time / Stretching before and after." For Wilbur it is "the punctual rape of every blessed day." But before he wakes, he cries:

> Oh, let there be nothing on earth but laundry,
> Nothing but rosy hands in the rising steam
> And clear dances done in the sight of heaven.

Yet the soul does rejoin the waking body and, realistically, advises all to bring the clothes in from the clothesline to clothe thieves and lovers and nuns:

> Let there be clean linen for the backs of thieves;
> Let lovers go fresh and sweet to be undone,
> And the heaviest nuns walk in a pure floating
> Of dark habits,
>   keeping their difficult balance.[6]

In other words—the mundane—clothes—clean clothes—which afforded the speaker the glimpse of heaven and of God—are in this fallen world "put on" by all of us—even the meanest—thieves—and even the immoral lovers—those who do not in all probability recognize the transcendent in the midst

---

[6]Richard Wilbur, *New and Collected Poems* (San Diego: Harcourt Brace Jovanovich, 1989), pp. 233-34.

of the mundane. But then there are the "heaviest nuns," who attempt a more enlightened knowledge of the soul, who attempt to keep the vision of God alive. Even they "walk in a pure floating Of dark habits, / keeping their difficult balance."

The Romantic poets were extremely optimistic about humankind's ability to receive revelation through glimpses of God in the Book of Nature. Recall Wordsworth's "Tintern Abbey" in which he describes his youthful, exuberant connection with Nature:

. . . And I have felt
A presence that disturbs me with the joy
Of elevated thoughts; a sense sublime
Of something far more deeply interfused,
Whose dwelling is the light of setting suns,
And the round ocean and the living air,
And the blue sky, and in the mind of man:
A motion and a spirit, that impels
All thinking things, all objects of all thought,
And rolls through all things. Therefore am I still
A lover of the meadows and the woods,
And mountains; and of all that we behold
From this green earth; of all the mighty world
Of eye, and ear—both what they half create,
And what perceive; well pleased to recognize
In nature and the language of the sense
The anchor of my purest thoughts, the nurse,
The guide, the guardian of my heart, and soul
Of all my moral being.[7]

But this vision fades as he moves away from childhood, he complains later, and for later modernist poets its ring is absolutely hollow. Recall T. S. Eliot's description in "The Love Song of J. Alfred Prufrock" of the "evening . . . spread out against the sky like a patient etherized upon a table." This sky is certainly incapable of being, in Wordsworth's words, "the guide, the guardian of my heart, and soul / Of all my moral being." In fact, Wordsworth's claim sounds to our jaded and postmodern ears and sensibilities nothing less than exaggerated and dubious. We have no doubts about God's presence and even his revelation in and through creation. It's just that for

---

[7]William Wordsworth, *Selected Poems and Prefaces* (Boston: Houghton Mifflin, 1965), p. 110.

those who have received the insights of special revelation through Christ, resting in nature and not the triune God of nature is not enough. This triune God takes us places that are not always comfortable. And this God's answers are not always forthcoming in the forms in which we request them. This God is frequently silent or speaks in a small, still voice when we would have him speak loudly, clearly and directly.

And thus is born an unsettling aspect of the beauty of God—his inscrutableness. Gerard Manley Hopkins, the late-nineteenth-century Jesuit poet that Jonathan Culler quoted, wrote that "the world is charged with the grandeur of God. / It will flame out, like shining from shook foil." He wrote of the starlit night, of spring, of the windhover, of pied beauty. But he also wrote a number of poems called the terrible sonnets in which he confronted a largely silent and distant God with his suffering. "No worst, there is none," he writes in one of these poems.

> . . . Pitched past pitch of grief
> More pangs will, schooled at forepangs, wilder wring.
> Comforter, where, where is your comforting?[8]

He ends this poem with what he calls the only comfort he knows: "all / Life death does end and each day dies with sleep." He finds no solace. In one of these poems of anguish he turns to nature for solace and all he finds is an almost frivolous beauty. He observes the thick leaves, the lacy parsley, the busy birds building nests and all he can see is the contrast with his own fruitless and dry spirit. "O thou lord of life, send my roots rain," he begs.[9]

One recalls the suffering and anguished picture of Christ that O. E. Parker in Flannery O'Connor's story "Parker's Back" has tattooed on his back. His eyes are all demanding, and there is no soft comfort here. But it is this Christ who takes Parker's sufferings alongside him when Sarah Ruth picks up the broom and beats him across the back with it, the welts forming on the face of Christ as they form on Parker's back—the Word most clearly become flesh.

It is this Christ—the Christ of Good Friday and the cross—the Christ of hideous suffering, pierced and bleeding—the Christ not like Eliot's patient

---

[8]Gerard Manley Hopkins, "No Worst, There Is None. Pitched Past Pitch Of Grief," *The Poetical Works of Gerard Manley Hopkins,* ed. Norman H. Mackenzie (Oxford: Clarendon, 1990), p. 182.
[9]Gerard Manley Hopkins, "Thou Art Indeed Just, Lord," *The Poetical Works of Gerard Manley Hopkins,* ed. Norman H. Mackenzie (Oxford: Clarendon, 1990), p. 201.

etherized against the sky but a Christ with all of his nerve endings exposed —not the Romantic picture of Sallman's *Head of Christ* with its flowing locks and sensitive face—but the Christ Hopkins describes with "darksome devouring eyes"—it is this Christ that reveals the beauty of a God that we in this post-Holocaust age can hold onto by our fingernails. This is a God who on the cross cried to God—Why have you forsaken me?—and was met with the silence of God. This is the God that any Christian poet with credibility must encounter face to face.

The poems of Sydney Lea are often torrents of words, creating longer lines and therefore longer poems. His poems, heavy in images and strong on narrative, require the space; in fact, they often tell stories that catch you by surprise with their striking oddness and the frequent pattern that moves the subject from degeneracy to hints of redemption.

The second part of his most recent collection, *Ghost Pain,* is titled "A Man Walked Out," with an epigraph from Psalm 40: "and He hath put a new song in my mouth." But the journey from the first poems to the "new song" of the psalm is, in e. e. cummings's words, "banged with terror." A suite of ten poems, it begins in depression and fear:

> A man walked out much later into something awful   every thing
> 　reminding him of some other thing
> 　　and this each last thing and that private last other
> 　　　equally laden with freight of dread   And yet the dread was not
> 　　　　a common or garden type

But even amidst this alarm and dread, even in spite of the man's "bodily deafness / and his longstanding other sorts of torpor," there is a small sign, maybe even a still voice, at any rate "a tiny bell . . . there to be heard it seemed heard in its minuscule clangor." Even though the man cannot quite remember what that tiny bell is, he responds to it with lessening fear. In the next poem called "666: Father of Lies" he fights the devil, but once again at the end, a "delicate ringing in our man's left ear. / His tinnitus? His angelus?" Each poem in the series traces this trajectory from the knowledge of total depravity to the recognition of grace. At one point he asks, "Where did hope ever come from? Knowing the facts, / how might anyone ever opt for joy?"

> His mother would go down into the earth with Speed [their dog],
> her liver large as a toilet seat, a bag
> girt to her turgid flank to catch her waste.
> His father would go with actual speed: infarction,

said someone to all his dazed children. The manchild that summer—

even with nightfall, even with swimmings up
of planet, star—sprawled wet with sweat and despair.
And now again. This was the tableau Forever,
which some dull teacher made him study forever.
Stunned museum. Miasma of dust unrelenting.
There must be more to life, he thought back then.

The poem ends with, if not images of resurrection, then at least the hint of
a pleasant freshness in the air and the rustling of a spirit not yet recognized
as holy.

A change seemed bound to come: not his mother risen,
intact, not his father, his heart and innards quick,
but something. The passing of birds. More scent than sound.

A part of the process of conversion is the conviction of guilt, and so half-
way through the cycle of poems the man remembers and relives in graphic
images his years of predatory behavior. All of the faces "line up on this new
horizon to glare at him." Another poem describes a moment of road rage
conquered, when he for the first time through the sheer act of will simply
forgives and pulls over to the side of the road. In the penultimate poem of
the series for the first time the man experiences grace in its fullness:

. . . in that moment, the man felt forgiven
for each unpardonable word and deed,
even the worst, which he couldn't name.
Everything out in the Yankee woods
recalled the hour of its creation,
and even dying, declared it good.

In the final poem the man walks out into the October landscape one Sunday at noon (here the familiar bells faintly chime in the distance) with the
memory of the previous evening's Psalm reading in his head: *Make me to
hear joy and gladness that the bones / which thou has broken may rejoice.*"
His prayer is on his lips: "Forgive my little postures." And then he catches a
scent of something he cannot define on a wind blowing softly to him, as if
fanned by the wings of a passing hawk.

All easy parable was gross.
And yet the hawk was coasting now,
with assured wing was fanning

this wind that softly flew
to him, that coursed a flank of hill on which he stood *Selah*

he actually stood, it seemed a miracle, or poem,
a grand ongoing one he smelt as much as felt
and touched as much as heard—a bird retreating
and in retreating moving
the man thus quietly home.[10]

So moves the Holy Spirit, his holy muse, nudging him toward miracle and poetry.

What Lea has accomplished in "A Man Walked Out" is terribly difficult to do. The Christian poet attempts one of the most challenging endeavors, revitalizing the language, the common language, which all of us have heard for years both in Scripture and in the church. It is why at one point in the final poem in the series Lea writes:

. . . one hadn't known god
(though damn the terminology)
was all he needed till god was all he had.

Language, especially familiar language, seems almost insufficient to capture the transcendent, to reflect truth in all of its complexity. But language is what the poet has to work with and so the poet is forced to take sometimes exaggerated, sometimes extreme steps to pierce the mundane, breaking up lines, using words in odd new contexts, relying on sound effects and packing the stanzas with sensuous images and fragments from Scripture, and the common language of our faith which suddenly takes on new meaning through these odd juxtapositions. The poem for Lea and for any poet who is trying to capture religious truth in language is a miracle, a journey home for all of us who, because we are human, have at some time or other been terribly lost.

But poets like Sydney Lea are in the minority in today's literary culture. The problem is—it is difficult to find poets interested in making connections to something larger than themselves. This seems to be a peculiarly American problem. Terrence Des Pres identifies it as an unhealthy preoccupation with self encouraged by the abiding influence of Emerson in our time. He quotes lines from Emerson's "Ode":

---

[10]Sydney Lea, *Ghost Pain* (Louisville: Sarabande, 2006), pp. 29-65.

I cannot leave
My honeyed thought
For the priest's cant,
Or statesman's rant.

Des Pres explains:

> Founded on Emersonian principles, our poetry has drawn much of its strength
> from an almost exclusive attention to self and nature. Typically, we have con-
> ceived of the self *as* a world rather than of the self *in* the world. Things be-
> yond the self either yield to imagination or else they don't matter, and the
> world becomes a store of metaphor to be raided as one can. The "strong" poet
> turns any landscape to private use, and solipsism wins praise as the sign of
> success.[11]

Another ominous trend is that certain theoretical influences have made
both inaccessibility and solipsism—related characteristics—popular traits in
poetry. In fact, one recent winner of a prestigious poetry award admits that
the strongest influences on his work are Julia Kristeva, Slavoj Žižek, Giorgio
Agamben and Jacques Lacan, none of whom write poetry themselves, but
all of whom have left lasting imprints on literary theory. This phenomenon,
of the poet grounded more in the tradition of philosophy or psychoanalysis
or feminism than in the tradition of poetry and poets that T. S. Eliot described in his classic essay "Tradition and the Individual Talent" is, unfortunately, creating a class of poets speaking not even to each other. The recent
Iowa Anthology of New American Poetries presents example after example
of this phenomenon. One reviewer writes, "Despite the poems' intellectual
surfaces, their actual domain is the self and the idiosyncratic thought processes of the singular mind. Their authors find themselves infinitely fascinating, and the tricks of their memory and sense the best possible material."[12]

For example, try out "The Sickness & the Magnet" by Christine Hume:

Cursing his eyes' erasing motion
His face caught snow & his horse
Prevented falling sickness
Diadems & degrees echoed
Every red electricity spit out

---

[11]Terrence Des Pres, "Self/Landscape/Grid," *The Pushcart Prize IX: Best of the Small Presses* (New York: Avon, 1984), pp. 46-47.
[12]Danielle Chapman, *Poetry* 185, no. 4 (2005): 320.

He starved a beast & became full of tricks
Now a lightning maker could feel
What a lightning of metal tasted like
It hammered at him & joined disease
He felt the storm new magnets in hems
He felt fevers of wept railings
Amazed how hot an animal is
So sorry so chattered so scat sorry so strung
Sweated horse light excruciating sweat
Birds went in & out of his mouth
He lived out of his mouth
Sucking the slap backwards
Then everything wanted to be
Killed at the rural spot[13]

This is not difficult poetry, like Sydney Lea's; this is a collection of obscure ramblings. Difficulty is not anathema; obscurity is. As the reviewer said, "These poems fail not because they are too erudite, but because they are narcissistic." They never travel beyond the self and the self's desire to hear itself talking. There is no communication attempted and therefore no connections are made outside of the tiny world of the individual and self-referential poem.

So how does a poet orient him- or herself in order to avoid the traps of narcissism? As a poet I have confronted the narcissistic trap, which for many also comes in the form of a temptation to become overly confessional, to focus attention on struggles, needs and personal predicaments. The poet must keep in mind that poetry is not all about the journey, as one so often hears. On the contrary, poems must take you some place—and that place should be, in one form or another, the cross. Even when the subject is personal grief, the poet must attempt to get beyond the self to make connections and to answer bigger questions. A vehicle which I have found helpful is the liturgy.

Requiem was written in the weeks and months following two events: the sudden death in August 2001 of my godson at age twenty-one, and the terrorist attacks of September 11, 2001. The cycle of poems was incorporated into a commemorative "Service of Remembrance and Healing" at Grace

---

[13]Christine Hume, "The Sickness & the Magnet," in *The Iowa Anthology of New American Poetries,* ed. Reginald Shepherd (Iowa City: University of Iowa Press, 2004), p. 96.

Lutheran Church, River Forest, Illinois, on September 11, 2002, and published in *Christianity and Literature* the following spring. The twelve poems in the cycle are based on "The Burial of the Dead" service in the *Lutheran Book of Worship,* which itself has roots in the ancient Requiem Mass. I was looking for some means, some structure, some way to put a handle on the overwhelming fears and sadness of that time.

So I wrote these poems, following closely the structure of the funeral service, attentive to the Scripture the liturgy contained, trusting that experts in worship and liturgy knew something I could learn from following that structure. The first poem, "The Procession," follows the coffin down the center aisle of the church, "the procession of anguish" for the mourners who now confront only loss and unfinished business, and who are uncertain about the destination of this journey and even about next steps.[14]

The Procession

The world teeters to contain
the images: stone, metal, glass
dissolving into dust,
a building dropping into itself,
the chalky air breathed in like smoke
by those who will live
on these ashes forever.

This is a progress of the living,
fragile with grief.
One woman calls home
several times a day to hear
the flash of his voice.
There—his breath, his tongue
and lips form syllables,
electrons on an endless
loop of magnetic tape.

Two stand at the window
stupefied—What do we do now?—
they think, the hour blank,
the pages empty, disconnected
from narrative.

---

[14]Permission to reprint these poems was graciously granted by *Christianity and Literature.* The poems first appeared in volume 52, no. 3 (2003): 409-16.

This is what is left:
a hamper of laundry,
a recorked bottle of wine,
a lamp on an electric timer,
a Franck sonata opened on a music stand,
asters and ferns in a vase of dwindling water.

The list of images,
the procession of anguish,
the fleeting walk from here to there,
from narthex to the chancel steps,
the coffin or the urn no effort for the dead,
the walk the living take,
uncertain,
brief.

Near the end of the service, after the Communion, the "Nunc dimittis" is
sung—the words of Simeon after he saw the Christ child in the temple.

Nunc Dimittis

Reaching for the child, a light bundle of grace,
Simeon says, "I can go in peace. I have seen."
Jesus gazes at the ancient man, all beard and bristle,
rheumy eyes intent on his small face.
These are not his mother's arms that fold him
to her heartbeat. With Simeon he is both clutched
and barely held at all, precarious in the old man's
trembling joy. The baby squirms, unsettles.
His parents marvel at the man's odd words.
How can it be both promise and dissent?
Both light of revelation and the sword?

We step away from the table, return to our pews,
our current sorrow, our old vexations.
We have for those few seconds with the host
in our palm and the chalice at our lips
lived in anticipation of—what exactly?
A new vision? A better way of handling
what we do not want to hold? Immediate
resurrection of the newly dead? Can we now
bear more than we know how, the cross in sight?
Having seen and tasted, is it ever possible

to live as if we had never seen at all?

We will follow the coffin back down the aisle
trusting the dead to the extravagance of dust
from which they came, knowing God breathed
dust to life and will so do again.

Finally, at the end of the service is the benediction. Here my poem "Benedictus" tries to provide a gentle push back into the world for mourners heavy with autumnal dying but looking forward to spring.

Benedictus

We turn back to our lives,
plot lines altered,
palimpsests: characters erased,
lines overwritten.
We will never be the same.
Burned clean of illusion,
we face the cross,
finding there the exacting cost of grace.

We lift our faces to the softer light
we sense beyond the treetop shadows.

We step onto the path,
thick with fallen leaves,
the earth beneath sheltering
the tight fists of bloom
spring will uncurl.

It was through living inside the liturgy, the structure of the funeral service, the way of worship, the words of worship so bound to Scripture that I began to understand something new about the resurrection. I was able to go on an intense journey of mourning—a journey inward—and then move out into the world again. And it was poetry and the Word which took me there. Let me return to an earlier point. We cannot respond to creation as moral beings if we do not have a language that names creation and our experiences, even our terrible experiences, in it. In fact, our experience of death links us directly to Christ and his suffering. Through the poems I wrote during the fall of 2001, I was learning the language of grief, of the atonement, of redemption. My experience of the beauty of God had everything to do with the cross and suffering, and it was poetry that took me there.

8

THE BEAUTY OF THE WORD RE-MEMBERED

Scripture Reading as a Cognitive/Aesthetic Practice

James Fodor

Reading Scripture is the life-blood of Christian existence.[1] This observation is so obvious that it hardly warrants a mention. Yet sometimes stating the obvious can have the fortuitous and surprising effect of casting important light on crucial aspects of our world, dimensions of reality that we tend to overlook. "Overlooking the obvious" tends to be particularly true when it comes to understanding the relationships between Scripture reading practices, theological reflection and artistic imagination. To be sure, for most Christians it seems intuitively right and "natural" that the reading of Scripture and theological reflection should go together—that is, a reciprocal, mutually constructive relation obtains here: Scripture "informs" theology and theology, in turn, helps "explicate" Scripture. But within this relation of mutual illumination we don't often give recognition to artistic creativity or aesthetic sensibility. For most of us, the latter seem to have nothing essential to do with either Scripture reading or theological reflection.

I wish to make the case that the kinds of aesthetic judgment Christians

[1]I am grateful for the kindness of friends and colleagues who read, commented on and directed my attention to overlooked resources in the writing of this essay, especially Kevin Hughes, Oleg Bychkov, Xavier Seubert, Mary-Beth Ingham and Thomas McKenna. Each in their own way has encouraged me to think more deeply and carefully about the issues raised and, not least, saved me from some small but embarrassing mistakes. Their kind help notwithstanding, whatever errors or infelicities that remain are entirely my own.

make are in fact intimately bound up with the Scripture reading practices we promote and the modes of theological inquiry we engage in.[2] Indeed, I will argue that any shift or evolution or transformation in one will necessarily be accompanied by a shift or alteration in the other two. This is so because modes of reflection, forms of artistic "making" and ways of Scripture reading are *at once cognitive and affective*—reading, reflection and aesthetic judgment are concomitants of one another.

In order to set forth my case I avail myself of the work of two medieval theologians—Augustine and Bonaventure—and the work of one contemporary scholar, Mary Carruthers, who has contributed singularly important insights on the role of memory *(memoria)* in medieval culture, with implications for our own time concerning how imagination (aesthetic sensibility) and memory are constitutive of the craft of theological thinking.

I will trace in a very general and schematic way how Scripture reading practices and protocols once dominant in medieval monastic culture—with its attendant hierarchically ordered, multiple senses of Scripture (literal, allegorical, tropological and anagogical)—gave way to modern reading regimes. And here I have in mind primarily the historical-critical method, which has dominated our reading practices since the Enlightenment, but also more recent literary, social-scientific and assorted postmodern methods of Scripture reading, all clashing and jostling for position within universities and academic culture. I want to show why it is not by accident that shifts in aesthetic sensibility and modes of theological reflection track exactly, over time, the shifts and changes observable in reading practices. In the transition

---

[2]Paul J. Griffiths, in *Religious Reading: The Place of Reading in the Practice of Religion* (Oxford: Oxford University Press, 1999), offers a helpful typology of "consumerist" and "religious" modes of reading. Nonetheless, it is not altogether clear how, according to Griffiths's account, the religious modes of reading can be inculcated among readers in ways that leave its formative practices largely immune from the negative features of consumerist modes of reading. Indeed, Griffiths's critique of consumerist reading provokes one to thinking about what exactly is lacking in modern reading practices. For the reading practices of all of us—not simply the specialized methodological reading practices instilled by the academy more generally and that of biblical studies in particular—have been corrupted/impaired/diminished in significant ways. And it may be that this more general corruption is not reducible to the "trickle-down" effect of historical/critical/social-scientific/literary methods. Indeed, one may wonder if both consumerist and academic/critical reading practices are both symptomatic of some deeper cause. In his forthcoming book Matthew Levering contends that this deeper cause amounts to the loss of a metaphysics of participation. For a constructive, suggestive and hopeful account of how Christian reading might be reimagined and reestablished, especially in conjunction with liturgical reading practices, see Peter M. Candler Jr., *Theology, Rhetoric, Manuduction: Or Reading Scripture Together on the Path to God* (Grand Rapids: Eerdmans, 2006).

from the medieval to the modern we observe not only an attenuation—a contraction, a shrinking—of the multiple senses of Scripture, but we also note a correlative diminishment of the role of aesthetic judgment (or at least its cordoning off into the private realm of the subject)[3] as well as a certain hardening of theological reflection, the result of which is that it tends to be less supple and often devoid of any kind of "symphonic power."[4] I suspect that the conference organizers' concerns about the relative neglect of the sense of Beauty in recent theology—a concern which I too share—arises from this deeply felt but infrequently articulated awareness that the aesthetic quality of theological reflection has been reduced, diminished and perhaps in some cases even lost altogether.

We want to retrieve and renew that vital dimension for reflective Christian faith, and rightly so. But if my hypothesis is correct that modes of reflection, forms of artistic "making" and ways of Scripture reading are *at once cognitive and affective,* then we cannot—indeed we dare not—attempt to initiate and fund that renewal by focusing solely on "the arts" per se, least of all by taking some refresher course in aesthetics! Rather we must somehow repair and renew *all three* of these modes *together,* simultaneously—Scripture reading, theological reflection and artistic engagement. And one way to begin is through a sound understanding of their mutual, deeply interfused relationships. Part of my suggestion for renewal—and this may sound paradoxical after what I have just said—is that "neglect" of aesthetics may well be a good thing here. For a proper kind of forgetfulness of the beautiful (construed in a certain manner) is a precondition both for doing theology well and for reading Scripture faithfully and fruitfully. But in order to make good on that claim I first need to set forth a theological understanding of Beauty as refracted through Scripture reading practices and particular styles of theological reflection.[5]

---

[3]See Fergus Kerr, "Aesthetics," in *The Blackwell Encyclopedia of Modern Christian Thought,* ed. Alister E. McGrath (Oxford: Basil Blackwell, 1993), pp. 1-2.

[4]Robert J. O'Connell, *Art and the Christian Intelligence in St. Augustine* (Cambridge, Mass.: Harvard University Press, 1978), p. 91.

[5]I share Alejandro García-Rivera's position that what contemporary theology—along with the wider culture more generally—needs to retrieve is a renewed "sense of Beauty." See Alejandro García-Rivera, "On A New List of Aesthetic Categories" in *Theological Aesthetics After von Balthasar,* Ashgate Studies in Theology, Imagination and the Arts, ed. Oleg Bychkov and Jim Fodor (Aldershot, U.K.: Ashgate, forthcoming). I use the terms *Beauty* or *sense of Beauty,* or *beauty* or *the beautiful* somewhat loosely in this essay. The former pair of terms suggests, with García-Rivera, "a belief in the human capacity to know and love God." While this sensibility

Augustine and the Reading of Scripture

Augustine models for us just how profound and indissociable are the connections between Scripture reading, theological reflection and aesthetic judgment. It was Augustine, after all, who in the garden famously heard the chant—seemingly issuing from children at play: *Tolle lege,* "take up and read, take up and read." And heeding that cry, Augustine hurries back to his Scripture, to where he left it with his friend Alypius, sitting under a tree in the garden, and he picks up the book of the apostle and proceeds to read from Paul's letter to the Romans: "Not in reveling and drunkenness, not in debauchery and licentiousness, not in quarreling and jealousy. Instead, put on the Lord Jesus Christ, and make no provision for the flesh" (Rom 13:13-14). Augustine's conversion—his "turning back" to the Christian faith of his mother—is marked by this well-known scene from the *Confessions.*[6] But of course Augustine's reading of Scripture neither began nor ended with this episode.

Reading was a constant feature of Augustine's life both prior to and after this pivotal turning point.[7] His meditations and commentaries on Scripture nourished his preaching and his pastoral endeavors. His prayers are steeped in the Psalms—not only in language and expression but in rhythm and tone and image as well.[8] Moreover, the ancient pedagogy of the liberal arts indelibly formed his intellect and imagination; he excelled in the art of rhetoric—indeed he made his living for a time as a teacher of rhetoric. His reading

---

is clearly *human* in character it is not however exclusively "subjective"—i.e., rooted in the human subject along the lines of the modern autonomous self. Moreover, the *sense of Beauty* is not to be equated with *Beauty* itself, for the latter always outstrips and exceeds the former. It would therefore be incorrect to say that the *sense of Beauty* is reducible to *the beautiful,* for that would render *Beauty* exclusively in terms of human "judgment or as mere experience." Beauty would thereby be construed as a mere attribute of subjective, human understanding, which would deserve the designation *the beautiful* rather than *Beauty.* What is in view here, when using the term *Beauty* or *a sense of Beauty,* is, to use García-Rivera's words, "a marvelous sensibility that brings us into encounter with that dimension of the divine that mystics and theologians have known as Beauty" (ibid.).

[6]Augustine, *Confessions,* trans. Henry Chadwick, Oxford World Classics (Oxford: Oxford University Press, 1991), pp. 152-53.

[7]Of course, Augustine's reading repertoire was considerable, and not restricted exclusively to Scripture.

[8]"Closer study reveals how much not only Augustine's expression, but his powers of observation, sensibility, and artistic conception owe to the way of images, music, and poetry of the *Psalms,* the mighty images of the Bible, had penetrated into the deepest recesses of his being" (*Art and the Christian Intelligence,* p. 127; cf. Rowan Williams, "Augustine and the Psalms," *Interpretation* 58, no 1 [2001]: 17-27).

practices were also deeply shaped by, infused with and drawn toward a profound sense of Beauty—inherited, no doubt, through his exposure to Neo-Platonic philosophy but later translated into and recalibrated according to a Christian understanding of creation and incarnation.[9] By rightly reading the signs of God's Beauty in the created order—both in the book of creation and in the book of Scripture—the fallen, wandering soul is led back to God, its original source.[10] "Our heart is restless until it rests in you." Thus Augustine introduces the overarching theme of the *Confessions.*

But what impels the soul, what converts its futile wanderings into pilgrimage and quest and destination, is its first being awakened to a sense of Beauty—initially through earthly forms of beauty which, if followed correctly, order one's life and lead to union with that Beauty which is God himself. As Robert O'Connell puts it:

> The soul must be awakened to the reach of its profoundest yearning: for the "Beauty, ever ancient, ever new," "holy delight," form beyond all the grace of created forms, most beautiful of beings, and Beauty of all beauties. Once glimpsed, the charm of God's Beauty *[decus]* can sweep the heart upward, to Himself, the swelling fountain of unfailing sweetness that alone can satiate the soul's deep thirst for beauty.[11]

Not only are the trajectories of the soul's journey "upward," leading toward union with God, but also "outward," extending across space and time, and "inward," away from a fragmented toward a whole, unified self. Indeed, what translates the lost soul's wandering into a journey is this ability to read signs—the traces, if you will—of God's Beauty in the world.[12] So Augustine's anthropology and soteriology (his understanding of human being and of salvation) are thoroughly semiotic and hermeneutical in nature (i.e., concerned

---

[9]See, for example, Emmanuel Chapman, *Saint Augustine's Philosophy of Beauty*, St. Michael's Mediaeval Studies Monograph Series (New York and London: Sheed & Ward, 1939); and O'Connell, *Art and the Christian Intelligence.*

[10]To be sure, reading humanmade, linguistic signs is distinct from the reading of creation or natural signs. My contention is that although distinct they are nonetheless analogous activities. However, for present purposes it is suffice to make the observation, not demonstrate its validity—which would take us beyond the scope of this essay.

[11]O'Connell, *Art and the Christian Intelligence in St. Augustine,* pp. 114-15.

[12]Indeed, the relation between semiotics and aesthetics is complex. It is not my intention in this essay to attempt to parse what I see as their interrelationship. My only claim is that semiotics (a facility in using—reading, manipulating and interpreting—signs) is an essential aspect of developing an aesthetic sensibility necessary to Scripture reading and theological reflection. Although intimately related, semiotics and aesthetics are, of course, not reducible to the other. I owe this insight to Oleg Bychkov.

with signs—linguistic and nonlinguistic—in their manifold, interconnected complexity and interpretation). This is the backdrop against which "virtually all of Augustine's observations on the function and value of art become readily understandable."[13]

While the Beauty of God's signs in creation and in his Word is without question *the* indispensable means of salvation, these are also potentially impediments to the soul coming to itself and to God. The power accorded to "the beauties of nature and of art" "to mediate God's Beauty to our fallen state" is efficacious only if they are continually relativized (*hierarchicalized* is a more apt, albeit cumbersome, term) and made subservient to their true end in God. Indeed, Augustine is acutely aware of the special power of the beautiful: the "lovely created things" can both liberate and entrap the soul.

> Late have I loved you, beauty so old and so new; late have I loved you. And see, you were within and I was in the external world and sought you there, and in my unlovely state I plunged into those lovely created things which you made. You were with me, and I was not with you. The lovely things kept me far from you, though if they did not have their existence in you, they had no existence at all. You called and cried out loud and shattered my deafness. You were fragrant, and I drew in my breath and now pant after you. I tasted you, and I feel but hunger and thirst for you. You touched me, and I am set on fire to attain the peace which is yours.[14]

In these poignant, stirring lines, Augustine is cognizant of just how easy it is to become distracted by and immersed in the signs themselves, beautiful as they may be, and to exchange ultimate delight for penultimate satisfaction. Augustine would persuade us—in retracing our steps along the way of memory—that we must be vigilant in extricating "our entangled hearts from the 'fornication' of taking this world as an object of terminal love." For whatever is beautiful in nature or in art is capable of "laying a spell upon the soul, seducing it to cease from its restless journeying, and luxuriate in the embrace of languorous delights." The artist, therefore, is in need of continual reminding that his or her "creations must be made to serve the soul's interior pilgrimage of return from this image-world to the radiant homeland of divine Light." "The God Who is Beauty is also our highest Good: He alone is large enough for our hearts' desire; He alone is to be enjoyed."[15] All of

---

[13]O'Connell, *Art and the Christian Intelligence,* p. 113.
[14]Augustine, *Confessions* 10.28 (38), p. 201.
[15]O'Connell, *Art and the Christian Intelligence,* p. 115.

this is to say that although Augustine readily endorses what we understand as "the arts"—which include, among other things, reading and writing and speaking—he does so on condition that they be put to use in God's service. He remains, in other words, "profoundly suspicious of the distracting power of poetry, myth, theater, even of the sweet-sounding melodies of the Ambrosian psalms."[16]

This last point is worth comment. Scripture itself—sung, chanted, prayed—can, if improperly engaged and performed, lead one *away* from God.[17] The reason for this diversion, apparently, does not reside in the signs themselves but in *how they are used* or, better, *how they are ordered.* Augustine's distinction between "use" *(uti)* and "enjoyment" *(frui)* suggests that "God alone is the terminal object in whose vision the soul must find restful enjoyment; all other beings are to be used in pursuit of that beatific vision."[18] This is not to say that created beauty is never to be enjoyed as such. On the contrary, created beauty *is* to be enjoyed—but with the important qualification: only "in God," that is, in such a way that our enjoyment does not impede or deflect our journey to God.[19] Again, Augustine avails himself of the

---

[16]Ibid., p. 116.

[17]O'Connell argues that this as a characteristic feature of Augustine's early aesthetic rather than of his more mature reflections. "Augustine's primary reflex makes him think of Scripture as obscuring our direct vision of the divine splendor. That obscuring function is, however, providential: the 'natural man, like a babe in Christ' does not have eyes 'strong' enough to 'gaze at the sun'; the firmament of Scripture has been established to bring aid to this weakness of the lower race we have become in consequence of our fall. By means of it, the radiance of God's truth 'reaches down to the clouds'—*to* them, but not, at this juncture, precisely *through* them. His word appears to us, not 'as it is,' but in the dark image those 'clouds' of Scripture provide; we glimpse it only darkly, indirectly, in the mirror of the heavens. But we must keep our hopes alive, for the clouds will eventually pass away, leaving only the spiritual heavens to endure forever" (*Art and the Christian Intelligence,* p. 113).

[18]Ibid., p. 137.

[19]As important as this distinction is, one wonders whether Augustine's *uti/frui* differentiation is all that effective in helping "rein in" the excesses of spiritual exegesis in the ways suggested. For if God is really the only proper object of enjoyment, then "use" and "enjoyment" cannot really delineate, for example, the distinction between literal and spiritual. Rather, *uti/frui* would help identify a different way in which Scripture might "lead one away from God." In other words, according to Augustine's distinction it would be possible to fall in love with the letter—not simply the literal sense here but the text itself—in such a way that would distract from the love of God. Augustine does not have this concern, but one can find it arising later in Hugh of St. Victor. For example, in the *Didascalicon* 5.7, Hugh writes: "I remember that I was once told of a man of praiseworthy life who so burned with love of Holy Scripture that he studied it ceaselessly. And when, with the growth of his knowledge day by day, his desire for knowledge also grew, finally, consumed with imprudent zeal for it and scorning the simpler Scriptures, he began to pry into every single profound and obscure thing and vehemently to insist upon untangling the enigmas of the Prophets and the mystical meanings of sacred

master trope of the journey to describe this ordered pursuit of Truth and Beauty. In this earthly life, "we are still on a road toward ultimate happiness, but just as the foot can be said to rest at each step of its continuing progress, so too the will may find restful delight in another creature even while pursuing its onward course toward God: resting, that is, not like a pilgrim finally arrived at his native land, but like a traveler taking refreshment, even temporary lodging, in view of his further journeying."[20]

This distinction between "use" and "enjoyment" casts some helpful light on how the multiple senses of Scripture—the literal, allegorical, tropological and anagogical—are meant to work. As an important antidote against the excessive spiritualization of Scripture, Augustine's *uti/frui* distinction not only allows for but actually insists that the literal sense of Scripture be respected—that is, "enjoyed in God" for what it signifies—as well as "used" as a stepping stone to its higher and fuller senses.

> The letter of Scripture's sacred text must be respected for itself, not treated all too prematurely as a trampoline, occasion for an impatient leap into the disincarnate realms of spiritual interpretation. But if the letter deserves that respect, then the things the letter designates must in their turn be acknowledged as real, historical things: the earth and sun, the trees and birds, the man and woman of Genesis' creation account cannot be sublimated into symbols.[21]

Created beauty invites from its readers, then, the kind of attention that would recognize the ontological status and peculiar singularity of those things to which signs refer, thereby honoring the object and indeed the sign itself, all the while not losing sight of the higher reality to which they point.

---

symbols (*sacramentorum*). But the human mind, unable to sustain such a burden, soon began to tire from the greatness of the task and the constancy of the tension. . . . [W]hoever studies the Scriptures as a preoccupation and, if I may say so, as an affliction to his spirit, is not philosophizing but is making a business out of them, and so impetuous and unwise a purpose can hardly avoid the vice of pride." (*The Didascalicon of Hugh of St. Victor: A Medieval Guide to the Arts*, trans. Jerome Taylor [New York: Columbia University Press, 1991], pp. 129, 130. I owe this reference to Kevin Hughes.) The issue is not so much that the Scriptures come to be seen as inherently sacred (the text itself, or the actual materials comprising the page and the words), but that the one who reads or studies Scripture is in danger, by his or her mode of reading, of becoming driven more by pride than by a desire for communion with and love for God whose revelation it is.

[20]O'Connell, *Art and the Christian Intelligence*, p. 138.
[21]Ibid., p. 140.

Bonaventure and the Hierarchical Order of Beauty

Augustine's theme of the soul's ascent to God is appropriated and developed—some eight hundred years later—by Bonaventure in "a stunningly original treatise" called *Itinerarium Mentis in Deum,* "Journey of the Soul into God."[22] "For clarity of expression, mastery of organization, and density of thought, the *Itinerarium* ranks as one of the purest gems of medieval theology."[23] Indeed, this elegant treatise is perhaps "the closest thing we have to a medieval *summa* of Christian mysticism."[24]

Even a cursory treatment of Bonaventure's "stunningly original treatise," the *Itinerarium,* cannot be offered here. For present purposes, however, I will consider two of its central images: the seraph and the tabernacle.[25] I do so in order to illustrate Mary Carruthers's insights concerning the thoroughly memorial—which also means, as will shortly be noted, imaginary, cognitive and aesthetic—character of medieval reading practices.[26] That is, these reading practices utilize mnemonic techniques not only as a way of storing material for later recall but, more importantly, as devices or tools for crafting thoughts, composing ideas. For the rhetorical-compositional work of the human memory is ex-

---

[22]Steven F. Brown, "Reflections on the Structural Sources of Bonaventure's *Itinerarium Mentis in Deum,*" in *Medieval Philosophy and Modern Times,* ed. Ghita Holmström-Hintikka (Dordrecht: Kluwer Academic, 2000), pp. 6, 10. The continuities and dependencies of Bonaventure on Augustine are treated by Frederick Van Fleteren, "The Ascent of the Soul in the Augustinian Tradition," in *Paradigms in Medieval Thought Applications in Medieval Disciplines: A Symposium,* ed. Nancy van Deusen and Alvin E. Ford, Medieval Studies 3 (Lewiston, N.Y.: Edwin Mellen Press, 1990), pp. 93-110.

[23]Bernard McGinn, "Ascension and Introversion in the *Itinerarium mentis in Deum,*" in *S. Bonaventura 1274-1974* (Rome: Collegio S. Bonaventura Grottaferrata, 1973), 3:535.

[24]Ewert H. Cousins, "Bonaventure's Mysticism of Language," in *Mysticism and Language,* ed. Steven T. Katz (New York and Oxford: Oxford University Press, 1992), p. 239.

[25]Bonaventure's theology, like Augustine's, is informed by, deeply indebted to, the sense of God's Beauty. For a careful, illuminating and comprehensive account of Bonaventure's theological aesthetics, see Thomas Jefferson McKenna, "Delight in the Cross: The Beautiful, the Agreeable, and the Good in St. Bonaventure's Spiritual Treatises" (Ph.D. diss., Yale University, 2004).

[26]Mary Carruthers's work on medieval conceptions and uses of memory is to be found in two important books, but also in dozens of essays and chapters. *The Book of Memory: A Study of Memory in Medieval Culture,* Cambridge Studies in Medieval Literature 10 (Cambridge: Cambridge University Press, 1990); *The Craft of Thought: Meditation, Rhetoric, and the Making of Images, 400-1200,* Cambridge Studies in Medieval Literature 34 (Cambridge: Cambridge University Press, 1998). See also her helpful anthology, coedited with Jan M. Ziolkoswski, *The Medieval Craft of Memory: An Anthology of Texts and Pictures* (Philadelphia: University of Pennsylvania Press, 2002). For a marvelously instructive discussion of how the medieval locational memory was used in respect to architecture—in particular temples but also amphitheaters, citadels, strongholds and other monastic buildings—see Mary Carruthers, "The Poet as Master Builder: Composition and Locational Memory in the Middle Ages," *New Literary History* 24, no. 4 (1993): 881-904.

actly an interfusing of the cognitive and the aesthetic, the rational and the affective. By showing how the affective and the intellective aspects of the mind *(mens)* are operative in even the most mundane, everyday practice of reading signs, I wish to underscore (with Mary Carruthers) the key aesthetic features intrinsic to medieval Christian reading practices. Drawing attention to the ways in which Scripture reading is an inherently and inescapably aesthetic practice will take us a long way toward redressing the neglect of Beauty in recent theology without the need or the desirability—and this is the key point—of focusing on aesthetics as such (i.e., in isolation from other aspects of human life).

The *Itinerarium* is occasioned by Bonaventure's meditation at Mount Alverno on the ecstatic vision that St. Francis of Assisi received there in 1224. According to accounts of the life of Francis, two years prior to his death Francis received an amazing vision of a seraph. Bonaventure himself offers an account of this event in his *The Life of Saint Francis*. There is of course an extraordinary wealth of images in honor of Francis, several of which depict the experience of Francis's vision of the seraph on Mount Alverno.[27] For my purposes one of these images will suffice—a sixteenth-century woodcut (fig. 8.1)—which can be taken as a helpful accompaniment, indeed a "pictorial display," of the following text from Bonaventure.

> Francis saw a seraph with six fiery and splendid wings descending from the
> highest point in the heavens. When the vision in swift flight came to rest in

---

[27]One of the earliest images of the stigmatization of Francis is by Bonaventura Berlinghieri of Lucca in 1235. It is an episode in the Pescia vita icon. The Seraph in the scene is not nailed to a cross as in later depictions, especially after Bonaventure's *Legenda maior,* "but its hands and feet, the only part of its body visible other than its face, have wounds." Another early image (circa 1245) is by the Master of St. Francis in the Bardi Dossal in Santa Croce in Florence. Again, it is an episode in a vita icon and the Seraph here also is not nailed to a cross. A third figure of the stigmatization on a separate panel is in the Uffizi in Florence (circa 1250) by an artist who is either thought to be the same as the one who did the Bardi Dossal or is somehow connected to him. The artist is usually listed as the Bardi St. Francis Master. Here in this image the seraph figure is nailed to a cross and inclines its head toward Francis, who is kneeling and looking upward. Despite variations among these images, one consistent feature of all of them is that the seraph is consistently depicted as having three pairs of wings. One pair descends below the Seraph, one extends laterally and one extends above. The placement of the sets of wings is a key feature of their use as a mnemonic device. These seraph images can be found respectively in William R. Cook, *Images of St. Francis of Assisi in Painting, Stone and Glass from the Earliest Images to ca. 1320 in Italy: A Catalogue* (Florence: Leo S. Olschki Editore, 1999), pp. 165-168, 98-102, 108-9. I am grateful to Xavier Seubert for pointing me to this invaluable resource. The woodcut in figure 8.1, although from a much later time (1511), is offered as a representative image here not because it is among the earliest images but because of its simple, clean lines—which effectively illustrate the aesthetic/imaginative/cognitive aspects of its mnemonic "reading."

Figure 8.1. Alfonso de Casarrubios, *Compe[n]dium priuilegiorum Fratrum Minorum: necnon [et] aliorum fratrum mendicantiu[m] ordine alphabetico congestu[m]* **(Venice: Per Joan. Antonium: Fratres De Sabio, 1532). Title Page. The image comes from the Franciscan Institute Library holdings located in St. Bonaventure University's Rare Book Collection, St. Bonaventure, New York, 14778.**

the air near the man of God, there appeared in the midst of the wings the image of a man crucified, with his hands and feet stretched out and nailed to a cross. Two of the wings were raised above his head and two were stretched out in flight, and two shielded his body. Seeing this, Francis was overwhelmed, and his heart was flooded with a mixture of joy and sorrow. He was overjoyed at the gracious way Christ looked upon him under the form of the seraph, but the fact that he was nailed to a cross pierced his soul with a sword of compassionate sorrow. . . . As the vision disappeared, it left his heart burning with a marvelous ardor and impressed upon his body an image of the signs which was no less marvelous. There and then the marks of nails began to appear in his hands and feet, just as he had seen them in his vision of the crucified man.[28]

In the prologue to the *Itinerarium,* Bonaventure returns to this event but rather than relating it as an incident in the life of Francis he takes it as a heuristic—a mnemonic device, a mental image—around which his understanding of the soul's ascent to God is organized. With a prayer to God that he might "enlighten the eyes of our mind to guide our feet into the way of that peace which surpasses all understanding," Bonaventure offers the following description/interpretation of the seraphic figure:

> It happened that, thirty-three years after the death of the Saint, about the time of his passing, moved by a divine impulse, I withdrew to Mount Alverno as to a place of quiet, there to satisfy the yearning of my soul for peace. While I abode there, pondering on certain spiritual ascents to God, there occurred to me, among other things, that miracle which in this very place had happened to the blessed Francis—the vision he received of the winged seraph in the form of the Crucified. As I reflected on this marvel, it immediately seemed to me that this vision suggested the uplifting of Saint Francis in contemplation and that it pointed out the way by which that state of contemplation can be reached.
>
> The six wings of the seraph can be rightly understood as signifying the six uplifting illuminations by which the soul is disposed, as by certain grades or steps, to pass over to peace through the ecstatic transports of Christian wisdom. . . . The figure of the six wings of the Seraph, therefore, brings to mind the six steps of illumination which begin with creatures and lead up to God, Whom no one rightly enters save through the Crucified.

---

[28]Bonaventure *Legenda maior* 13.3; 8:543, cited in Zachary Hayes, *Bonaventure: Mystical Writings* (New York: Crossroad, 1999), p. 30.

The six wings of the seraph constitute the overall structure to the *Itinerarium,* each wing signifying one of the six stages or grades of the soul's ascent. The overall movement is upward but it involves three vectors or directions: the things outside us (*extra nos:* the external world, the whole created universe), our own interiority (*intra nos:* the image of God resident within us in terms of memory, intellect and will), and those things which surpass us (*supra nos:* transcendent realities, the absolute Being and Goodness of God). Bonaventure's ascent, then, is first outward to the physical world, then inward to the interiority of the self, which in turn becomes the means to transcend oneself to God.[29]

While Bonaventure's schema can certainly be understood as a development of Platonic and Neo-Platonic speculations about "procession-return" or "emanation," it is a development profoundly transformed within a Christian, biblical context.[30] The controlling tropes and images of Bonaventure's schema, in other words, are biblical-philosophical rather than philosophical *illustrated by the Bible.*

The vision of the soul's ascent is an ancient one, going back most funda-

---

[29]As Van Fleteren puts it, "The movement of Bonaventure's ascent is from the physical world into oneself as a means to transcend oneself to God" ("The Ascent of the Soul in the Augustinian Tradition," p. 105).

[30]In what follows I am indebted to the work of Adriaan Peperzak, "Platonian Motifs in Bonaventure's *Itinerary of the Mind to God,*" in *Christian Spirituality and the Culture of Modernity: The Thought of Louis Dupré,* ed. Peter J. Casarella and George P. Schner (Grand Rapids: Eerdmans, 1998), pp. 50-62. It is important to recognize that Bonaventure is indebted to Francis as much as (if not more so) than he is to Plotinus and the Neo-Platonic tradition through Augustine. As Ewert Cousins notes, Bonaventure's sense of beauty draws heavily on Francis's "nature mysticism."

> In beautiful things
> He saw Beauty itself
> and through his vestiges imprinted on creation
> he followed his Beloved everywhere,
> making from all things a ladder
> by which he could climb up
> and embrace him who is utterly desirable.

("The Life of St. Francis," in *Bonaventure,* Classics of Western Spirituality: A Library of the Great Spiritual Masters, trans. Ewert Cousins, pref. Ignatius Brady [Mahwah, N.J.: Paulist Press, 1978], p. 263). Similarly, Francis's own *The Canticle of Brother Sun* praises God in and through creatures: the sun, moon, stars, earth, air, fire and water.

> Praised by you, my Lord, with all your creatures,
> Especially Sir Brother Sun,
> Who is the day and through whom you give us light.
> And he is beautiful and radiant with great splendor,
> And bears the signification of you, Most High One.

mentally to Plato's allegory of the cave in the *Republic*.[31] And even within Christian tradition prior to Bonaventure the idea of the soul rising up through different stages of contemplation was a common one.[32] Bonaventure's originality, however, lies in the way he doubles each of the three levels or dimensions of the journey: the external world, the internal world and the transcendent world.[33] He does so through "the application of a distinction between a seeing *per speculum* (through the mirror) and a seeing *in speculo* (in the mirror): each level of reality mirrors some other reality in two different ways."[34]

> Finite realities, such as . . . a tree, or a mountain, can be taken as points of departure for the ascent insofar as each of them, in its own way, mirrors God as the creator—and therefore also, in some sense, shows God to be the "formal cause" *(causa formalis)* of all things. In concentrating on the tree [for example], . . . we can discover certain traits in it that suggest an essential reference to its first cause, and thus, by way of conclusion, direct the mind to God. Having found God *per speculum,* the mind can then enjoy its discovery by realizing that the reference of finite realities to God entails a certain presence of God *in* those realities, not only behind them or deep down, concealed at the bottom of or underneath their being, but also *in and as* their ultimate

---

[31]Perhaps a better passage in Plato concerning the ascent of the soul is *Symposium* 210. Augustine copied it almost exactly (probably following Plotinus), and Pseudo-Dionysius quotes this passage in the *Divine Names*. Both Augustine and Pseudo-Dionysius were, of course, sources for Bonaventure. Given the cognitive-aesthetic emphasis of my argument, it strikes me that both of Plato's texts are appropriate here: the *Republic* (which concerns itself in the passage noted with epistemological and ontological matters) and the *Symposium* (which concerns itself more with the role of beauty in the epistemological and erotic ascent of the soul), jointly address the themes central to my argument. I am grateful to Oleg Bychkov for alerting me to the passage in Plato's *Symposium*.

[32]St. Bernard, Boethius and Hugh and Richard of St. Victor are but several Christian thinkers who employed hierarchies of contemplation (of varying numbers of steps). See Brown, "Reflections on the Structural Sources," pp. 1-16.

[33]Bernard McGinn articulates Bonaventure's originality in relation to the two themes of introversion and ascension. "The Seraphic Doctor's use of ascension and introversion in the *Itinerarium* provides a brilliant example of his relation to his theological heritage. Almost nothing in his evocation of the two themes can be said to be original, except for the form and genius of the whole. The law of symbols and of the mystical themes associated with the soul is one of the combination and interaction of previously disparate elements into new, more complex, and sometimes more adequate wholes. The architectonic character of the *Itinerarium*, the way in which the ancient symbols are not only appropriated and combined, but also placed within the framework of a mystical theory based upon the experience of Francis and of the profound systematic mind of Bonaventure, is the mark of the creativity of the Saint's relation to the tradition" (McGinn, "Ascension and Introversion," p. 542).

[34]Peperzak, "Platonian Motifs," pp. 56-57.

and primordial truth and "essence." God's infinite being then becomes visible, audible, touchable as displayed (be it in a finite, limited manner) in the mirror of finite entities *(in speculo)*.[35]

Bonaventure describes the universe as "a beautifully composed poem in which every mind may discover, through the succession of events, the diversity, multiplicity, and justice, the order, rectitude and beauty, of the countless divine decrees that proceed from God's wisdom ruling the universe."[36] His outlook is—like Augustine's—a profoundly aesthetic one. Comparing the universe to a beautiful poem means that Bonaventure discovers in it not only Beauty but *meaning*. As God's poem the universe as such not only *is* but it also *means*, it bears *significance*. "The creature is not merely a creature; the creature is a sign that points to something beyond itself. Every creature, having an ordered, internal relationship to its Creator, exhibits this relationship in some way. The universe of things is also a universe of signs, whose ultimate significance is the Sign-Giver."[37]

Like Augustine, Bonaventure believes that the human mind can be "led back" *(reductio)*—through God's creatures, God's poem—to God himself (to whom Bonaventure refers, among other designations, as the Supreme Creative Artist). The right perception and understanding of Beauty is, above all, an operation of the intellect—in particular, the faculty of judgment.[38] The problem, however, is that the soul in its present fallen condition is in need of grace to recover its spiritual senses. Because our minds

---

[35]Ibid., p. 57.

[36]Bonaventure, *The Breviloqium,* prologue 2.4, in *The Works of Bonaventure*, trans. José de Vinck (Paterson, N.J.: St. Anthony Guild Press, 1963), 2:11. See also Peter J. Casarella's treatment of the theme of the universe as a beautifully composed poem in the works of Augustine, Bonaventure and John Polkinghorne in "*Carmen Dei*: Music and Creation in Three Theologians," *Theology Today* 62 no. 4 (2006): 474-500.

[37]David E. Ost, "Bonaventure: The Aesthetic Synthesis," *Franciscan Studies* 14 (1976): 234. Bonaventure uses *imago* (image) in conjunction with representational art, defining it as "an expressed similitude." "And just as an artistic representation bears an expressed similitude to its prototype, so natural objects, the creations of God, bear an expressed similitude to their Creator. It is this similitude, in its variety of manifestations, that makes the Bonaventurian *reductio* possible. Implicit (or incarnate) in each thing as it is in itself is a spiritual meaning, a similitude to God by which the thing manifests the character that it has in itself" (ibid., p. 239).

[38]Thomas McKenna argues that Bonaventure is "the first to introduce the distinction between the beautiful, the agreeable and the good. Bonaventure argues that the mind perceives an object through the five senses, delights in its beauty, agreeableness, from the sensible species, in order to know it. The delight in beautiful things, as well as agreeable and good things, is a stimulus to know and love them, not an end in itself" (see dissertation abstract to "Delight in the Cross" in n. 25.).

are darkened, we wander aimlessly, unable to discern true Beauty and the significance of creatures—that is, we are incapable, on our own, of "leading ourselves back" through these created realities to their source. Hence a proper understanding of their purpose eludes us. The reawakening of the spiritual senses comes, for Bonaventure, by the illuminating power of the Holy Spirit through the book of Scripture. Scripture is ordained as a way of restoring to humanity the proper way of reading created objects— that is, as signs.[39] Beauty is the mark of God's presence in creation as revealed through the Spirit of God by means of God's Word, the Scriptures. Bonaventure says:

> But as no one can appreciate the beauty of a poem unless his vision embraces it as whole, so no one can see the beauty of the orderly governance of creation unless he has an integral view of it. And since no man lives long enough to observe the whole with his bodily eyes, nor can anyone by his own ability foresee the future, the Holy Spirit is given to us the book of the Scriptures, whose length corresponds to the whole duration of God's governing action in the universe.[40]

Hence for Bonaventure the fact that creatures are corporeal and material does not present an obstacle, as it might for Plato, to the soul's ascent to God. On the contrary, the creaturely reality is precisely the indispensable means of upward illumination, without which we could not even take the first step on the ladder of ascent. What we must flee, then, is *not* matter per se but "a wrong manner of concentrating on and relating to God and the universe."[41] Yet at the same time Bonaventure is, like Augustine, cognizant of the fact that beautiful things may impede our ascent not because they are beautiful but because of *our* failure (aesthetic-cognitive) appropriately to order them to the Supreme Creative Artist, who is the source and end of all.[42]

From what I have argued to this point, I hope that it has become evident

---

[39] Ost, "Bonaventure," p. 241.

[40] Bonaventure, *Breviloqium,* pp. 11-12.

[41] Peperzak, "Platonian Motifs," p. 57.

[42] Bonaventure, like Augustine, is cognizant of the power of the beautiful in nature or in human art to seduce us into ceasing from our restless journeying, preventing us from moving from the external world into ourselves and from thence ascending to God. See the opening paragraph of chap. 4 of Bonaventure's *Itinerarium* (quoted and discussed in the main text on p. 181). Bonaventure reiterates the same point in his lesser-known edition of the *Collations in Hexaemeron:* "Of course, everyone wants to be wise and knowledgeable, but it happens to

just how deeply and pervasively aesthetic are the theologies of Augustine and Bonaventure. Both give careful, exacting attention to the signifying character of creatures, both theologies are framed in terms of schemas of "ascent," and both accord considerable weight to the practice of reading and interpreting signs that comprise the book of Scripture and the book of creation. Bonaventure and Augustine also assign a special role to memory *(memoria)* in the soul's return—its being *reduced* (lead back)—to God. The complex, subtle ways in which reading, memory and a sense of Beauty interweave in this kind of aesthetic theology is convincingly recounted in the work of Mary Carruthers—and it is on her work that I am largely reliant in what follows.

The Beauty of Reading: The Poet as Master Builder

The concept of *memoria* in medieval Western culture is, by comparison with our own, a much more rich and expansive notion. While it clearly includes the power of recall (short- or long-term memory, as we understand these terms), *memoria* denotes additionally "the essential roles of emotion, imagination, and cogitation *within* the activity of recollection."[43] In modernity the tendency is to think of the imagination as the highest creative power, but for ancient and medieval people this power was reserved for memory. Memory is a faculty most closely associated with the art of rhetoric: writing and composition, reading and meditation.[44] Seen in this context of rhetoric and the pedagogy of the liberal arts, memory was far more than a matter of storing facts by rote without comprehension—a sort of passive receptacle for information. On the contrary, it was active. Memory was used to absorb material, to analyze it and divide it in ways that made it easy to retain, so that it became part of one's thinking and imagination and could be retrieved and used where pertinent in an ongoing dialogue. Continuously meditating on these memories increases and revises our thoughts.

---

them as it happened to the woman: 'She saw that the tree was beautiful and sweet to the taste.' [Gen. 2:9] They see the beauty of the knowledge of passing things and, so smitten, they linger, they taste, and they are beguiled" (*Collationes in Hexaëmeron,* ed. F. Delorme [Florence: Ad Claras Aquas, 1934]). I am indebted to Kevin Hughes for this last reference.

[43]Carruthers, *Craft of Thought,* p. 2 (emphasis added).

[44]*Memoria* is an integral part of the tradition of liberal arts, the *trivium* (logic, grammar and rhetoric). Monastic culture conceived of meditation more in terms of composition than of persuasion. After all, medieval monks were not in need of being convinced of what they already believed!

The practice of meditation is, of course, a rhetorical exercise, one of the arts of invention. It exemplifies memory's dual role of retaining information and actively organizing, manipulating and fashioning "the stuff of memory" in ways that make it conceptually fruitful. Indeed, memory's compositional character—as expressed in the term *inventio*—is to be understood in its two-fold sense of (1) *inventorying* (i.e., orderly arranging and locating discrete "bits" of information within a storeroom of memory), and (2) *inventing* (i.e., a "making" *(poesis)* or "creating," an activity which is neither separable from nor opposed to but rather in dialectical relation with "discovery").[45] The whole point of medieval memory training, then, was heuristic: a trained or educated memory aided composition by furnishing it with shared meta-phors, clever associations, tropes and various other mental images. Scripture was perhaps the most immediate and ready source of such images—but the liturgy, the artistic productions and the architectural layout of monastic buildings themselves also served this function. By means of these mental structures, which the monks created in their minds and linked together through schemas or other ordering devices, they were able to collect and hold together in a coherent, systematic order an immense and diverse uni-verse of materials.[46]

What readily comes to mind in this connection are the monastic practices of *lectio divina* and *sacra pagina,* where the scriptural texts were prayerfully meditated on, slowly and thoroughly chewed, digested and then regurgi-tated from the "stomach of memory" to be ruminated and redigested. Medi-eval readers were trained to move from *lectio* (the primary level of reading for sense) to *meditatio* (the process of reflection and memory processing, sometimes termed *ruminatio,* chewing over the text, in which the text is "made one's own," internalized as part of one's ethical character), to *con-templatio* (moments of ecstatic self-loss and spiritual union with God). If reading and meditation are the systole and the diastole—the heartbeat—of monastic scriptural practice, then memory is the intricate network of vessels

---

[45]Memory is thus both a mode of imagination and cogitation.

[46]These "devices" of thinking are designated by the term *rationes* (see Carruthers, *Craft of Thought,* p. 33). What medieval monastic culture was known for, indeed excelled in, was the filling in of the interior spaces of memory through a system of spatial and visual mnemonic designs. Monks were taught to meditate by learning to store their memories first with the syl-lables of the fundamental texts (e.g., the Psalms) and then to build on that foundation a men-tal edifice of connections, parallels, associations and linked chains of thought, which could be recalled at will and elaborated and enlarged over time. Again the key point is that memory was not mere recollection, but an "active recycling."

and arteries supplying blood to the whole body. Memory, in other words, not only gives the body structure and form, it also animates it, moves it, supplies it with orientation and a telos.

According to Carruthers these texts and mental images are designed to transport the reader to and through a series of places understood, not just as *topoi* but as stepping stones along variable paths to wisdom, insight and salvation. The medieval craft of memory supplied the rules of reading and composition, themselves understood as vehicles that induced forms of viewing. Reading was a type of "seeing" and seeing a kind of "reading."[47] Together they were intended to impel the monk along an *itinerarium* culminating in the vision of the heavenly Jerusalem. Memory's "inventorying" and "inventing" dimensions are thus active; they impel movement, journey and ascent of the soul—outward, inward, upward. Prayerful, meditative Scripture reading involves both the making and the following of different routes, circuits within and among memory's images, pathways at once emotional and rational. Indeed, these memorial pathways are comparable to the routes of liturgical processions and pilgrimages, stations of the cross—external, bodily movements which are themselves forms of prayer grounded in arts of remembrance.

The Seraph-Temple Image as a Bonaventurian Mnemonic Device

What I have tried to show—with Mary Carruthers's help—through the exploration of medieval memorial practices is how the woodcut image of Bonaventure's cruciform seraph (fig. 8.1) can also be construed as one such medieval mnemonic device. It wonderfully exhibits how the craft of mem-

---

[47]The relation between reading and seeing is too complex to be treated here even in a cursory manner. There are important similarities, to be sure, just as there are also important differences between reading and seeing. It would be a mistake to ignore these differences. Nonetheless, it is instructive to observe the several ways in which linguistic and artistic activities are mutually implicated and, to a certain extent, mutually illuminating. Robert Sokolowski, for example, argues that learning to "read" or understand words/texts and learning to "see" pictures/images involves a common set of "artful combinatorics." Indeed, Sokolowski contends that there is an important formal analogy between verbal/linguistic composition and artistic/imagistic presentations, whereby the three linguistic levels of syntax, phonemes and prosody essentially parallel the three pictorial levels of configuration, line and color, and cadence. If Sokolowski is generally right in his analysis—and there is good reason to believe that he is—then the question "What kind of intelligence is at work when we thoughtfully read a portrait?" might just as easily and accurately be posed as "What kind of aesthetic is at work when we read a text?" (see Robert Sokolowski, "Visual Intelligence in Painting," *The Review of Metaphysics* 59, no. 2 [2005]: 333-54).

ory works, simultaneously conceptually fecund and aesthetically pleasing. Moreover, it demonstrates how in a premodern context there is no hard and fast distinction between craft-making (the work of artisans) and what we tend to refer to as the "fine arts" (the work of artists).

The cruciform seraph (introduced in the prologue to Bonaventure's *Itinerarium*) is an exquisite mental image precisely because it is fecund: it invites multiple associations—multiple readings, if you will—which is, of course, how medievals read their Scriptures.

The central seraphic figure "interprets" two key biblical motifs or images: seraph and temple. The source of the seraph image is without question scriptural—deriving principally from the throne vision of the prophet recounted in Isaiah 6 (see also Ezek 1). The key hermeneutical device is the human figure in the center of the seraph, whose direct and immediate allusion is to the temple where Isaiah was standing when he received the angelic vision. But the cruciform figure alludes to another temple, namely, the body itself—proximately Isaiah's body and the body of the people of Israel, to be sure, but ultimately Jesus' own body and the body of his followers, the church.

> The Jews then said to him, "What sign can you show us for doing this?" Jesus answered them, "Destroy this temple, and in three days I will raise it up." The Jews then said, "This temple has been under construction for forty-six years, and will you raise it up in three days?" But he was speaking of the temple of his body. (Jn 2:18-21)

The setting of the seraphic vision is clearly the temple—the temple in Jerusalem where Isaiah stood when he beheld the vision. But the temple is a peculiarly polyvalent symbol in Christian Scripture. It evokes not only place and presence, but also body—corpus—in all its figurative and scriptural multidimensionality: the fleshly body of Jesus (creation and incarnation), the eucharistic body of Christ (ascension and transfiguration, sacraments), but also the wounding of that body, and hence the marks impressed on the flesh of his followers (ecclesiology). As the soul retraces its steps by means of this mental image, turning first to the outward world to discern the traces of God's Beauty in created things, before being drawn inward on its ascent to God, the cruciform seraph provides a sort of mental-aesthetic map for the soul. In places the seraphic image reverberates most strongly with the temple image, as Bonaventure indicates in the opening lines of the fifth chapter of the *Itinerarium*.

It is possible to contemplate God not only outside us and within us but also above us: outside, through vestiges of Him; within, through His image; and above, through the light that shines upon our mind. This is the light of Eternal Truth, . . . Those who have become practiced in the first way of contemplation have already entered the atrium before the Tabernacle; those who have become practiced in the second have entered into the Holy Places; and those are practiced in the third, enter with the High Priest into the Holy of Holies, where the Cherubim of Glory stand over the Ark, overshadowing the Seat of Mercy.[48]

The movement is simultaneously inward and upward, the imaginative pathways diverse and dynamic, as the figure oscillates between seraph, temple, body and then—through the cherubim—back to seraph again. Despite the beauty of these signs individually and in their proportionally coordinated arrangement, Bonaventure is cognizant of how easily the soul's ascent may become impeded by or even ensnared in the beautiful signs/things themselves.

It seems strange indeed that after what has been shown of God's closeness to our souls there are so few concerned about perceiving the First Principle within ourselves. Distracted by many cares, the human mind does not enter into itself through the memory; beclouded by the sense images, it does not come back to itself through the intelligence; and drawn away by the concupiscences, it does not return to itself through the desire for interior sweetness and spiritual joy. Therefore, *completely immersed in the things of sense*, the soul cannot re-enter into itself as the image of God.[49]

The image of the six-winged, cruciform seraph is clearly a hybrid of sorts. What I have argued here is that, in addition to its many other uses, it can also be seen as a mnemonic instrument that holds together in fruitful tension a number of fundamental biblical images and theological motifs—each invented by and inventoried (located) in the memory. But as one can appreciate, that cognitive-aesthetic "holding together" mutually enhances and extends those biblical motifs of temple and seraph, which together are—for Bonaventure in the *Itinerarium*—principally the ascension and the introversion of the soul. The seraph, an exterior symbol, signifies height—the uplifting of the soul, while the temple is interior and portrays depth—suggest-

---

[48]Bonaventure, *Itinerarium Mentis in Deum*, *Works of Bonaventure*, trans. Philotheus Boehner (St. Bonaventure, N.Y.: Franciscan Institute, 1956), 2:81.
[49]Ibid., p. 73.

ing that to ascend is also in some way to go deep within.[50] The cruciform body—unquestionably the christological focus of Bonaventure's reflection—is the central figure that appropriately sets in motion, arranges and orchestrates these images in such a pleasing and inviting harmony.

Conclusion

What I have argued in this paper—with the help of Augustine and Bonaventure, but also Mary Carruthers's fascinating work on memory—is that theological aesthetics is more pervasive and fundamental to Christian existence than we often care to acknowledge. Furthermore, it is not restricted to or even a privileged prerogative of what is now typically designed by the "fine arts." Traces of God's created Beauty are everywhere, even in the seemingly lowly art of Scripture reading and meditation on Scripture—the crafting of thought by means of mnemonic techniques. These rhetorical arts may seem servile, even mechanical and preliminary, in light of the "higher" or "fine" arts; but if understood as indissociably cognitive-aesthetic practices they are clearly not so. At least that has been the burden of my argument.

What I have tried to demonstrate is that today we need to find ways of fostering a properly theological-aesthetic attunement to Beauty which does not exacerbate the already deep divide between the arts and the rest of life. Giving more attention to or valorizing the "fine arts"—or even aesthetics as a discipline—will, I fear, only further confuse our present wanderings; they will not yet convert them into a journey. What is needed, rather, is a reexamination and retrieval of a broader, more expansive understanding of "art"—something like what we have seen in the memorial practices of monastic culture where art was construed as "a skill of producing proportionate things everywhere exercised."[51] And there the universal qualifier "everywhere exercised" was taken in earnest! The medievals did not privilege in

---

[50]McGinn, "Ascension and Introversion," p. 546.

[51]The egalitarianism of art and craft, characteristic of a medieval outlook, is largely absent in our time for reasons too complex to recount here. However, Bonaventure and Hugh of St. Victor both offer discussions of the arrangement of all the arts: Hugh in the *Didascalicon* and Bonaventure in the *de reductione artium ad theologiam (On the Reduction of the Arts to Theology)*. Indeed, the categories that both Bonaventure and Hugh use have interesting dimensions: e.g., theater for both is a mechanical art, because mechanical arts move things, and theater moves the affect. I am not suggesting that we simply exchange a modern (or late-modern) understanding of art and craft for a medieval one. What I am suggesting, rather, is that we reconsider the logic of our own modern and late-modern distinctions in light of a medieval rationale. I am indebted to Kevin Hughes for referring me to Hugh and Bonaventure in this regard.

any absolute sense one domain over all the others. Quite the contrary; the lowlier forms of art—especially the art of memory as embodied in Scripture reading and meditation, liturgy and prayer, pilgrimage and bodily comportment—took its rightful, acknowledged place in the overall scheme of life. But in assuming its rightful place, these humble arts also placed—that is, relativized—the "fine arts." For "the 'fine arts' are only valid when they see themselves as intensifying . . . art which is proper to humanity as such."[52]

We are, then, at a time of great challenge—as the "Beauty of God" conference organizers have well articulated. The sense of Beauty has suffered diminishment, distortion and neglect in recent theology. But in our efforts to redress and put right this carelessness and deformation we also face a danger—which a glance back at our medieval forebears has, I hope, helped us be alert to. That danger is one of losing sight of "the medieval advantage in *not* recognizing any special domain of fine art, nor any special region of understanding dubbed the 'aesthetic.' " The benefit, of course, is that in refusing to recognize a special region of life called "the arts," we can once more

> allow *arts* to be silently operating everywhere, in democratic ubiquity and with a self-forgetting absorption. . . . Equally, [we] can allow beauty that 'looks after herself' silently to mediate between the will, the understanding and material things in a way that disallows the tyranny of either desire, logic or the sheerly and inertly given. Just because there was no aesthetics in Aquinas's theological philosophy [and, one might add, Bonaventure's], the aesthetic is therein everywhere present.[53]

Past vital resources for the formation of the present are urgently needed, indeed!

I began this essay with the seemingly paradoxical claim that a proper kind of forgetfulness of aesthetics and the arts—understood in a post-Kantian sense of a "regional dimension of reality" rather than in a medieval sense of Beauty as a transcendental—may in fact be the very precondition in our time both for doing theology pleasingly and for reading Scripture fruitfully. I hope that I have made good—if only in a preliminary way—on that claim.

---

[52]John Milbank, "Scholasticism, Modernism and Modernity," *Modern Theology* 22 no. 4 (2006): 669. As Milbank reminds us, "art is *not* in the first place the kind of stuff that might end up in art-galleries." Rather, it is also and equally "architecture and house-decoration and gardening . . . before it is novels and stage plays and contextless sculpture and the re-performance of old operas" (ibid., pp. 665-66).

[53]Ibid., p. 669.

9

The Beauty of Belief

Roger Lundin

Like many things we take for granted and assume to be timeless—such as the notion that each of us possesses a faculty called the imagination or the view that the purpose of writing poetry is self-expression—beauty as we know it was born in the eighteenth century. That said, in case you wonder, I am not claiming that until then no lover's heart raced at the sight of his beloved or that no voice gasped in the presence of the sublime. On these matters I am a realist of the kind Isak Dinesen had in mind in one of her remarkable stories, "The Supper at Elsinore." If we doubt the persistence of beauty, she suggested, we only need to take a minute to look around us in a crowd and consider what a central character in her story observes: "What a strange proof, [Fanny De Coninck] thought, are these . . . bodies here tonight of the fact that young men and women, half a century ago, sighed and shivered and lost themselves in ecstasies."[1]

Yes, beauty has been around for a while, and even if we were to fail to recognize the proof of it that we carry in our bodies, we would know this fact from the remarkable history of reflection on its meaning. Plato worked this theme ceaselessly and set beauty near the good at the peak of his scale of values, and in the history of the Christian church, from Augustine to Aquinas and beyond, beauty has been a source of wonder and a path to the divine.[2]

---

[1]Isak Dinesen, *Seven Gothic Tales* (1934; reprint, New York: Vintage, 1991), p. 238.

[2]Under the pressure of political events and social change, beauty was significantly eclipsed as a subject of academic interest in the last decades of the twentieth century, but in the past decade that interest has begun to rise once again. Works such as Elaine Scarry's *On Beauty and Being Just* (Princeton, N.J.: Princeton University Press, 1999), and Denis Donoghue's *Speaking of Beauty* (New Haven, Conn.: Yale University Press, 2003), are representative of a vibrant, renewed emphasis on the centrality of beauty in literary and cultural studies.

In that sense beauty was not born in the eighteenth century, but what did come into being at that time was the concept of beauty as a unique discipline within the larger philosophical enterprise. The development of this new disciplinary understanding was sudden—unfolding as it did over the brief span of several decades at mid-century—yet its influence proved lasting and extensive. From the concept of a separate discipline of aesthetics, there soon followed the idea of beauty as a surrogate for a seemingly discredited system of Christian belief. For many of the nineteenth century's most ardent apologists for beauty, what Emily Dickinson called "the abdication of belief" made urgent the need to press the case for beauty.

My subject in this chapter is "the beauty of belief," and in the closing section I will address that theme directly, but to reach that point we have historical ground to cover and a correlative theme—beauty as belief—to explore. We will begin in the eighteenth century with the birth of aesthetics as a discipline; we will see how modern cosmology and historical consciousness propelled the creation of this discipline. We will then move into the nineteenth century, which in retrospect can be seen as the age of beauty's ascendancy and reign; our focus will be on what the poets and critics made of the shift to "beauty as belief." We will conclude in the company of Karl Barth, who along with several others, including Hans Urs von Balthasar, convincingly brought the subject of beauty back within belief in the twentieth century.

The Birth of Aesthetics

We begin in 1735, when a young German scholar, Alexander Baumgarten, published a treatise called "Philosophical Meditations on Some Requirements of the Poem," and in it introduced for the first time the idea of aesthetics as an independent philosophical discipline. At first, Baumgarten had a modest goal: to defend the relevance of sensory perception and to demonstrate that it could produce valid knowledge. Only later would he and others expand the scope of aesthetics to make it a rigorous "investigation of art and a [general] theory of beauty and ugliness."[3]

Why at this particular point in history did the likes of Baumgarten and Moses Mendelssohn feel driven to defend sensibility and secure a special domain for art? A number of extraordinary books over the past hundred

---

[3]Kai Hammermeister, *The German Aesthetic Tradition* (Cambridge: Cambridge University Press, 2002), p. 4.

years—from Martin Heidegger's *Being and Time* to Hans-Georg Gadamer's *Truth and Method* to Charles Taylor's *Sources of the Self*—have sought to answer that question, but for our purposes I want to turn to a poet rather than a philosopher to clarify the issues at stake.[4] The poet is W. H. Auden, and his critique of modern aesthetics can be found in an essay titled "The Poet & The City," in which he examines "four aspects of our present *Weltanschauung* which have made an artistic vocation more difficult than it used to be."[5]

The second of those four aspects provides the backdrop for understanding the eighteenth-century emergence of aesthetics. Auden speaks of this development as *"the loss of belief in the significance and reality of sensory phenomena."* To explain what he means by the use of this term, he cites two towering figures from the early modern era: Luther and Descartes. The father of the Reformation drove a wedge between the inner dynamics of the spirit's experience and the outer realm of public deeds; he did so, Auden claims, by questioning the significance of sensory phenomena through his denial of "any intelligible relation between subjective Faith and objective Works." To use a distinction borrowed from Dietrich Bonhoeffer, it was hardly Luther's primary motive to sever the ties between inward spirit and outward nature, but it did prove to be a troubling secondary consequence of his thought.[6]

A century after Luther, "with his doctrine of primary and secondary qualities" Descartes struck an even more devastating blow against the senses and the evidence they provide to the human mind and spirit.[7] For Descartes the primary qualities of objects were such things as extension in length, width and depth, along with the properties of substance and duration; the secondary qualities—what our senses, and the arts, consider the "good stuff," such as sound, light, color, taste and touch—may either exist in the object or be pro-

---

[4]See Martin Heidegger, *Being and Time,* trans. Joan Stambaugh (Albany: State University of New York, 1996); Hans-Georg Gadamer, *Truth and Method,* trans. and rev. Joel Weinsheimer and Donald G. Marshall, 2nd ed. (New York: Crossroad, 1989); and Charles Taylor, *Sources of the Self: The Making of the Modern Identity* (Cambridge, Mass.: Harvard University Press, 1989).

[5]W. H. Auden, *The Dyer's Hand and Other Essays* (1962; reprint, New York: Vintage, 1989), p. 78.

[6]Dietrich Bonhoeffer, *Letters and Papers from Prison,* ed. Eberhard Bethge (New York: Collier, 1972), p. 123: "One wonders why Luther's action had to be followed by consequences that were the exact opposite of what he intended, and that darkened the last years of his life, so that he sometimes even doubted the value of his life's work."

[7]Auden, *Dyer's Hand,* p. 78.

jected from the subject. We simply can't know for certain which is the case.[8]

Auden says a conception of "sacramental analogies" had governed thinking about the phenomenal world for centuries before Luther and Descartes, and it had served efficiently the needs of the saint as well as the demands of the artist. In that system of analogies, the senses offered outward evidence of inward and invisible realities, and both the inner sign and the outer manifestation were taken to be real, valuable and substantial. That is not to say that the testimony of those senses was clear and unambiguous. On the contrary, for as literary historian Erich Auerbach argues, the history of Christian interpretation has been marked by a persistent "antagonism between sensory appearance and [spiritual] meaning." This antagonism has its roots in the doctrines of revelation and providence, both of which depend upon a distinction between what Auerbach calls "sensory occurrences" and the "figural meanings" that are foreshadowed by those occurrences.[9]

Still, despite the tension between the evidence of the senses and the meaning to be gleaned from that evidence, for medieval men and women, a basic spiritual assurance remained. It was that a measure of truth about the God whom the heart worshiped could be discovered in the wonders that the eyes observed. According to Auden, it is precisely this confidence which has been undermined over the past two centuries, as science, abetted by philosophy and theology, "has destroyed our faith in the naïve observation of our senses" by informing us we cannot know what the world really *is like*. We can only know our subjective notions about reality, and those have more to do with the "particular human purpose[s] we have in view" than with the nature of things.[10]

In turn, this view of the self and reality "destroys the traditional conception of art as *mimesis,* for there is no longer a nature 'out there' to be truly or falsely imitated." As a result, the poet or artist can only be *true* to his or her "subjective sensations and feelings." To highlight this point Auden cites William Blake's famous remark that "some people see the sun as a round

---

[8]Charles Taylor says of the Cartesian "objectification of nature": "[According to Descartes] we also have to clear up our understanding of matter and stop thinking of it as the locus of events and qualities whose true nature is mental. And this we do by objectifying it, that is, by understanding it as 'disenchanted,' as mere mechanism, as devoid of any spiritual essence or expressive dimension" (*Sources of the Self,* pp. 145-46).

[9]Erich Auerbach, *Mimesis: The Representation of Reality in Western Literature,* trans. Willard R. Trask (Princeton, N.J.: Princeton University Press, 1953), p. 49.

[10]Auden, *Dyer's Hand,* p. 78.

golden disc the size of a guinea but that he sees it as a host crying Holy, Holy, Holy." Blake may have abhorred Newton's science, but he accepted its division "between the physical and the spiritual." The poet simply turned the tables on the physicist, as he lauded the spiritual imagination, consigned the material universe to the status of "the abode of Satan," and refused to attach "any value to what his physical eye" looked upon.[11]

In the early eighteenth century Baumgarten found himself thrust into the middle of this debate about the senses. He not only had to work against the influence of naturalist philosophy, but he also faced the considerable challenge of Protestant Pietism and its denigration of the splendors of the outer world. If Descartes had dismissed their evidence as episodic, unmethodical and subjective, and if people such as Blake were to take them to disclose little more than the measurements of Satan's dwelling place, how were they to be defended?

To rehabilitate sensory perception Baumgarten set about analyzing the obscure images and unfocused reflections that fall somewhere between the disjointed world of private perception and the ordered domains of science and rational thought. Following the lead of Leibniz, he called this the realm of *confused cognition,* and to account for the activities within its borders he proposed a "science of sensual cognition" called aesthetics. This new discipline would work the night shift, sifting through and making sense of the mass of rough, raw perceptions that pour into the mind each day. To Baumgarten this confusion "is a necessary condition for the discovery of truth, because nature does not make leaps from obscure to distinct thought. Out of the night dawn leads to daylight."[12]

The sensations of dawn needed a theory to explain the rules governing them, and the aesthetic doctrine of beauty was intended to provide this. To be sure, for Baumgarten the beauty revealed in art paralleled the harmony to be found in the mind of God and the order of the world. Yet he was not greatly concerned with questions of theology or apologetics, for his primary focus was on the power of art to shelter, organize and preserve the immediacy of experience and the intricacy of perception. According to Kai Hammermeister, in the end the "truth of art for Baumgarten is not a mere preparation for logical truth, nor . . . is it accessible by means of logic." Instead, it remains "sensual" and "unconceptualized." At first, aesthetics may

---

[11]Auden, *Dyer's Hand,* pp. 78-79.
[12]Alexander Baumgarten, quoted in Hammersmeister, *German Aesthetic Tradition,* pp. 7, 8.

have been meant by Baumgarten to "be a prop for the perfection of rationality," but in his wake the discipline "no longer defended its usefulness by reference to its helpfulness for logical modes of thought. Instead, it presented itself both as independent of and even productively opposed to rationality."[13]

The separation of aesthetics and rationality—of art and reason—soon became a commonplace. To use the terms of Immanuel Kant, the preeminent figure of late-eighteenth-century aesthetics, both reason and art worked with the sensory manifold, that array of unorganized particulars furnished to the mind by the experience of the senses. Rationality worked upon these phenomena for its own particular purposes, unifying them through the synthesizing powers of the understanding and organizing them for the purposes of scientific description and technological control.

In the meantime, as reason charted the workings of the kingdom of necessity, art was busy building a separate fortress of freedom. In his *Critique of Judgment,* Kant defined art as being "distinguished from nature as doing is from acting or producing in general"; the product of artistic activity proves to be a "work," whereas nature only produces "effects." "By right," Kant argues, "only production through freedom, i.e., through a capacity for choice that grounds its actions in reason, should be called art."[14] This power of choice is a sign of consciousness freely at labor, and it marks the distinctiveness of art. Here, at least, freedom is alive and vital, and the human mind and affections have their chance to make a mark, to leave a durable and indelible impression on an indifferent universe.

In this same passage Kant draws a sharp distinction between *art* and *handicraft,* or between what we might call the *fine* and the *useful* arts. In his words, the first (fine art) "is called liberal" and the second, the useful, is termed "remunerative art." The first (fine art) can be successful "only as play, i.e., an occupation that is agreeable in itself; the second (useful art) is regarded as labor, i.e., an occupation that is disagreeable (burdensome) in itself" and is attractive only because it brings payment.[15] Once again, we have a world of freedom—the playful domain of art that does not look beyond itself for its ground or purpose—and a province of bondage, that being the

---

[13]Hammermeister, *German Aesthetic Tradition*, p. 13.

[14]Immanuel Kant, *Critique of the Power of Judgment*, ed. Paul Guyer, trans. Paul Guyer and Eric Matthews (Cambridge: Cambridge University Press, 2000), p. 182.

[15]Ibid., p. 183.

realm of the crafts in which we labor with the tools of our trade.

For Kant, as for Baumgarten and countless others who were to come after them in the nineteenth century, beauty was the central category for understanding the "fine arts." "Only that which has the end of its existence in itself," Kant wrote in the *Critique of Judgment,* that is, "the human being, who determines his ends himself through reason, . . . this human being alone is capable of an ideal of beauty." Animals may find things agreeable, but only human beings can appreciate them for their beauty, which is an end in itself and serves as a marker of the unique supremacy of art: "Beauty is the form of the purposiveness of an object, insofar as it is perceived in it without representation of an end."[16] For Kant, in the end "experience of the beautiful is . . . an experience of 'purposiveness without purpose,' a sense that things fit together according to a purpose that we cannot state."[17]

By the end of the eighteenth century, then, a new and powerful understanding of beauty and the arts had planted its flag on the Western intellectual landscape and staked its claim to a sizeable plot of cultural ground. The aesthetic realm was governed by a set of interlocking assumptions that had at their base the belief that science disclosed a cosmos governed by law and necessity, while the spirit's inner drama played itself out in oppositional freedom. Yet as highly as modernity prized this inner realm, it worried about its epistemological status and struggled to reaffirm the *"significance and reality of sensory phenomena."* The creation of an aesthetic domain and the elaboration of a doctrine of the fine arts were meant to establish the epistemological authority of sensory perception and to secure the spiritual rights of beauty. To that end the eighteenth century placed the arts side by side with the sciences in a setting in which each was to become increasingly impervious, even incomprehensible, to the other.

It was no coincidence that the dream of a domain of beauty came at the same time that new intellectual and social realities were causing a great deal of unrest for Christians across the West. Over the course of the eighteenth century, a number of new forces brought sharp challenges to the Christian tradition, as rationalism subjected the concept of miracles to a withering critique, the historical-critical method called the trustworthiness of the Scriptures into question, and Enlightenment ideals of universality and fairness

---

[16]Ibid., pp. 117, 120.
[17]Terry Pinkard, *German Philosophy 1760-1860: The Legacy of Idealism* (Cambridge: Cambridge University Press, 2002), p. 72.

questioned the particular and exclusive claims of Christian revelation.

In these events of the late eighteenth century, Hans Frei sees clear evidence of "the centrifugal pressure of modernity," as the religious thought of northwestern Europe moved toward a "complete polarization" between those who saw revelation as a "unique, salvific, miraculous occurrence" and those who "denied positive revelation altogether, and opted instead for something else, such as a straightforward theism or 'natural religion.' "[18] In the late eighteenth century, among those who embraced this natural religion were almost all who championed the realm of the aesthetic and found in beauty a rich alternative to the poverty of a material world. The harder it became to trust in the God of Abraham, Isaac and Jacob—and Jesus Christ— the more beguiling it became to believe in beauty, entire and alone.

Beauty as Belief

At first the advocates of beauty worked to secure it to a concept of reality, divine or natural, and keep it from being carried away by any gusts of human subjectivity. For some, such as Samuel Taylor Coleridge, Christian belief provided the anchor. The poet remained to the end of his life convinced that religious belief could be reconciled with "nineteenth-century scientific thought," and he believed it possible to reconcile historic Christianity with modern selfhood and its passion for vocational and technological control.[19] For William Wordsworth and others it was not Christian orthodoxy so much as ordinary nature that would secure the rights of the spirit in an increasingly material world; to them, Christian belief and the Bible comprised "the grand store-house of enthusiastic and meditative Imagination" that pointed to the primary revelation to be found in the interaction of the human mind and nature.[20]

As the nineteenth century unfolded, however, art's ties to both Christian belief and the natural world continued to fray, and by century's end they began to snap. The poetry and letters of John Keats show a brilliant mind working to maintain the bond between beauty and nature early in that century. Trained for a career in medicine and intuitively drawn to the secular

---

[18]Hans W. Frei, *The Eclipse of Biblical Narrative: A Study in Eighteenth and Nineteenth Century Hermeneutics* (New Haven, Conn.: Yale University Press, 1974), pp. 62-63.

[19]Richard Holmes, *Coleridge: Darker Reflections, 1804-1834* (New York: Pantheon, 1998), p. 539.

[20]William Wordsworth, quoted in M. H. Abrams, *Natural Supernaturalism: Tradition and Revolution in Romantic Literature* (New York: Norton, 1971), p. 32.

skepticism that was in the cultural air of his day, Keats had little interest in Christian thought and practice per se. Yet he retained a passionate concern for the questions of truth that had occupied Christian thought for centuries and intuitively understood the debate about beauty in his own day. Specifically, like Baumgarten and Kant, he had a strong spatial sense of beauty and believed it might offer a retreat from the world of mortal toil and sorrow. The opening lines of his long poem, *Endymion,* capture this sense well:

> A thing of beauty is a joy for ever:
> Its loveliness increases; it will never
> Pass into nothingness; but still will keep
> A bower quiet for us, and a sleep
> Full of sweet dreams, and health, and quiet breathing.[21]

If the foxes have holes, and the birds of the air have nests, may not beauty offer those who bear the burdens of consciousness a place to lay their heads?

In "Ode on a Grecian Urn," Keats offered one of his most extensive—and certainly most well known—poetic treatments of beauty and belief. This is the first poem by Keats that I remember having read. I came upon it in high-school English during my senior year, and I came to it fresh from a two-year struggle over the death of my brother and the division of my family. Because I was seeking anything that offered beauty, order and the promise of last-ingness, the ode tapped into some of the deepest wellsprings of my heart. I was drawn to its portrayal of art's capacity to capture and preserve beauty, and the Spirit of God began to lead me to wonder whether there could be a power or person even greater than this "cold pastoral."

The poem opens with a tribute to the "still unravish'd bride of quietness," the "foster-child of silence and slow time" that is the urn.[22] After posing a series of questions—"What men or gods are these? What mad pursuit? What struggle to escape? What wild ecstasy?"—it unfolds as a meditation on human mutability and historical process. Everything depicted in the second stanza fades or fails in the course of ordinary experience, but in the extraordinary timeless world of the urn, these things endure. Here the "fair youth's" song never ends, and the trees never stand bare. The bold lover may never

---

[21]John Keats, *Selected Poems and Letters,* ed. Douglas Bush (Boston: Houghton, 1959), p. 39.
[22]All references to the text of "Ode on a Grecian Urn" are taken from *Selected Poems and Letters,* pp. 207-8.

win his beloved, but "do not grieve," the speaker instructs him, for "she cannot fade" and "for ever wilt thou love, and she be fair!"

Walter Jackson Bate notes that at this point the poem's sympathies begin
"to desert the urn for the painful world of process, of which the urn is obliv-
ious."[23] The urn may preserve mutable experience, but it always will remain
a "cold Pastoral." There is a limit to the powers of preservation, for in the
words of one of Keats's greatest poetic descendants, William Butler Yeats,
"the mountain grass / Cannot but keep the form / Where the mountain hare
grass has lain."[24]

Still the power of this beautiful "silent form" remains:

> When old age shall this generation waste,
> Thou shalt remain, in midst of other woe
> Than ours, a friend to man, to whom thou say'st,
> "Beauty is truth, truth beauty,—that is all
> Ye know on earth, and all ye need to know."

According to Bate these final words are meant to convey what Keats called
the "greeting of the Spirit," that dynamic encounter of the imagination with
nature which "is itself as much a part of nature, or reality, as is its object."
With the "harmony ('beauty,' 'intensity') of the greeting mind and its object,"
writes Bate quoting Keats, "we have a fresh achievement altogether within
nature: a 'truth—whether it existed before or not' in which reality has been
awakened further into awareness."[25]

A year before he wrote this ode, Keats had outlined in a letter his view
of religion and the theory of poetry that followed from it. "You know my
ideas about Religion," he told Benjamin Bailey, who was concerned about
his friend's religious uncertainty. Keats had "a mind so left to itself—an or-
phan mind," Bailey was to write decades after the poet's death, that it
seemed hardly surprising he was given to skepticism, "yet he was no scoffer,
& in no sense was he an infidel," Bailey wrote of his friend.[26] In his letter to
Bailey, Keats explained, "I do not think myself more in the right than other
people and that nothing in this world is proveable," but he also admitted

---

[23]Walter Jackson Bate, *John Keats* (Cambridge, Mass.: Belknap Press of Harvard University
Press, 1963), p. 513.
[24]William Butler Yeats, *Selected Poems and Four Plays,* ed. M. L. Rosenthal, 4th ed. (New York:
Scribner, 1996), p. 63.
[25]Bate, *John Keats,* pp. 517-18.
[26]Benjamin Bailey, quoted in Bate, *John Keats,* p. 217.

that he could not, even for a "short 10 minutes," enter into this subject as eagerly as his friend was able to do. He was too skeptical of the outmoded doctrines of Christianity and too committed to his own "system of Salvation" to take the Bible's claims seriously.[27]

At times, Keats confessed to Bailey, he even looked skeptically upon poetry itself and considered it to be "a mere Jack a lanthern to amuse whoever may chance to be struck with its brilliance." Since, "as Tradesmen say everything is worth what it will fetch," it may be that "every mental pursuit takes its reality and worth from the ardour of the pursuer—being in itself a nothing." Still, despite the conjuring powers of ardent pursuit, there are many "Things real" and "things semireal" in the world. Substantial realities, such as the "Sun Moon & Stars and passages of Shakespeare," can stand on their own without the support of human willing or imagining, but many things of value, "Things semireal such as Love, the Clouds" do "require a greeting of the Spirit to make them wholly exist." These things are not called out of nothing by the mind but made vital through their contact with it. They require the vivifying power of the imagination to bring to life their latent form and vitality, and without a "greeting of the Spirit," these things remain mute and incomplete, because they are objects in desperate need of the subjects that make them whole. In turn, they are to be distinguished from what Keats identifies as a third class of "things." These are the fantasies of human imagining, the "Nothings which are made Great and dignified by an ardent pursuit —Which by the by stamps the burgundy mark on the bottles of our Minds, insomuch as they are able to *'consecrate whate'er they look upon.'*"[28]

This celebration of the "greeting Spirit" follows a series of similar observations Keats had made in previous letters to Bailey and to his own brothers. Even as he was writing his great odes and entering his death struggle with tuberculosis, Keats was forging in his vision of beauty as belief a romantic variation on the aesthetics of Baumgarten and Kant. "What the imagination seizes as Beauty must be truth," he wrote to Bailey. "The Imagination may

[27]Keats, *Selected Poems,* pp. 268-69. The reference to "system of Salvation" is quoted in Abrams, *Natural Supernaturalism,* p. 67.

[28]Keats, *Selected Poems,* pp. 268-69. Keats was troubled by such a mind-centered understanding of poetry, but many of his poetic descendants thrilled to the prospect of such powers. For example, in 1936, William Butler Yeats memorably wrote that once the mind had discovered its power, it had to press even further: "that soul must become its own betrayer, its own deliverer, the one activity, the mirror turn lamp" (quoted in Richard Ellmann, *Yeats: The Man and the Masks* [1948; reprint, New York: Norton, 1978], p. 284).

be compared to Adam's dream—he awoke and found it truth. . . . O for a Life of Sensations rather than of Thoughts!"[29] A few weeks later he told his brothers of his conviction that "the excellence of every Art is its intensity, capable of making all disagreeables evaporate, from their being in close relationship with Beauty & Truth." Keats cherished most of all a quality he believed "Shakespeare possessed so enormously." He called it "Negative Capability" and defined it as the capacity for remaining "in uncertainties, Mysteries, doubts, without any irritable reaching after fact & reason."[30] This was Kant's disinterestedness given a Keatsian twist, just as the theory of the Imagination was an intuitive variation upon the Kantian theme of synthetic judgment.[31]

What Keats held together at the start of the nineteenth century—the countervailing demands of spirit and nature—began to come asunder as the century progressed. Romanticism depended on a spiritualized view of nature to drive its system. It relied, after all, on spirit's complex courtship of nature, and in theory the romantics considered nature a spouse capable of responding to the intricate demands and growing powers of the imagination. If beauty was to be something more than one of those "Nothings" made great by an ardent pursuit, there had to be a *Something* in nature with which spirit could unite.

What that "something" was varied for the romantic poets and essayists. For Wordsworth it was something like the Spirit of God that brooded over the world and coursed through nature and the human soul alike. Why should paradise be a "history only of departed things, / Or a mere fiction of what never was?" the poet asked:

> For the discerning intellect of Man,
> When wedded to this goodly universe
> In love and holy passion, shall find these
> A simple produce of the common day.[32]

In the early works of Ralph Waldo Emerson, a similar intimacy was taken to be a given. For the American essayist, spirit and nature were all but iden-

---

[29]Keats, *Selected Poems*, pp. 257, 258.
[30]Ibid., pp. 260, 261.
[31]Walter Jackson Bate notes that it was during his brief but intense friendship with Benjamin Bailey that Keats first began to use the term "disinterestedness," and within a year "the word and all it represented were to become something of a polar star" (*John Keats*, p. 202).
[32]Wordsworth, preface to *The Excursion*, quoted in Abrams, *Natural Supernaturalism*, p. 467.

tical, for "nature is the opposite of the soul, answering to it part for part. One is seal, and one is print. Its beauty is the beauty of his own mind. Its laws are the laws of his own mind."[33] And if in the poetry and letters of Keats the sense of nature often seemed more material than spiritual, he nonetheless labored to keep imagination and nature wedded to one another and to make certain that the spirit stayed faithful to its partner. As long as that relationship held, beauty could claim a lineage both in nature and in spirit and confidently pursue the myriad tasks that lay before it as a surrogate of belief.

To this point I have been describing a historical drama of sorts, and in it Kant, Keats and others have played key parts. We have reached the point, however, where Charles Darwin comes on stage, and with his entry, the scene changes, the story takes a new direction entirely, and the actors find their roles transformed in the middle of the play. There were others, such as Charles Lyell in biology, who had appeared in scenes before him and many others who came after him, but in the drama of spirit and nature, Darwin did more than anyone else to break up the marriage by discovering the irreconcilable differences between the workings of nature and the aspirations of the spirit. As John Dewey explains, with Darwin intellectual "interest shifts from the wholesale essence back of special changes to the question of how special changes serve and defeat concrete purposes." It shifts from a preoccupation with a divine "intelligence that shaped things once for all" and turns its attention to "the particular intelligences which things are even now shaping."[34]

Although some sentimentalists and popularizers would try to do so, it was hard to romanticize the survival of the fittest, and if the romantics had relied on the marriage of spirit and nature to produce a sanctuaried beauty, their union was now being dissolved. If beauty was to have permanent strength and status, by the latter decades of the nineteenth century, it would be that of a "Nothing" whose dignity was a gift bequeathed to it by the "ardent pursuit" that had conjured it into being ex nihilo.

The poetry of Emily Dickinson provides a clear guide to the transition from Kant and Keats to the contemporary world. Dickinson was an avid student of science, a keen reader of intellectual culture and a brilliant artist

---

[33]Ralph Waldo Emerson, *Essays and Lectures*, ed. Joel Porte (New York: Library of America, 1983), p. 56.

[34]John Dewey, *The Influence of Darwin on Philosophy and Other Essays* (1910; reprint, Amherst, N.Y.: Prometheus, 1997), p. 15.

who treasured her poetic prerogatives and longed to believe in the spirit's possibilities. In her childhood and adolescence she took comfort in the argument from design and eagerly studied the evidence nature offered for everything from the existence of God to the resurrection of the body.[35] Even more than Keats, she lamented the changes that had left the present age bereft of belief:

> Those - dying then,
> Knew where they went -
> They went to God's Right Hand -
> That Hand is amputated now
> And God cannot be found -
>
> The abdication of Belief
> Makes the Behavior small -
> Better an ignis fatuus
> Than no illume at all – (1581)[36]

Many Christian readers of this poem assume that *abdication* serves as a synonym for "abandonment" and take the poem to be blaming modernity for having discarded belief. But Dickinson's sense of things is less clear, for it seems that belief itself has abdicated the throne and left the ungoverned human race to its own devices.

To Dickinson, it often appeared that only the poets could compensate for the loss of belief. In 1863 she composed a poetic hymn in praise of the poets of beauty. "I reckon - When I count at all -" she wrote, "First - Poets," then the sun, summer and the heaven of God. But why value all these different things equally, when one—poets—"comprehends the whole." They create a summer that never falls away, and their sun is "extravagant" by any standard. And even if the "Further Heaven" proves to

> Be Beautiful as they prepare
> For Those who worship Them -

---

[35]In her educational training Dickinson was strongly influenced by the work of Edward Hitchcock, a preeminent antebellum geologist who taught at the Amherst Academy and served as president of Amherst College. Much later in life the poet wrote to a friend: "When Flowers annually died and I was a child, I used to read Dr Hitchcock's Book on the Flowers of North America. This comforted their Absence—assuring me they lived" (*The Letters of Emily Dickinson*, ed. Thomas H. Johnson and Theodora Ward [Cambridge, Mass.: Belknap Press, 1958], 2:573).

[36]Emily Dickinson, *The Poems of Emily Dickinson*, ed. R. W. Franklin (Cambridge, Mass.: Belknap Press of Harvard University Press, 1999); hereafter each poem will be cited in the text by the number assigned to it in the Franklin edition.

It is too difficult a Grace -
To justify the Dream – (533)

The poets, as another poem would have it, have the "Essentials Oils" wrung from their lives through that suffering which is "the gift of screws." Their lives will perish, but their works will last:

The General Rose - decay -
But this - in Lady's Drawer
Make Summer - When the Lady lie
In Ceaseless Rosemary – (772)

If "The Definition of Beauty is / That Definition is none," Dickinson concludes in another poem, then all we can know is that it is "Of Heaven, easing Analysis, / Since Heaven and He are one" (797).

But that's not all. Or as is so often the case with Dickinson, that is only half the story. For every poem of hers that lauds poetry and declares it to be an everlasting boon, another draws art back within the circuit of mortality. The most famous of such poems is a commentary on the "Beauty is truth, truth beauty" lines of Keats's ode. Dickinson's ironic take-off begins with the poetic speaker announcing

I died for Beauty - but was scarce
Adjusted in the Tomb
When One who died for Truth, was lain
In an adjoining Room -

These two chatter into the night, declaring "Themself are One." This sibling talk would go on forever, were it not for the stubborn fact of death, which claims their lives, their lips and at last their names:

And so, as Kinsmen, met a Night -
We talked between the Rooms -
Until the Moss had reached our lips -
And covered up - Our names – (448)

Dickinson's confidence in poetry as beauty's sanctuary was shaken by post-Darwinian science, which undermined the idea of intelligent design, on which romantic poetics and Protestant apologetics had been grounded. In a poem from early adulthood she took a stock theme of nineteenth-century evangelical apologetics—the emergence of the butterfly from its cocoon—and gave it a skeptical slant. In her treatment of the theme, the butterfly is a mindless winged creature that emerges on "a Summer Afternoon - / Repairing Everywhere - Without Design - that I could trace." The butterfly flutters in a field "Where Men made Hay-" and struggles "hard / With an opposing Cloud - ." There is nothing to meet in nature but "Parties - Phantom as Herself - " which

> To Nowhere - seemed to go
> In purposeless Circumference -
> As 'twere a Tropic Show -

Upon this carnival of random beauty in senseless motion, God looks down without interest: "This Audience of Idleness / Disdained them, from the Sky - " (610). Deprived of its divine audience the "phantom" self can only play its part in a "Tropic Show," this endless play of signs without design. No longer a *type* of a higher spiritual reality, nature in this poem can only prompt *tropes* of human longing.[37]

The silence of this God who is the "Audience of Idleness" is mirrored by the silence of nature. Nature had shouted to Wordsworth and Henry David Thoreau and spoken softly to Keats, but it now stood silent, having been rendered mute by a process that had taken several centuries to unfold. "About two hundred years ago, the idea that truth was made rather than found began to take hold of the imagination of Europe," Richard Rorty notes. It was in the nineteenth century that men and women began to realize that the world outside themselves had nothing to say to them. The idea of a truth that is "out there" in the world is the legacy of an era when "the world was seen as the creation of a being who had a language of his own." According to Rorty, by the end of the nineteenth century, some of the more enlightened among us came to realize such a being—God—does not exist. And in light of this fact, we can only conclude "the world does not speak. Only we do."[38] Nature may endure, but for Dickinson, as for Rorty, she has nothing to say:

> We pass, and she abides.
> We conjugate Her Skill

---

[37] In this study of the "purposeless Circumference" that is "a Tropic Show," Dickinson uncannily anticipates poststructuralist views of language as a system of endless tropes and infinite differences. In the latter decades of the twentieth century, such a vision of language was often employed to attack or dismantle modernist notions of beauty and aesthetic form.

[38] Richard Rorty, *Contingency, Irony, and Solidarity* (Cambridge: Cambridge University Press, 1989), pp. 3, 5, 6.

While She creates and federates
Without a syllable – (798)

According to Albert Gelpi, throughout her life Dickinson kept raising the same fundamental questions: "Do I know myself only in connection with, even in submission to, something beyond self? Or must I make my own meaning in a murky universe?" And "when I behold Nature," is there some inherent connection between "the phenomenon and its significance, between the concrete thing and its universal relevance, between physics and metaphysics?" In the terms of poetry and aesthetics, "the question is whether Nature is type or trope."[39]

If nature is a *type,* it is grounded in a higher reality, and each of its elements points to that reality. This was the Puritan view of nature in the New World, just as it had been, in modified form, the dominant understanding of reality in medieval Catholic Europe. By the early nineteenth century, however, Puritanism had all but disappeared as a vital intellectual force, and at the same time, idealist philosophy and literary romanticism had begun to trumpet the newly discovered powers of the imaginative self. As we have seen, nineteenth-century romanticism initially attempted to balance its emerging view of nature as a *trope* anchored in the creative human mind with the more ancient understanding of it as a *type* of transcendent reality. Over the course of the century the balance shifted, and by the time Dickinson began to write poetry, *types* had all but given way to *tropes.* In Rorty's categories, *types* are truths as they are supposedly found; *tropes* are truths as they are actually made.[40]

We recall Auden's observation concerning the way in which the modern understanding of the cosmos destroys the idea of "art as *mimesis,* for there is no longer a nature 'out there' to be truly or falsely imitated." Although Dickinson did not give up on the idea of design entirely and finally, she did question the viability of beauty as a surrogate for belief. If what some of her poems were beginning to imagine—that truth and beauty are "Nothings" spun off by the energy of "ardent pursuit"—it would be difficult for the heavy laden to find rest in them. Along with others in the late nineteenth

---

[39]Albert J. Gelpi, *Emily Dickinson: The Mind of the Poet* (1965; reprint, New York: Norton, 1971), p. 153.

[40]For a fuller discussion of these issues and their implications for poetics and aesthetics, see my *Emily Dickinson and the Art of Belief,* 2nd ed. (Grand Rapids: Eerdmans, 2004), pp. 44-48, 218-20.

century, she foresaw what has developed into a central dilemma of contemporary cultural life: How are we to believe in anything if we consider truth to be something that has been *created* entirely by our desire to believe rather than something that has been *discovered* through our capacity to learn and to receive?

Friedrich Nietzsche set this challenge more clearly than anyone in the nineteenth century. In *Twilight of the Idols,* he wrote bluntly about the origins of beauty in the will to power and scuttled all efforts to ground it in nature or the transcendent self or in the offspring of their union. There is nothing essential about beauty, he claimed, for "nothing is so conditional, let us say *circumscribed,* as our feeling for the beautiful." We may believe "the world itself is filled with beauty," but our belief is based on our forgetfulness, for we are the ones who have created this beauty. We alone have "bestowed beauty upon the world—alas! only a very human, all too human beauty."[41]

To Nietzsche beauty was not a product of the marriage of spirit and nature but a matter of "man . . . [transforming] things until they mirror his power—until they are reflections of his perfection. This *compulsion* to transform into the perfect is—art." In analyzing what he terms "the psychology of the artist," Nietzsche describes the process by means of which the artist fabricates the beautiful: "From out of this feeling [of plenitude] one gives to things, one *compels* them to take, one rapes them—one calls this process *idealizing.*"[42]

There is much we can learn about beauty from this nineteenth-century journey from the imagery of intimacy to that of violation. "Is the world actually made beautiful because *man* finds it so?" Nietzsche asks rhetorically. His answer to his own question is simple: "Nothing is beautiful, only man:

---

[41]Friedrich Nietzsche, *Twilight of the Idols* and *The Anti-Christ* (London: Penguin, 1990), p. 89.
[42]Nietzsche, *Twilight,* p. 83. With Nietzsche the persistent question has long been, and will likely remain, to what degree we are to take his pronouncements seriously. Should we accept them as relatively harmless exercises in ironic suggestiveness? Or should we consider them to be earnest, angry efforts at self-assertion? Although I favor the latter interpretation, I believe Charles Taylor is on target with his balanced judgment: "One after the other, the authoritative horizons of life, Christian and humanist, are cast off as shackles of the will. Only the will to power remains. The power and impact of Nietzsche's work come from his fierce espousal of this destructive movement which he pushes to the limit." Nevertheless, Nietzsche "also seems to have held that the will to power of self-defining man would be disastrous. Man as a purely self-dependent will to power must be 'overcome', to use Zarathustra's expression" (Charles Taylor, *Hegel* [Cambridge: Cambridge University Press, 1975], p. 563). That Nietzsche's rhetoric celebrated violence and violation is unquestionable; it is less clear that he found a way of "overcoming" disastrous self-will.

on this piece of naiveté rests all aesthetics, it is the *first* truth of aesthetics." The second truth, which follows upon it, is that "nothing is ugly but *degenerate* man—the domain of aesthetic judgment is therewith defined." In language that sounds haunting after Auschwitz, Nietzsche boasts of being able to measure ugliness "with a dynamometer." When a man feels depressed, he can assume "the proximity of something 'ugly,'" and this ugliness represents a clear threat to "his will to power, his courage, his pride." In the presence of degrading ugliness, "a feeling of *hatred* then springs up; what is man then hating?" The answer is the *decline of his type*. And this he hates "out of the profoundest instinct of his species." Indeed, "it is the profoundest hatred there is. It is for its sake that art is *profound*."[43]

Nietzsche had contempt for Kant's ideal of aesthetic perception as a disinterested apprehension of the beautiful, just as he did for the views of art-for-art's sake that had flowed from the Kantian source. He rejected the idea that aesthetics had to do with a unified experience set apart from science and granted the right to rule over its own limited domain. Nietzsche had no desire to rest in any Keatsian bowers or gaze disinterestedly upon any Grecian urns, for he was too busy trying to establish the rule of aesthetics over every domain of knowledge and action. From epistemology to ethics and beyond, everything became for Nietzsche a matter of art, and beauty was no longer a surrogate for belief but simply one more product of the will to power, that source and substance of all beliefs.

The Beauty of Belief

In his recent study of the German aesthetic tradition, Kai Hammermeister calls Nietzsche's endeavor a "remarkable" attempt to effect "nothing less than an aestheticization of philosophy at large" and of all moral, cultural and spiritual endeavors.[44] For art, Nietzsche sought not provincial rule—with the aesthetic serving as a kind of Switzerland of the spirit—but centralized control.

In claiming this ground for aesthetics, Nietzsche hardly acted alone. In analyzing the Nietzschean declaration of war against Christianity ("Hear me, for I am he; do not at any price mistake me. Am I understood?—Dionysius versus the Crucified"), Karl Barth says the philosopher was merely saying "with less restraint" and "greater honesty" what "Goethe, Hegel, Kant and

---

[43]Nietzsche, *Twilight*, pp. 89-90.
[44]Hammermeister, *German Aesthetic Tradition*, p. 146.

Leibniz" had long been arguing, and indeed, what "the spirit of all European humanity as fashioned and developed since the 16th century" had been intimating with increasing boldness. If Nietzsche is to be blamed for everything from reactionary fascism to leftist perspectivalism, according to Barth the fault ultimately lies with "the European spirit during the last centuries." In its most distinguished representatives, that spirit has lustily promoted the belief that the human mind in its "last and deepest isolation" is alone "the eye and measure and master and even the essence of all things. What Goethe [and others] quietly lived out, Nietzsche had to speak out continually with the nervous violence of ill-health."[45] Nietzsche simply harvested and marketed the cultural crops that others had been tending for several generations.

Yet what was it that Nietzsche, gleaning from the European tradition, found "absolutely intolerable and unequivocally perverted" in the Christian faith? The answer, Barth says, can be discovered in his declaration of war: "Dionysus versus the Crucified." Dionysus, Zarathustra, Nietzsche himself, as he wished to envision himself—this was the ethical and spiritual ideal, "the lonely, noble, strong, proud, natural, healthy, wise, outstanding, splendid man." In contrast to this lofty figure—a real beauty, so to speak—Christianity has offered a far different ideal, of which Nietzsche says, "this ideal we contest."[46]

The Christian faith sets against the Dionysian ideal what Barth calls the gospel's "blatant claim that the only true man is the man who is little, poor and sick, . . . who is weak and not strong, who does not evoke admiration but sympathy, who is not solitary but gregarious—the mass-man." Christian belief goes a step further and speaks of a crucified God; it identifies "God Himself with this human type" and demands of all men and women "not merely sympathy with others but that they themselves should be those who excite sympathy and not admiration."[47] Nietzsche found it disgusting that in Christianity "the neighbour is transfigured into a God." He concluded that if God had indeed chosen "what is weak and foolish and ignoble and despised in the eyes of the world" as his standard of beauty and virtue, there is nothing for us to do but to resist Christianity, which "is the greatest misfortune of the human race thus far."[48]

---

[45]Karl Barth, *Church Dogmatics: The Doctrine of Creation* 3/2, trans. H. Knight et al., ed. G. W. Bromiley and T. F. Torrance (Edinburgh: T & T Clark, 1960), pp. 236, 232.

[46]Ibid., p. 239.

[47]Ibid.

[48]Nietzsche, quoted in ibid.

Once again, Barth says, the context is important, for in his aestheticizing opposition to the crucified One, Nietzsche was only trumpeting at the close of the nineteenth century what a host of others had been murmuring in muted tones for decades. "Goethe, too, had no great time for Christianity," but he made his repudiation of it "cool and good-tempered and mild." The same was true "of the philosophical Idealists of the time, of Kant, Fichte, Schelling and Hegel," according to Barth. They had little use for the Christianity of the New Testament but were "restrained and cautious and sparing" in their critiques, and even their materialist descendants, such as Strauss and Feuerbach, stopped short of proposing that Dionysus take on the Crucified.[49]

What Barth calls the "new thing in Nietzsche" was "the development of humanity without the fellow-man," which was, after all, the secret humanity of the post-Cartesian ideal. Christianity confronts this Nietzschean "superman" with "the figure of suffering man." It places before the Olympian man the "Crucified, Jesus, as the Neighbour," and in his person "a whole host of others who are wholly and utterly ignoble and despised in the eyes of the world (of the world of Zarathustra, the true world of men), the hungry and thirsty and naked and sick and captive, a whole ocean of human meanness and painfulness." Christianity audaciously informs Dionysus-Zarathustra that he is not a god and says that if he wishes to be redeemed, he must belong to the crucified One and be in "fellowship with this mean and painful host of His people."[50]

Barth credits Nietzsche with having recovered Christian truths that modernity had been content to misconstrue or ignore. Nietzsche uncovered the gospel, he explains, "in a form which was missed even by the majority of its champions, let alone its opponents, in the 19th century." This advocate of Dionysus did the servants of the crucified One a service by "bringing before us the fact that we have to keep to this form [of the gospel] as unconditionally as he rejected it, in self-evident antithesis not only to him, but to the whole tradition on behalf of which he made this final hopeless sally."[51]

To Barth, "keeping to the form" meant holding to Christ at the center of the theological enterprise. The christological turn in twentieth-century theology has several implications for the story I have told and for a contemporary Christian understanding of the arts. The first has to do with overcoming

---

[49]Ibid., p. 240.
[50]Ibid., p. 241.
[51]Ibid., p. 242.

the dichotomies that Auden uncovered in modern views of the arts. If we
believe in the incarnation and accept that the same mind is to be in us that
was in Christ Jesus

> who, though he was in the form of God,
>   did not regard equality with God
>   as something to be exploited,
> but emptied himself,
>   taking the form of a slave,
>   being born in human likeness.
> And being found in human form,
>   he humbled himself
>   and became obedient to the point of death—
>   even death on a cross (Phil 2:6-8)

—and if, as Yeats's Crazy Jane tells the bishop, it is true that "Love has
pitched his mansion in / The place of excrement"—then who are we to deny
"the significance and reality of sensory phenomena?"[52]

In addition, the Barthian revival of christological thought and trinitarian
theology addressed the problem of impersonal power that had led to the
birth of aesthetics in the first place. The turn to beauty took place in reaction
to a rising view of nature as an intricate mechanism ruled by impersonal
laws. In the words of H. Richard Niebuhr's stinging critique of the "Christ
against culture" position—a position embraced by, among others, the fundamentalist ancestors of contemporary evangelicalism—this view led to "an
ontological bifurcation of reality." The position was built on a deep "suspicion of nature and nature's God," and it readily gave way to a temptation
"to divide the world into the material realm governed by a principle opposed to Christ and a spiritual realm guided by the spiritual God." For, as
Niebuhr says, "at the edges of the radical movement the Manichean heresy
is always developing" as the "relation of Jesus Christ to nature and to the
Author of nature" is obscured or denied.[53] One could argue that the history
of aesthetics from Baumgarten to Nietzsche is the story of the slow but
steady rise of a thoroughly modern Manicheanism.[54]

---

[52]Yeats, *Selected Poems,* p. 149.
[53]H. Richard Niebuhr, *Christ and Culture* (New York: Harper, 1951), p. 81.
[54]For a brilliant discussion of the connections between Christian belief and materialistic pagan-
ism, both ancient and modern, see Charles Norris Cochrane, *Christianity and Classical Culture: A Study of Thought and Action from Augustus to Augustine* (1940; reprint, London: Oxford University Press, 1944), pp. 399-516.

Although Wordsworth, Keats and others had tried to sustain the tie between spirit and nature, in the end, beauty as a surrogate for belief depended on a Manichean view that posited, in the words of Hans Jonas, "an absolute rift between man and that in which he finds himself lodged—the world."[55] With its renewed emphasis on the "relation of Jesus Christ to nature and to the Author of nature," the robust Christology of Barth, Dietrich Bonhoeffer and others sought to repair that rift and to reject the idea of a radical opposition between outward banality and inward beauty.

The christological vision enabled the likes of Barth and Hans Urs von Balthasar to reestablish and enact for the contemporary world what might be called a *dramatic* understanding of the architectonic beauty of Christian belief. To explain what I mean, we can refer to terms established by C. S. Lewis in *The Discarded Image,* where he brilliantly compares the felt differences between a medieval and a modern vision of the universe. In describing what it meant to "see the sky in terms of the old cosmology," Lewis depicts the cosmos as an immense spatial structure that is undeniably intricate in its complexity but unmistakably finite in its totality. It has an architectural harmony that the eye can see and the heart can dwell in. To gaze at "the towering medieval universe" is like looking up "at a great building." We behold "an object in which the mind can rest, overwhelming in its greatness but satisfying in its harmony."[56]

The modern view of the universe is something else entirely. One cannot rest in the spatial dimensions of this cosmos, nor is it feasible to construct a satisfying structural model of the whole of it, for in the words of Lewis, "to look out on the night sky with modern eyes is like looking out over a sea that fades away into mist, or looking about one in a trackless forest—trees forever and no horizon." This "space" of modern astronomy can "arouse terror, or bewilderment or vague reverie," but it cannot offer a satisfying structural or visual harmony.[57]

For that harmony, we must turn to other models, in which the structural intricacy of God's creative and redeeming love can be told, can be sung and can be heard. In twentieth-century theology the most powerful models proved to be those that employed metaphors of drama or patterns of nar-

---

[55]Hans Jonas, *The Gnostic Religion: The Message of the Alien God and the Beginnings of Christianity,* 2nd ed. (Boston: Beacon, 1963), p. 327.

[56]C. S. Lewis, *The Discarded Image: An Introduction to Medieval and Renaissance Literature* (Cambridge: Cambridge University Press, 1964), pp. 98, 99.

[57]Ibid., p. 99.

rativity to capture the majesty of God's activity. The greatest systematic expressions of the faith in the past century—Hans Urs von Balthasar's multivolume *Theo-Drama* and *The Glory of the Lord: A Theological Aesthetics* and Karl Barth's *Church Dogmatics*—display an architectural brilliance of the kind Lewis attributes to the medieval picture of the universe. In their own way they are "objects in which the mind can rest, overwhelming in their greatness but satisfying in their harmony."

The *Church Dogmatics* may be the St. Peter's Basilica or St. Paul's Cathedral of Barthian thought, but I want to conclude by looking at a passage from one of the outlying structures he put up in preparation for that larger project of a lifetime. It comes near the close of his *Ethics,* has to do with the arts and evidences Barth's passionate concern to situate all human activity in a christological and eschatological context.

"Art must be considered in an eschatological context," Barth argues, "because it is the specific external form of human action" in which our deepest ethical duties "cannot be made intelligible to us except as play." Along with humor, art is an activity of which "only the children of God are capable," and like humor, it is "born of sorrow" and "sustained by an ultimate and very profound pain." Art is the creation of children (1 Jn 3:2-10) who play away in a world "whose corruptibility they cannot overlook or ignore. . . . Only those who have knowledge of the future resurrection of the dead really know what it means that we have to die," Barth reminds us.[58]

He sees art as accepting the essential homelessness of human experience east of Eden. "The artist's work is homeless in the deepest sense," Barth says, and he presses the case so far as to claim that it is "precisely in their strange and rootless isolation from all the works of present reality [that works of art] live so totally *only* by the truth of the promise" of God. By means of art, we learn "not to take present reality with final seriousness in its created being or in its nature as the world of the fall and reconciliation." In Barth's words, "true aesthetics is the experiencing of real and future reality." And to this extent, "Art *plays* with reality" by refusing to let present reality "be a last word" in its fallen and partial state.[59]

> [Art] transcends human words with the eschatological possibility of poetry, in
> which speech becomes, in unheard-of fashion, an end in itself, then to a

---

[58]Karl Barth, *Ethics,* ed. Dietrich Braun, trans. Geoffrey W. Bromiley (New York: Seabury, 1981), pp. 506, 507.
[59]Ibid., pp. 507, 508.

higher degree—although we are still dealing only with the sound and tone of the human voice—with the eschatological possibility of song, and then—still with the intention of penetrating to what is true and ultimate, of proclaiming the new heaven and the new earth, but now using the voices of the rest of creation—with the eschatological possibility of instrumental music.[60]

In case the eschatological gravity of all this singing and versifying threatens to make us too serious, Barth reminds us that to the end of our lives we remain the *little* children of God. Whether we envision a transformed world in our poetry or seek to bring it into being through political struggle, we "must not try to view our work as a solemnly serious cooperation with God." Instead, we forever "play in the peace in the father's house that is waiting for us." At all costs we strive to avoid allotting "final seriousness to what we do here and now." We play and we wait, "because the perfect has still to come beyond all that we do now. . . . We cannot be more grimly in earnest about life than when we resign ourselves to the fact that we can only play."[61]

But play we do, and play we will, throughout time and in eternity. At least that's what the Reverend John Ames believes we will do. He is the central character in Marilynne Robinson's recent, much-lauded novel, *Gilead*. Near the close of his life Ames reports that he feels like "a child who opens its eyes on the world once and sees amazing things it will never know any names for and then has to close its eyes again." He knows this world is only a "mere apparition" compared to the one to come, "but it is only lovelier for that. There is a human beauty in it." In fact, Ames refuses to believe that when we have all "put on incorruptibility" we will somehow forget the fantastic drama of mortality and impermanence, "the great bright dream of procreating and perishing that meant the whole world to us. In eternity this world will be Troy," he believes, "and all that has passed here will be the epic of the universe, the ballad they sing in the streets." However great the future will be, he says, "I don't imagine any reality putting this one in the shade entirely, and I think piety forbids me to try."[62]

That is the beauty of belief. So it always has been and so it always will be, world without end.

---

[60]Ibid., p. 508.
[61]Ibid., pp. 504, 505.
[62]Marilynne Robinson, *Gilead* (New York: Farrar, 2004), p. 57.

10

THE APOLOGETICS OF BEAUTY

Edward T. Oakes, S.J.

In 1974, Chris Burden had himself crucified on the roof of a Volkswagen. He was creating a work of art. A decade later, Hermann Nitsch staged a three-day performance in which participants disemboweled bulls and sheep and stomped around in vats, mixing the blood and entrails with grapes. Another work of art. Rafael Ortiz cut off a chicken's head and beat the carcass against a guitar. Ana Mendieta, who had a retrospective at the Whitney last year, also decapitated a chicken and let its blood spurt over her naked body. As one commentator has observed: "animals are not safe in the art world." Neither are the artists. They have sliced themselves with razor blades, inserted needles in their scalps, rolled naked over glass splinters, had themselves suspended by meat hooks and undergone surgical "performance operations" during which spectators could carry on conversations with the artist-patient.[1]

I have just quoted the opening paragraph of a review of several books on contemporary art that appeared in the December 11, 2005, *New York Times Sunday Book Review*. When the *New York Times* starts sounding like Jesse Helms and Rudolf Giuliani, something must be afoot.

Nor is this reviewer's lament an isolated one. A few years ago the French historian of the Soviet Union, Alan Besançon, published a history of iconoclasm called *The Forbidden Image,* a book that was first prompted by a visit he paid to the Paris Biennial, when he came to see how reliant contemporary artists have become on what museum marketing staffs like to call "the Shock of the New." Like the Venice Biennale or the Whitney Museum's bi-

---

[1] Barry Gewen, "State of the Art," *New York Times Sunday Book Review,* December 11, 2005 <www.nytimes.com/2005/12/11/books/review/11gewen.html?ex=1141448400&en=dd547980 0dlf683f&ei=5070>.

annual display of contemporary art in New York or the Brooklyn Museum's
notorious show *Sensation,* the Paris version displayed works whose only
purpose was to offend the very society whose support the artist was seeking. The results apparently were quite harrowing for Besançon, and he describes the Paris exhibition in vivid and telling detail:

> I walked through rooms capriciously strewn with debris, little piles of sand,
> roaring machines. On the walls were charred objects, the macabre remains of
> some death camp, obstetrical objects to turn your stomach, a neon tube in a
> corner. I could strike up a song on the death of art, take the side of the hag-
> gard guard, sitting overwhelmed in a corner of the room. But let us be cau-
> tious. The theme of the decadence of art is as old as art itself: Plato already
> lamented it, and, as in Baudelaire's poem "Beacons," that heart-felt sob has
> rolled from age to age, arriving on our doorstep. This time, it might be for
> good. I will not venture to say so, even though, like everyone else, I some-
> times believe it.[2]

My title is "The Apologetics of Beauty," and, as you can see, I have set
myself quite a challenge. The working assumption of this essay I have
drawn from the twentieth-century Swiss Catholic theologian Hans Urs von
Balthasar, who made beauty the starting point of his apologetics. But he also
knew the difficulties he was facing. In fact, his doctoral dissertation, *The
Apocalypse of the German Soul,* set out in harrowing detail, over the course
of three large volumes, the roots of Europe's nihilistic creed. And in his later
works he frequently depicted the devastating scene of European civilization
in the twentieth century, pockmarked by two wars of near annihilation and
whose rebuilding efforts led to further desolation:

> Before the dawn of the technical age it was easier to create genuine culture
> from genuine recollection. Life was more peaceful, man's surroundings ex-
> pressed eternal values more directly. . . . How immediately can a landscape
> absent of men unite us to God, for example high mountains, a large forest, or
> a freely flowing river! . . . In the cities, however, only man's handwriting is
> everywhere visible. . . . Concrete and glass do not speak of God; they only
> point to man who is practically glorified in them. The cities do not transcend
> man; hence they do not guide to transcendence. Quickly and greedily they
> devour the surrounding countries and turn it into a dirty, defiled forecourt of
> cities. For some years now the Roman Campagna has ceased to exist, the Swiss

---

[2]Alan Besançon, *The Forbidden Image: An Intellectual History of Iconoclasm* (Chicago: University of Chicago Press, 2000), p. 3.

landscape likewise. The Rhine has long "had it." Overnight, "nature" will be turned into a reservation, a "national park" within the civilized world; and besides, in national parks—mostly crowded—it is not very easy to pray either.[3]

This situation has rendered the project of apologetics extraordinarily difficult, but of course even more so for anyone who wishes to make aesthetics the touchstone of Christian efforts to bring our contemporaries to the gospel. How can anyone accept the gospel who has never prayed, never sensed the hunger for prayer, never felt like someone who has been endowed with an *anima naturaliter christiana* whose hungers can only be sated with the gospel?

> Many, not to say most, within this technical world, have capitulated interiorly by giving up prayer. The Christians who are determined to persevere in it groan under the great burden of external demands made on them if they want to compete with others who neither have nor allow time for prayer and thought. A synthesis between prayer and godless overactivity, between interior culture demanding a world of silence and external rush and ever-increasing speed, is more and more becoming an extraordinary attainment of the heroic few, and even so only for a limited time; it seems an impossible demand to make on a larger number of people.[4]

Contrast that landscape, so dourly depicted in these sad lines, against the high hopes of the nineteenth-century's Pope Leo XIII for Europe's re-Christianization through a revival of Thomism! Needless to say, that stark contrast meant for Balthasar that Leo's project had failed. Why? Because, according to Balthasar, the Neo-Thomist program was too rational, too based on philosophical demonstrations, too bloodless, and too, well, scholastic.

Instead, he proposed another approach, one that sounds eminently plausible when set down on paper but which is very hard to realize in practice. He begins simply with the concept of beauty. Now no one calls something "beautiful" without asserting at the same time that he or she is *attracted* to it. That does not mean that statements about beauty refer solely to one's subjective feelings (*de gustibus non est disputandum,* and so forth). But *if* one considers something beautiful and says so, one is also thereby asserting one's attraction to that beautiful object.

Now here's the point: people do not usually let themselves be *argued into*

---

[3]Hans Urs von Balthasar, *The God Question and Modern Man*, trans. Hilda Greaf (New York: Seabury Press, 1967), p. 57.
[4]Ibid.

recognizing that something is beautiful (another reason for the popularity of the *de gustibus non est disputandum* maxim); rather, it's just a matter of *seeing* it or not. Thus for Balthasar what apologetics should really be doing is not so much *arguing* as *showing*. In other words, proofs for the existence of God won't do much good (or any good actually) for those who do not already perceive the beauty of revelation from the outset. As he says in his monograph on Dionysius the Areopagite: "No explanation can help him who does not see the beauty [of revelation]; no proof of the existence of God can help him who cannot see *what* is manifest to the world; no apologetic can be any use to him for whom the truth that radiates from the center of theology is not evident."[5]

For that reason, in the 1940s Balthasar conceived the project not just of sketching a vast theological presentation of Christian revelation under the rubric of the three Platonic transcendentals: the beautiful, the good and the true (these three features of being are called "transcendental" because they are to be found in any being whatever, transcending their own particular identities that make them the specific beings they are), but also of starting with the transcendental of beauty. For it was Balthasar's conviction that the *order* in which these transcendentals are approached is utterly determinative for the way theology can credibly present the mysteries of the Christian religion to an increasingly skeptical public. In fact, that skepticism is, for Balthasar, largely due to the habit modernity has adopted of looking at being through the wrong end of the telescope.

From at least the time of René Descartes, and certainly by the time of Immanuel Kant, the focus of philosophers and theologians alike began with concerns over epistemology, that is, with the question of truth, with how minds might come into contact with the truth of beings. Unfortunately, to start with the question of truth means, as subsequent history would prove, never attaining it. Picking up both from the Thomistic axiom that nothing exists in the mind that was not first put there by the senses and from the Husserlian axiom that all philosophy is first and foremost a phenomenology (that is, a study of beings only as they appear to us and not as they "really are" in themselves independent of our perception of them), Balthasar insisted that, in theological terms, we will never come to affirm the truth of revelation unless we first perceive it as beautiful. This perception of the beauty of revelation will then elicit a quasi-erotic response (since the beau-

---

[5]Hans Urs von Balthasar, *The Glory of the Lord: A Theological Aesthetics*, vol. 2, *Studies in Theological Style: Clerical Styles*, trans. Andrew Louth et al. (San Francisco: Ignatius, 1984), p. 166.

tiful is that which is inherently attractive), which response will pull us out of ourselves into lives of committed action, and, finally, only in that action we will come to see how theology is thereby true.

Hence, his theological trilogy would reflect these views (and would, incidentally, take four decades to complete: the last volume was completed a year before his death in 1988). The first part, in seven volumes, constitutes his theological aesthetics and was called in German *Herrlichkeit,* which literally means "splendor" but is etymologically related to the German word for "Lord," a nice play on words that had to be expanded in the English translations as *The Glory of the Lord.* Here the focus is on the contrast between worldly beauty and divine glory, between, that is, the *kalon* of Plato and God's *kabod* in the Old Testament, together with its full manifestation as the *doxa* of Christ in the New Testament (as portrayed above all in the Gospel of John, the most crucial of the Gospels for Balthasar).

Despite the obvious contrasts between Hellenic *kalon* and Hebrew *kabod,* beauty and glory have in common this crucial feature: both are *enrapturing.* But the difference between them is also crucial: for the perception of the divine epiphany to Israel results in *mission,* another key term in Balthasar's theology, whereas Platonic beauty tends to terminate in static contemplation without further ado. *Mission* is the Latinate term for "sending"; that is, mission is a literal apostleship into the world of salvation history, and the response to that mission results in a drama: the drama of the soul saying yes or no to God, certainly; but above all the drama already effected by God when he first *sent* his Son to redeem the world. Thus the seven volumes of the *Aesthetics* seamlessly lead to the five volumes of the *Theo-Drama* (in German *Theodramatik,* a neologism of Balthasar's). Here the encounter with Christ is no longer treated so much under the rubric of his beauty/glory but instead under the rubric of his high priestly role as Judge and Redeemer of the world; in other words, under the rubric of the good, of action, of teleology: of the goal of creation and redemption.

Only then, in the course of committed action, is it possible to reflect on the truth of what that action has called us to, the exposition of which it is the task of the *Theo-Logic* (German, *Theologik*) to specify, published in three volumes. Here the focus is on the logic of exactly *why* God had to save us in just this kind of way. In other words, only by standing within the "hermeneutical circle" of a response *already made* to revelation and mission can one approach the truth of the triune God who plans to bring the whole of the world to his redemptive ends through the (to us) disconcerting means of the cross.

Note how the direction of this trilogy works in conscious opposition to the direction of Kant's trilogy, the *Critique of Pure Reason, Critique of Practical Reason* and the *Critique of [Aesthetic] Judgment*. By starting with the dilemma of the isolated ego, seemingly operating by rules quite at variance with the deterministic Newtonian laws governing the behavior of bodies, Kant had, by the same quick stroke that Descartes employed, rendered the ultimate reality of the world inaccessible to us, confining us to the world of phenomena only and relegating the unknown "noumenon" to a mere posited surd. The trouble is, ethical action requires notions of freedom and responsibility (quintessential noumenal realities), for which Kant could make room only on an "as if" basis: the human actor must act "as if" he were free, "as if" God existed, "as if" the soul were immortal and judged by that same posited God. Finally, when it came to beauty Kant stressed the serenity of disengaged contemplation of the "sublime" in place of the engaged moment of rapture when the soul directly encounters the beautiful. All of these presuppositions Balthasar denies, which is why his theology often strikes some readers as an antimodern throwback to earlier ages. (I happen to believe that such an interpretation is singularly obtuse, but that it occurs testifies to the pervasiveness of Kant's influence.)

Now, setting Balthasar and Kant over against each other in this way might make it sound as if Balthasar shared one characteristic with Kant: that the transcendentals can be compartmentalized in the way Kant had pigeonholed them (as many commentators have noted, Kant had the most schematic and architectonic mind in the history of philosophy). Such a view, however, ignores another important feature of Balthasar's trilogy: that he sees beauty, goodness and truth as always interrelated and interpenetrating; in fact their mutual interrelationship is for him a *vestigium trinitatis* of the *circuminsessio* of the three Persons of the divine Trinity:

> For the moment the essential thing is to realize that, without aesthetic knowledge, neither theoretical nor practical reason can attain to their total completion. If the *verum* lacks that *splendor* which for Thomas is the distinctive mark of the beautiful, then the knowledge of truth remains both pragmatic and formalistic. The only concern of such knowledge will then merely be the verification of correct facts and laws, whether the latter are laws of being or laws of thought, categories and ideas. But if the *bonum* lacks that *voluptas,* which for Augustine is the mark of its beauty, then the relationship to the good remains both utilitarian and hedonistic: in this case the good will involve merely

the satisfaction of a need by means of some value or object, whether it is founded objectively on the thing itself giving satisfaction or subjectively on the person seeking it.[6]

This mutuality and exchange of the three transcendentals can best be explained by an illustration that Balthasar makes about the daily life of every Christian apostle of the Word, whose life of fidelity to Christ will always be marked by three key moments: the contemplative, the kerygmatic and the dialogic. The argument goes like this: in order to preach the Word, the minister must first have heard it and taken it to heart (Rom 10:14-15); this is the contemplative moment, when the believer is lovingly enraptured by the message he has heard. So enrapturing is this message that the hearer/contemplator can do no other than proclaim to others the glorious and joyous message that has come to him; this is the kerygmatic moment. Finally, the proclamation of that message will elicit a variety of responses from the preacher's hearers, just as Paul's preaching to the Athenians on the Areopagus generated a variety of responses (Acts 17:23-34). What does the preacher do then? Perforce, he gets to know the mental worldview(s) of his listeners to see how their already-held presuppositions govern their responses. (Luke makes clear that the response to Paul's preaching on the Areopagus was determined by the philosophical doctrines already held by those who went to hear Paul preach; see Acts 17:16-21.) And this effort to engage listeners on their own terms is what Balthasar calls the dialogic moment.

Most every preacher of any Christian denomination, I suspect, will understand Balthasar here: first comes homily preparation, which entails prayer and reflection, then comes the sermon and finally comes the tricky task of dealing with the varied responses that will come from the congregation—often right after the service! But this example can be extended to all of theology, indeed to the life of the church as a whole: first prayer, then proclamation of the good news and finally dialogue with the world—not necessarily in that chronological order but always in mutual dependence on the other two moments.

So far I have tried to present Balthasar's views in all their internal plausibility. The trouble is—as he readily acknowledges—matters are not so simple. For, as my initial quotation about the situation of contemporary art

---

[6]Hans Urs von Balthasar, *The Glory of the Lord: A Theological Aesthetics,* vol. 1, *Seeing the Form,* trans. Erasmo Leivà-Merikakis (San Francisco: Ignatius, 1982), p. 152.

proves, ugliness faces us at every turn. That is why Balthasar had to spend
so much effort in the first three volumes of *The Glory of the Lord* doing a
kind of Nietzschean genealogy, tracing how we got to where we are, a genealogy I called in my book on Balthasar *Pattern of Redemption*, his "ar-
chaeology of alienated beauty." This is why he opens the first few pages of
volume one with a sad note of elegy when speaking of what his project intends to accomplish:

> Beauty is the word that shall be our first. Beauty is the last thing which the
> thinking intellect dares to approach, since only it dances as an uncontained
> splendor around the double constellation of the true and the good and their
> inseparable relation to one another. Beauty is the disinterested one, without
> which the ancient world refused to understand itself, a word that both imper-
> ceptibly and yet unmistakably has bid farewell to our new world, a world of
> interests, leaving it to its own avarice and sadness. No longer fostered by re-
> ligion, beauty is lifted from its face as a mask, and its absence exposes features
> on that face that threaten to become incomprehensible to man. We no longer
> dare to believe in beauty and we make of it a mere appearance in order the
> more easily to dispose of it. Our situation shows that beauty demands for itself
> at least as much courage and decision as do truth and goodness, and she will
> not allow herself to be separated and banned from her two sisters without tak-
> ing them along with herself in an act of mysterious vengeance. We can be sure
> that whoever sneers at her name as if she were the ornament of a bourgeois
> past—whether he admit it or not—can no longer pray and soon will no longer
> be able to love.[7]

Unfortunately, is that not our situation today? Again, think of my opening
citation from the *New York Times Sunday Book Review*. If apologetics first
depends on getting the unbeliever (or half-believer) to *see* the beauty of
God's creative and redemptive artfulness, how can that happen in the contemporary setting, so aptly described by Jacques Barzun in his Bollingen
Lectures, *The Use and Abuse of Art* (Princeton):

> Nowadays anything put up for seeing or hearing is only meant to be taken in
> casually. If it holds your eye and focuses your wits for even a minute, it justi-
> fies itself and there's an end of it. . . . The Interesting has replaced the Beau-
> tiful, the Profound, and the Moving. [But] if modern man's most sophisticated
> relation to art is to be casual and humorous, [if it] is to resemble the attitude
> of the vacationer at the fair grounds, then the conception of Art as an all-

---

[7]Ibid., p. 18.

important institution, as a supreme activity of man, is quite destroyed. One cannot have it both ways—art as a sense-tickler and a joke is not the same art that geniuses and critics have asked us to cherish and support. Nor is it the same art that revolutionists call for in aid of the Revolution.[8]

Barzun's book title deliberately alludes to Friedrich Nietzsche's essay "The Use and Abuse of History" (an essay that formed one of the four chapters in his early work *Untimely Meditations*), and for good reason. For it was Nietzsche who first recognized the connection between the beauty of art and the truth of belief. Admittedly, his witness is an ironic one, given his own fierce attacks on the Christian religion. But at least he recognized the loss for art in the loss of belief, especially in his essay *Human, All-Too Human:*

> *The Beyond in art.*—With profound sorrow one admits to oneself that, in their highest flights, the artists of all ages have raised to heavenly transfiguration precisely those conceptions which we now recognize as false: *artists are the glorifiers of the religious and philosophic errors of mankind,* and they could not have been so without believing in the absolute truth of these errors. If belief in such truth declines in general, then that species of art can never flourish again which—like the *Divine Comedy,* the paintings of Raphael, the frescoes of Michelangelo, the Gothic cathedrals—presupposes not only a cosmic but a *metaphysical* significance in the objects of art. A moving tale will one day be told how there once existed such an art, such an artist's faith.[9]

So the question I put to you is simple: can the sense for beauty lead us anymore to Christ? To answer that question we must return once more to a point I made earlier: no strategy will work that ends up isolating the Platonic transcendentals, whose mutual interplay constitutes, as we saw, a vestige of the Trinity in creation. So we must also look at what led Nietzsche—and Europe's post-Christian culture generally—to depart from the truth of Christ.

Take, for example, a key passage for Balthasar, the claim Jesus makes about himself in the Gospel of John: "I am the way, and the truth, and the life" (Jn 14:6). What can such a statement mean? Ignoring for a moment the knotty question of the historicity of the figure of Jesus presented in this most theological of the Gospels, Balthasar asks us first and above all to concentrate on what the statement is actually saying, logically. How can a human

---

[8]Jacques Barzun, *The Use and Abuse of Art,* Bollingen Series 35, 22 (Princeton, N.J.: Princeton University Press, 1974), p. 17.
[9]Friedrich Nietzsche, *Human, All Too Human,* in *The Nietzsche Reader,* selected and trans. R. J. Hollingdale (Harmondsworth, N.Y.: Penguin, 1977), p. 129.

being not just point *to* the truth but *be* the truth? Taking the statement on a purely phenomenological level, one notices immediately that other founders of world religions (as well as the founders of philosophical schools) *always* divorce their persons from the teaching they are imparting. Theoretically, Aaron could have received the tablets of Sinai as well as Moses; the Koran could have been revealed a generation earlier or later to a different prophet designated by God;[10] some other man could have come to the teachings of Confucius, Plato or the Buddha. Platonism might be an inevitable philosophical position, but Plato the man is not.[11] Abraham's father Terah could just as well have been told to leave Ur as his son Abraham was (Gen 11:31—12:2). As a Buddhist *koan* has it, "The finger that points to the moon is not the moon."

But what does it mean to *be* the truth? Against this other "koanic" background, the provocation represented in these words of Jesus to *be* the Truth becomes even more unsettling, as Balthasar explains in this key passage:

> The Greek mind found it absurd that one of the products of the all-pervasive *physis* should equate itself with the generative matrix. Jewish thought found it even more incredible that a created man should predicate of himself the attributes proper to the Creator of the world and the Covenant-Lord of Israel. It is still nonsense, but now to a modern evolutionary worldview of any persuasion, to assert that one wave in the river that has flowed on for millions of years and will continue to flow on unthinkably for yet more millions once the wave is no more, can be identified with the river. Nonsense, too, to assert that this wave has already comprehended all of that future and enclosed within itself the fullness of time and the end of time. On attempting to estimate the degree of provocation in such fantastic claims, we see clearly that any school of religious or philosophic thought must be surprised and further shocked by

---

[10]This, one gathers, is part of the reason for the storm of violence unleashed by the Danish cartoons of Muhammad; not only were the caricatures themselves offensive (as caricatures are meant to be); but according to Sunni majority doctrine, *any* pictorial depiction of the Prophet is forbidden, lest the pious believer be led into "idolatry," that is, into confusing the spokesman of God with the God who is speaking through him.

[11]This divorce between doctrine and the person advocating the doctrine was recently demonstrated in the case of Plato by Lloyd Gerson, who rightly points out: "It was fairly widely believed in antiquity that Plato was not the first Platonist, as we might put it. Aristotle tells us that Plato 'followed the Italians (i.e., the Pythagoreans) in most things.' Plotinus tells us that Plato was not the first to say the things that in fact we today widely identify as elements of 'Platonism,' but he said them best. . . . In trying to understand what Platonism is, we must, therefore, recognize that Platonism is, in a sense, bigger than Plato" (Lloyd P. Gerson, "What is Platonism?" *Journal of the History of Philosophy* 43, no. 3 [2005]: 256, 257).

another statement in the same context: "They hated me without cause" (John 15:25).[12]

Christians, in other words, have their own *koan*. Instead of "The finger that points to the moon is not the moon," they have: "The wave *is* the sea."

This passage explains both Balthasar's interpretation of the nature of the claim made by Jesus in his life and preaching and the reasons why such a claim would provoke a reaction that would bring about his execution, which represents in a sense the refutation of that claim by the human race, a refutation that can itself only be counter-refuted by God in the resurrection. Thus the triad of claim-crucifixion-resurrection (or in another formulation, provocation-execution-validation) represents the central *Gestalt* of the Christ event, so that no part of the triad can be omitted without distorting the overall saving pattern that the Christ event means as a whole.

But if the resurrection means God's own validation of the claim made by Jesus in his earthly life, *what* exactly is being validated? Or in other words, what did Peter mean in his first sermon preached on Pentecost that "God raised him [Christ] to life, freeing him from the pangs of Hades, for it was impossible for him to be held in its power" (Acts 2:24 Western text)? Why couldn't Hades "hold" Christ in its power?

To answer this question Balthasar varies the image of wave and sea slightly by now comparing Jesus to a stone dropped into the sea and whose ripple effects radiate outward. Now with all other human beings, one's ripple effects radiate only forward along time's future-bound direction, and even there one's effects eventually fade, to be overwhelmed by the effects of subsequent history. Perhaps no one's influence and impact entirely die out (history still feels the effects, for example, of Sennacherib's failure to conquer the city of Jerusalem in 701 B.C. even if that impact was later muted by Nebuchadnezzar's successful siege in 586 B.C.).[13] But if the saving effects of Jesus are to reach to the whole cosmos (Col 1:19-20), then his effects must not only be able to move backward in time, but also there must be something about the radiating power of the stone that prevents it from being

---

[12]Hans Urs von Balthasar, "Why I am Still a Christian," in *Two Say Why*, trans. John Griffiths (Chicago: Franciscan Herald Press, 1973), p. 18.
[13]On this point see William H. McNeill, "The Greatest Might-Have-Been of All," *New York Review of Books* 46, no. 14 (1999): 62-64: "This may be an odd thing to say about an engagement that never took place; yet Jerusalem's preservation from attack by Sennacherib's army shaped the subsequent history of the world far more profoundly than any other military action I know of" (p. 62).

swamped by later history. And that can only happen if somehow the claim is already true by virtue of the preexistence of the Logos and the reality of the incarnation, so that Christ's descent into hell is an event within the God-head, by which the entirety of the evil of the world has been fully plumbed:

> If the claim stands, the whole truth must also possess a ballast, an absolute counterweight [Schwergewicht] that can be counterbalanced by nothing else; and because it is a question of truth, it must be able to show that it is so. The stone in the one pan of the scales must be so heavy that one can place in the other pan all the truth there is in the world, every religion, every philosophy, every complaint against God *without counterbalancing it.* Only if that is true, is it worthwhile remaining a Christian today.[14]

The stone thus must land on the seabed with such a "thud," so to speak—indeed with such a continually reverberating thud—that it will continue to radiate outward *in both directions, past and future,* so that its effects can be fully appropriated by each conscious being of the cosmos as a fully contemporary event. And this for Balthasar is the meaning of the otherwise enigmatic line in 1 Peter 3:19 that Christ in his descent came to preach to spirits in prison "who disobeyed God *long ago.*" Nor can the effects of the Christ event be allowed to fade in the future; it must have power to make itself fully contemporaneous in the life of the church through its preaching and sacraments:

> The claim to be the overpowering weight on the scales—for all time and in all places, along with the whole scandal it contains—must be powerful enough (and this power is the Holy Spirit) to make itself intelligible "always, even until the end of the world" and "to all nations." This is not to deny the part played by hermeneutics ("you will be my witnesses" and "teach them to observe all things," which presumably includes teaching them to understand). But the claim, if justifiably upheld, is not dependent upon hermeneutical acuity.[15]

In other words, we must train ourselves to read the situation of contemporary art *christologically.* Art has become so dreadful precisely because contemporary man denies that he has been made in the image of Christ. Just as the Venus de Milo retains its serene beauty even after the accidents of history have broken off the goddess's arms, so too even the most perfectly preserved modern work bears witness to the truncated view of humanity

---

[14]Balthasar, "Why I Am Still a Christian," p. 29 (emphasis added).
[15]Ibid., pp. 37-38.

that now prevails almost universally throughout the artist's world, as again Barzun has explained so well:

> Today, when you are tempted to see human representation in art—in Picasso or Giacometti or in any example of the anti-novel—you are at once aware that the symbol is an angry distortion, a dismemberment and defamation of man, and not a reflection, much less a glorification, as it was from Phidias to the Pre-Raphaelites. Surgical remains are what we are invited to contemplate, as if the radical opposition between art and actuality were not yet clear enough. . . . Destruction by novelty becomes an incessant function of art.[16]

In that context I cannot help but think of the massacre at Littleton's Columbine High School on April 20, 1999, partly because the school is located in a suburb of Denver, where I used to teach. The day after the slaughter occurred, I found out that I had several students in my freshman class who had just graduated from there, all of whom spoke movingly of how their high school was simply too big for aberrant behavior to be noticed or for each student's talents to be fostered (many other students told me the same applied to their public high schools too). But one student, in response to my question about the causes that contributed to such mayhem, replied quite to my surprise: "Shopping malls."

This odd answer actually has a point, one that bears on this issue. After the massacre, one native of Littleton wrote an essay describing how the town had changed during his boyhood from a quiet village located well outside the urban environs of Denver into part of the suburban sprawl that now characterizes the entire national landscape, transforming his placid town into a seedbed for despair:

> I grew up in a town endowed, however humbly, with a character and a sense of place, and I had those things, too. What sense of place can there be in the Littletons of America now, in these mall-lands where each Gap and McDonald's is like the next, where the differences between things are neither prized nor scorned but are simply wiped from existence? Growing up in an anonymous landscape, how can anyone escape his own encroaching sense of anonymity? In this world, meaning evaporates. In a world of monotonous getting and spending, the need to shake things up, to make a mark—any mark—may overpower everything else, including sense. . . . The Trench Coat Mafia's particular brand of evil may have stemmed from a terrible absence—a loss of perspective

---

[16]Barzun, *The Use and Abuse of Art*, p. 47.

that might be one of the unforeseen consequences of a loss of place.[17]

What our civilization continues to forget is that we have souls, and when souls are not fed, they distort and warp themselves. And souls today go largely unfed. Everyday they must soak up the desolation of the contemporary landscape. Speaking in tones of a contemporary Jeremiah, Barzun observes in his last book, *From Dawn to Decadence,* that aesthetics has finally reached the crisis point toward which it has been hurtling for over two centuries:

> One cannot pour all human and material resources into a fiery cauldron year after year and expect to resume normal life at the end of the prodigal enterprise. . . . It was not long after the end of the Great War that farseeing observers predicted the likelihood of another, and it became plain the western civilization had brought itself into a condition from which full recovery was unlikely. The devastation, both material and moral, had gone so deep that it turned the creative energies from their course, first into frivolity, and then into the channel of self-destruction.[18]

So far, I seem to have left you with a rather grim picture. Let us for the moment assume that Balthasar is correct that only an apologetics of beauty will work. But given what I have said about the current moonscape of art, *how* can it work? How can we read art christologically when art gives us only distortions of what humans are called to be in Christ? I do not deny that the situation is grim. But lest I leave you with only the faintest glimmers of hope, let us return to what art—any art, whether bad or good—tries to be: both a reflection and a summing up of our image of ourselves. In other words, all art seeks to be, as it were, a *condensation* of reality. Think again of the image of wave and sea. While it might seem initially absurd or mad for a wave that foams up for its allotted years on earth to claim to be also the sea and the seabed, we in fact have analogues for that "condensation," so to speak, in some other forms of relative truth. And for Balthasar, that primary analogue can be found in art. We are able to understand and then to enter into that absolute singularity under the prior analogue of what he calls *relative* singularities, one of the most remarkable of which is the phenomenon of art:

---

[17]Stephen Schiff, "Littleton, Then and Now," *New York Times,* April 22, 1999, available online at <http://query.nytimes.com/gst/fullpage.html?sec=health&res=9C06E7DB153AF931A15757C0A 96F948260>.

[18]Jacques Barzun, *From Dawn to Decadence: 500 Years of Cultural Life, 1500 to the Present* (New York: HarperCollins, 2000), pp. 711, 712.

Great works of art appear like inexplicable miracles and spontaneous eruptions on the stage of history. Sociologists are as unable to calculate the precise day of their origin as they are to explain in retrospect why they appeared when they did. Of course, works of art are subject to certain preconditions without which they cannot come into being: such conditions may be effective stimuli but do not provide a full explanation of the work itself. Shakespeare had his predecessors, contemporaries and models; he was surrounded by the atmosphere of the theater of his time. He could only have emerged within that context. Yet who would dare offer to prove that his emergence was inevitable?[19]

The application of this image to biblical scholarship, I think, should immediately suggest itself: for it is one thing to *examine* all the necessary presuppositions and prior requirements that make possible the emergence of a work of art; but it is another thing entirely to claim that one has thereby *accounted* for that work of art. This is to mistake the sudden manifestation of the phenomenon for its presuppositions (a common mental habit called "the genetic fallacy"). And this fallacy is a perennial danger for scholars whose job it is to concentrate on narrating the history of origins until the story ends up at the termination point: the text itself. This movement of going from beginning to end in the narratives of historical critics can make it seem as if the beginning accounts for the end, rather than the end representing an astonishing fulfillment and supersession of what went before. But we can only fall into that illusory trap because we are already in possession of the work and so we know how our etiological narrative will conclude. Yet this is to fail to come to terms with the work itself, *which must itself determine how its own past is to be interpreted:*

At most we can point to or guess at the propitious moment—the *kairos*—but never what it is that flows into it and gives it that lasting form which, as soon as it emerges, takes control. *It speaks the word.* Its unique utterance becomes a universal language. A great work of art is never obvious and immediately intelligible in the language that lies readily available, for the new, unique language now emerging before us is its own interpreter. It is "self-explanatory." For a moment the contemporary world is taken aback, then people begin to absorb the work and to speak in the newly minted language (hence such terms as "the age of Goethe," or "age of Shakespeare," etc.) with a taken-for-granted ease as though they had invented it themselves. The unique word, however, makes itself comprehensible through its own self: and the greater a

---

[19]Balthasar, "Why I Am Still a Christian," p. 20.

work of art, the more extensive the cultural sphere it dominates will be.[20]

Moreover, this analogy also highlights how crucial faith is to the right understanding of the claim. For it has often been the (spoken or unspoken) presupposition of much biblical scholarship that faith is an obstruction to the neutrality of the historical-critical method, meaning both the faith of the scholar and the faith expressed in the biblical text. Faith is thus like a pair of sunglasses that irremediably tint the text being interpreted, and historical criticism explicitly doffs the glasses. In doing so, it notices how the biblical text is "layered" with the community's confession of faith, and this layering of course radically affects the narrative, transforming neutral history into a confessional text (a process that historical criticism claims to be able to reverse). But the aesthetic analogue, on the contrary, teaches the inner compatibility, indeed the essential symbiosis, of what the art work intends to say and the subjective readiness of the recipient to hear that message:

> A great work of art has a certain universal comprehensibility but discloses itself more profoundly and more truly to an individual the more attuned and practiced his powers of perception are. Not everyone picks up the unique inflection of the Greek in a chorus of Sophocles, or of the German of Goethe's *Faust,* or of the French in a poem of Valéry. Subjective adaptation can add something of its own, but that objective adequacy which is able to distinguish the noble from the commonplace is more important.[21]

Although he does not share Balthasar's theological freedom so radiantly on display here, and indeed is rather phobic toward Christianity, Harold Bloom echoes Balthasar's insistence on the primacy of the aesthetic and even comes close to seeing how resentment against aesthetic primacy is rooted in and arises from an ideologization of culture that will fear all true singularities, relative or otherwise. In other words, aesthetic contemplation, by its very nature as disinterested appreciation of the singular, refutes any and all ideologies, which is why Bloom hails Shakespeare as the single greatest refutation of all later ideal schemas, programs, reeducation camps and brainwashing propaganda. "We are all feminist critics," he quotes one professor as proclaiming, and then replies: "That is the rhetoric suitable for an occupied country, one that expects no liberation from liberation." No wonder, then, that in so many English departments in this nation "the teach-

---

[20]Ibid., p. 21.
[21]Ibid., pp. 21-22.

ing of poems, plays, stories, and novels is now supplanted by cheerleading for various social and political causes."

Even on the face of it, this project should strike everyone as absurd and self-defeating ("the idea that you benefit the insulted and injured by reading someone of their own origins rather than reading Shakespeare is one of the oddest illusions ever promoted in our schools"). But more crucially it begs the question in feeding off Shakespeare's preeminence precisely by attacking *him* and not, say, Ben Jonson or Christopher Marlowe, who presumably are equally the products of class myopia and imperial designs:

> Shakespeare's eminence is, I am certain, the rock upon which the School of Resentment must at last founder. How can they have it both ways? If it is arbitrary that Shakespeare centers the Canon, then they need to show why the dominant social class selected him rather than, say, Ben Jonson, for that arbitrary role. Or if history and not the ruling circles exalted Shakespeare, what was it in Shakespeare that so captivated the mighty Demiurge, economic and social history? Clearly this line of inquiry begins to border on the fantastic; how much simpler to admit that there is a *qualitative* difference, a difference in kind, between Shakespeare and every other writer, even Chaucer, even Tolstoy, or whoever. Originality is the great scandal that resentment cannot accommodate, and Shakespeare remains the most original writer we will ever know.[22]

By calling Shakespeare "non-ideological" and by joining Bloom in hailing him as a refutation of all those ideologies that offer us no hope of "liberation from liberation," I am not claiming that he passed his life in a hermetically sealed-off realm of pure aesthetics, blissfully unaware of the passions and ideas that were tearing apart the English nation. Quite the contrary, where Elizabethans were unanimous in their worldview (hierarchy, Great Chain of Being, immortality of the soul, etc.), Shakespeare was one with his contemporaries. But where his countrymen differed and hurled themselves into the conflict over ideas, Shakespeare participated by *dramatizing* the conflict, not by *contributing* to it. And that is the source of his greatness; for the aesthetic, properly understood, *subsumes* all ideologies by understanding them from within and by giving us true liberation through that understanding. Both Balthasar and Bloom converge at this point, one from a theological and the other from a literary perspective, but perhaps

---

[22]Harold Bloom, *The Western Canon: The Books and School of the Ages* (New York: Riverhead, 1995), p. 24.

Bloom can illustrate the point better because of the way Shakespeare has managed to liberate Bloom himself from his own previous excessive attachment to Freud:

> Here they [that is, the professional resenters] confront insurmountable difficulty in Shakespeare's most idiosyncratic strength: he is always ahead of you, conceptually and imagistically, whoever and whenever you are. He renders you anachronistic because he *contains* you; you cannot subsume him. You cannot illuminate him with a new doctrine, be it Marxism or Freudianism or Demanian linguistic skepticism. Instead, he will illuminate the doctrine, not by prefiguration but by postfiguration, as it were: all of Freud that matters most is there in Shakespeare already, with a persuasive critique of Freud besides. The Freudian map of the mind is Shakespeare's; Freud seems only to have prosified it. Or, to vary my point, a Shakespearean reading of Freud illuminates and overwhelms the text of Freud; a Freudian reading of Shakespeare reduces Shakespeare, or would if we could bear a reduction that crosses the line into absurdities of loss. *Coriolanus* is a far more powerful reading of Marx's *Eighteenth Brumaire of Louis Napoleon* than any Marxist reading of *Coriolanus* could hope to be.[23]

No doubt the resenters continue to rule, although I think their attacks are beginning to pall. I mean, how many times can you continue to paint moustaches on the Mona Lisa before the joke wears thin? But as Bloom points out, it really doesn't change the primacy of the aesthetic over the rage of the resenters, anymore than amateurish productions of Shakespeare can overthrow his greatness. In other words, he still remains a singularity, however relative in relation to Christ. But *as* a singularity he still gives us a conceptual and experiential *access* to Christ's singularity. And that at least can give us hope that the currently defaced visage of beauty will one day lead us back to Christ, and to a restoration of all things in Christ.

---

[23]Ibid.

Contributors

Roy Anker is professor of English at Calvin College and author of several books, including *Catching Light: The Search for God in the Movies*.

Jill Peláez Baumgaertner is dean of humanities and theological studies and professor of English at Wheaton College. Besides serving as poetry editor for *The Christian Century,* she is past president of the Conference on Christianity and Literature and an accomplished poet, with *Finding Cuba* among her collections.

Jeremy S. Begbie is honorary professor of theology at the University of St. Andrews, associate principal of Ridley Hall, Cambridge, and an affiliated lecturer in the faculty of divinity, University of Cambridge. He is a professionally trained musician and has taught widely in the United Kingdom, the United States and South Africa. His publications include *Voicing Creation's Praise: Towards a Theology of the Arts* and *Theology, Music and Time*.

Bruce Ellis Benson is associate professor and chair of the department of philosophy at Wheaton College (Illinois). He has written or coedited several books, among them a work on aesthetics, *The Improvisation of Musical Dialogue: A Phenomenology of Music* (Cambridge University Press).

James Fodor is associate professor of theology at St. Bonaventure University and edits the journal *Modern Theology*. He has written *Christian Hermeneutics: Paul Ricoeur and the Refiguring of Theology*.

Bruce Herman is professor and chair of the department of art at Gordon College. Among his artistic achievements is a major contribution to the exhibit and book *A Broken Beauty*.

Mark Husbands has been recently appointed to the position of the Leonard and Marjorie Maas Associate Professor of Reformed Theology at Hope College. He has completed the monograph *Barth's Ethics of Prayer* and has edited six books, including *The Community of the Word, Justification: What's at Stake in the Current Debates* and *Essays Catholic and Critical*.

Roger Lundin is the Blanchard Professor of English at Wheaton College. In addition to editing and coauthoring several volumes, he has written a number of books, including *From Nature to Experience: The American Search for Cultural Authority*.

Edward T. Oakes, S.J., is associate professor of systematic theology at the University of St. Mary's on the Lake, Mundelein Seminary. He is particularly known for his book *Pattern of Redemption: The Theology of Hans Urs von Balthasar* and his coediting of *The Cambridge Companion to Hans Urs von Balthasar*.

Daniel J. Treier is associate professor of theology at Wheaton College. He is the coeditor of several books, including *The Cambridge Companion to Evangelical Theology,* and the author of *Virtue and the Voice of God: Toward Theology as Wisdom*.

E. John Walford is professor of art at Wheaton College and, among other works, the author of *Jacob Van Ruisdael and the Perception of Landscape* (Yale University Press).

Index